FREEDOM
AND
DISCIPLESHIP

FREEDOM AND DISCIPLESHIP

Liberation Theology in an Anabaptist Perspective

Edited by
Daniel S. Schipani

WIPF & STOCK · Eugene, Oregon

Wipf and Stock Publishers
199 W 8th Ave, Suite 3
Eugene, OR 97401

Freedom and Discipleship
Liberation Theology in an Anabaptist Perspective
By Schipani, Daniel S. and Brown, Robert McAfee
Copyright©1989 Institute of Mennonite Studies
ISBN 13: 978-1-5326-8863-8
Publication date 4/15/2019
Previously published by Orbis Books, 1989

Grateful acknowledgment is made to the International Council for the Promotion of Christian Higher Education for permission to include the essay "Liberation Theology: An Appraisal" by C. René Padilla, originally published in *The Challenge of Marxist and Neo-Marxist Ideologies for Christian Scholarship,* © 1982; to Baker Book House for permission to use a major portion of "An Evangelical Theology of Liberation" by Ronald J. Sider from *Perspectives on Evangelical Theology,* © 1979; and to *Conrad Grebel Review* for permission to reprint "The Relevance of Anabaptist Nonviolence for Nicaragua Today" by C. Arnold Snyder (Spring 1984).

Contents

Foreword   vii
   Robert McAfee Brown

Acknowledgments   ix

1. Introduction: An Invitation to Dialogue   1
   Daniel S. Schipani

PART I
Perspectives on Liberation Theology

2. The Obedient Disciple: Agent of Liberation (John 8:31-32)   17
   C. Hugo Zorrilla

3. Liberation Theology: An Appraisal   34
   C. René Padilla

4. Anabaptism and Liberation Theology   51
   LaVerne A. Rutschman

5. Liberation Theology, Anabaptist Pacifism and Münsterite Violence: Hermeneutical Comparisons and Evaluation   66
   Willard M. Swartley

6. Withdrawal and Diaspora: The Two Faces of Liberation   76
   John H. Yoder

7. Mennonites and the Poor: Toward an Anabaptist Theology of Liberation   85
   Ronald J. Sider

8. The Anabaptist Vision and Social Justice   101
   John Driver

9. The Relevance of Anabaptist Nonviolence for Nicaragua Today   112
   C. Arnold Snyder

PART II
Dialogical Interface and Implications

10. On Discipleship, Justice and Power *José Míguez Bonino*	131
11. Response from a Baptist Biblical Scholar *George V. Pixley*	139
12. Responding to the Challenge: Renewal and Re-Creation *Richard Shaull*	147
13. Orientation in Midstream: A Response to the Responses *John H. Yoder*	159
14. Freedom, Discipleship and Theological Reflection *Gayle Gerber Koontz*	169
15. Implications for Peace and Justice Witness *LeRoy Friesen*	176
Contributors	185
Index	187

Foreword

ROBERT MCAFEE BROWN

In the late 1950s and early 1960s, dialogue was the big word in the Christian world. Embodied initially in the new and exciting Protestant-Catholic dialogue (or, as Catholics preferred to say, the Catholic-Protestant dialogue), it came on the scene as a welcome alternative to centuries of internecine warfare. Soon we began to hear about other dialogues as well: the Christian-Marxist dialogue, the Jewish-Christian dialogue, dialogue between the religions of east and west. As the 1960s heated up, however, and partners in the religious dialogue saw what was happening beyond the religious boundaries (the civil rights struggle, and protest against the war in Vietnam), dialogue was frequently forced to defer to another mode of interrelatedness, the posture of confrontation. Differences rather than similarities were now stressed, separation rather than unity was the agenda, either/or tended to replace both/and.

As a sometime participant in both of these phenomena, I begin to realize, retrospectively at least, that they needed each other. If the incipient danger of dialogue was fuzziness and allowing hearty amiability to replace hard analysis, the incipient danger of confrontation was a closing off of possible new insights from beyond one's own group and a rigidity that lost any sense of self-criticism.

There was the added factor that as new and threatening movements—black theology, feminist theology, even liberation theology—emerged on the scene it was initially necessary for their proponents to group in exclusivist fashion in order to forestall co-optation by representatives of the ecclesiastical *status quo,* and domestication into nothing more than interesting variants from the norm, variants that need not be taken too seriously, but from which (it was generously conceded) the representatives of the ecclesiastical principalities and powers could learn a few things about life on the periphery.

The present volume demonstrates that from the experiences of the earlier dialogue, tempered by the realities of confrontation so hard upon its heels, we are now re-entering a period of dialogue between different points of view that can be fruitful beyond anything that could have been imagined even a few years ago.

Here we have a series of appraisals of, and challenges to, Latin American liberation theology from a group of scholars who stand in the "Radical Reformation-believers' church tradition," what others call, perhaps too broadly, the "Anabaptist tradition," and what others refer to as the "leftwing of the Protestant Reformation." Before approaching these essays we need to absorb the fact that in the sixteenth century, the gulf represented by the Roman Catholic tradition (out of which some but by no means all liberation theology has come), and the radical sectarian movements at the other end of the spectrum, was absolutely unbridgeable. Anathemas, counter-anathemas and burnings at the stake were the order of the day. That particular history only heightens the significance of the present exchange. Some churches may still fire heretics, but at least we no longer burn them.

Many exchanges in our theological (and political) world are initiated to even old scores, and in such cases all instruments of battle are considered legitimate. A cheap victory is preferable to an honest draw, and infinitely preferable to a putative defeat. The present volume goes far beyond such easy maneuvering. The lengthy Part I, "Perspectives on Liberation Theology," combines a genuine effort to understand the opposing position on its own terms, with an equally forthright willingness to challenge those terms and to ask hard questions. There are no caricatures, and if there are some misunderstandings, ample opportunity is provided to the respondents in Part II, "Dialogical Interface and Implications," to set the record straight. No punches are pulled, but no histrionics are employed either. And just to keep the rules of the encounter fair and square, there is even "a response to the responses," along with (one of the genuinely new contributions) a frank setting forth of how participants on all sides must be faulted for their failure to consider feminist issues as part of a discussion on liberation. In such ways is progress measured.

It is not the task of this writer to assess the individual essays, for the contributors themselves do that. Nor is it to offer a kind of final word at the end of the exchange. (Forewords may come first, but they are always written last.) The final word will not be written in this volume but only in subsequent volumes growing out of it. Correction: were it to be written, it would not, of course, be a "final" word but only a "next" word, a word itself subject to scrutiny, critique and refinement.

Indeed, in the best tradition of both traditions, the truly significant "next" words will not be inscribed on sheets of paper, but will be enacted in lives dedicated to the liberation of all of God's children from the idols and the "principalities and powers" of this world that the contributors are willing to name directly, thus initiating their disempowerment. It is a happy prospect that after such "denunciation" (as Paulo Freire calls it), the writers will be closer to one another than they were before, because of the exercise of frank talk, and in a more united fashion, able to share in the holy task of "annunciation" of a gospel to which they are all committed.

Acknowledgments

The project leading to this book emerged from several conversations around the question of converging theological agendas. The focus of dialogue was the interface between Latin American liberation theology and theological reflection in the Radical Reformation-believers' church tradition. The settings were diverse, involving friends and colleagues in Central and South America, the Caribbean and North America. The proposal for the project was readily affirmed and endorsed, for which I am very grateful. Special encouragement was received from President Marlin E. Miller of Goshen Biblical Seminary, and Wilbert R. Shenk, Mennonite Board of Missions administrator and missiologist. Finally, I would especially like to thank Robert McAfee Brown for taking the time to read the manuscript and write the Foreword.

With few exceptions the essays in this collection have not been previously published. I am thankful for the willingness of contributors to participate in this endeavor to make public an ongoing theological dialogue which—regardless of differing views—we all deem pertinent for the hour.

The project was sponsored by the Institute of Mennonite Studies, the research agency of the Associated Mennonite Biblical Seminaries. Special thanks are due to its Director, Willard M. Swartley, for support and counsel, and to Elizabeth G. Yoder, Assistant Director, for assistance in preparing the manuscript. The skillful secretarial assistance of Sue DeLeón is also gratefully acknowledged.

It is our shared hope that many others may join this conversation on freedom and discipleship, not merely for the sake of advancing theological reflection, but also for the sake of recommitting ourselves to more faithful Christian praxis.

FREEDOM AND DISCIPLESHIP

1

Introduction:
An Invitation to Dialogue

DANIEL S. SCHIPANI

The title and subtitle of this book suggest the close connection between, first, Christian praxis—*Freedom and Discipleship*—and second, theological reflection—*Liberation Theology in Anabaptist Perspective*. That order is deliberate, of course, because a major assumption shared by all the participants in this project concerns the priority of faith lived out in the midst of the sociohistorical situation, theology being—in the words of Gustavo Gutiérrez—"critical reflection on Christian praxis in the light of the Word of God."[1]

Another general observation is that both the Anabaptist-believers' church tradition and liberation theology privilege a certain *pedagogical* orientation. That orientation is apparent in their sharing of key convictions and emphases such as the normative import of the teachings of Jesus, the view of the Bible as the text of the church and book of and for the people, the dynamics of faith as discipleship (that is, the committed following of Jesus Christ) and doing theology as—essentially—church education for the ministry and mission of the ecclesial community.[2] That accounts partially for the fact that the editor of this volume is a "practical theologian" especially interested in church education.[3]

It is precisely that acknowledged commonality that has facilitated the discussion presented in this book. However, before proceeding we must briefly state what is actually meant here by "liberation theology" and "Anabaptist perspective," and also why we assume that this project should be shared with a wider public.

A COMING TO TERMS

The established contours of this project on the one hand facilitate the discussion in terms of manageable sets of questions to be dealt with. On the other hand, a kind of contraposition results with the inherent risk of reification and polarization that John H. Yoder denounces in his second essay by contending that the two whole worlds of "liberation theology" and "Anabaptist perspective" overlap more than they collide and agree more than they differ. Granting that each "theology" or "perspective" is much broader and more heterogeneous than what is represented here, the following clarification is in order.

On "Liberation Theology"

In this project we have focused on *Latin American* liberation theology given the context of North and Latin American relations with the complex set of socio-economic, political, cultural and religious dimensions. This chosen partner for conversation happens to offer the most systematically articulated and developed—and widely translated and read—theological reflection among current liberation and Third World theologies.[4]

Several related issues underscore the pertinence of that focus: the question of refugees, immigrants and the growing Latin American community in the United States and Canada; and the character of relations between the United States and Latin America, including critical issues such as foreign debt and overall economic policy, perennial political interventionism and, at the point of this writing, outright aggression against Nicaragua. Further, one must take seriously the liberationist claim of a correlation between the impressive concentration of power and resources on the part of the rich, developed nations, and the widening gap with the so-called underdeveloped countries, including militarism and political repression, grinding hunger and poverty, and other indicators of marginalization, dependence and exploitation.[5] Together with the bankruptcy of the dependent capitalist paradigm, the collapse of the Christendom model of Roman Catholicism is another important factor.

We are especially interested in the fact that Latin American liberation theology purports to be *a new way of doing theology* that involves far more than a matter of alternative theologizing as an intellectual or academic endeavor. Traditional academic theology is in fact radically criticized by liberationists[6] who have moved even beyond the progressive contributions of European political theology.[7] Further, the critique and the alternative perspectives and corrective social action advocated by liberationists in light of the context of oppression within and from which they have reflected, have been reinforced in the last few years by the presence and praxis of the base ecclesial communities as *a new way of being the church*.[8] The resulting references to a *"new Reformation"* is not surprising in light of those developments.[9] Some of the parallels with the sixteenth-century Reformation movement include the emphasis of the base ecclesial communities on creative protest (the so-called Protestant principle), the "priesthood of all believers" motif, and the privileged place of the Bible for the church as hermeneutic community. It can also be noted that, historically, many of the Protestant churches that have become well-established institutions through a predictable sociological process can trace their origin to some kind of grassroots ecclesial community in Europe.[10] Actually, some striking analogies between socio-economic conditions at the close of the Middle Ages (feudalism and unequal land distribution; rudimentary forms of national and international capitalism; urbanization; a growing popular self-assurance; the ravages of war; newer means of communication) and present-day Latin America can be established, thus providing further backing to the idea of a "Reformation"—maybe a new *Radical* Reformation—in the making.[11] This suggestion takes us to the next section.

On "Anabaptist Perspective"

Our engagement with Latin American liberation theology has had an explicit bias. A number of terms are used in this book in reference to the Anabaptist perspective mentioned in the subtitle. The fact that those references are not very consistent or precise partially reflects the heterogeneous nature of both the ecclesio-theological sources as well as that of the present-day claims of identification with the tradition. The following brief comments will help to clarify meaning and connotations and to supplement related remarks made on the subject by several contributors to this collection, especially Rutschman, Swartley, Driver, Snyder and Yoder.

Anabaptist in its historical use refers to a sixteenth-century Radical Reformation movement that called for fundamental transformation in the church and society on the basis of a fresh understanding of the New Testament. Anabaptism was actually part of a larger movement of protest outside classical Protestantism and the so-called Magisterial Reformation.[12] It offered a more *radical* (in the twofold sense of "going to the root" and "far-reaching") biblical critique than Luther or any other major Reformer. This Radical Reformation movement, which Anabaptists integrated although not in a coordinated or systematic way, has been called the "left wing" of the Reformation by Roland H. Bainton. With Luther at the center and Roman Catholicism at the right, "left wing" Radical Reformers were characterized by a strong ethical concern, "primitivism" in the sense of a will to return to the patterns of the early church, a heightened sense of eschatology, anti-intellectualism and complete separation of church and government.[13] Although attempts have been made to establish and define the essential core of the movement, there was great variation among Anabaptists. The best-known definition of an "Anabaptist vision" is that of Harold S. Bender, who characterized its three major foci as, first, a new conception of the essence of Christianity as discipleship; second, a new conception of the church as a faith community; and third, a new ethic of love and nonresistance.[14]

Two other terms associated with historical Anabaptism and present-day heirs of the Radical Reformation are *free church* and *believers' church*. Alongside the parish system of medieval Catholicism and the territorial system of the Reformers, there emerged voluntary faith communities free from cultural and political coercion. Franklin H. Littell has listed a number of traits of the free church paradigm such as voluntarism, religious liberty, consensus, resistance or nonresistance to evil, missionary concern, and the disciplined and binding community.[15] The related concept of believers' church is broader than Anabaptism (historically, it applies to other movements such as the twelfth-century Waldensians); Donald F. Durnbaugh has provided a thorough characterization in terms of the issues of discipleship and apostolicity, mission and evangelism, church and state, mutual aid and service, and sectarianism and ecumenicity.[16] This is the preferred term for some of the writers (Gerber Koontz, Friesen), although all the representatives of the "Anabaptist perspective" share a nonviolence, pro-peace and justice stance consistent with their identification or affiliation with historic peace churches who claim a historico-theological link with the Anabaptist tradition and its pacifist and nonresistant orientation.[17]

Finally, we are in agreement with Gregory Baum, who has asserted that the sixteenth-century Anabaptist movement was inspired by a new imagination and a new vision that had the virtue of anticipating developments which were to occur centuries later in the history of the church and Christianity.[18] Actually, a case in point is the striking parallel between the legacy of the Radical Reformation and the contributions of the liberationist-base ecclesial community movement. They include, among other things, the prophetic critique of the social order, ecclesial as well as political-cultural; the emergence of grassroots Christian communities as "free churches" in terms of their voluntary association and also in their repudiation of the marriage altar-throne; the defense and promotion of religious freedom and the openness to ecumenical cooperation; and the understanding of Christian faith as the actual following of Jesus, that is, discipleship-orthopraxis.

WHY READ THIS BOOK?

A number of developments point to the relevance of our topic, beginning with the observation that the emergence of liberation theology is one of the most significant theological events of the last two decades. The massive impact of that "new way of doing theology" is particularly apparent in the United States as reflected in the production of numerous and diverse analyses, critiques and reformulations of liberation theology.[19] In a sense it could be argued that too much has been written already on the subject and there is no need for yet another volume dealing with Latin American liberation theology! However, it can also be claimed that this theological discussion correlates somehow with significant issues and experiences within the pluralistic North American scene of our time and is much more than an intellectual exercise or an academic game. A number of religious bodies have made important statements—notably the Catholic bishops' pastorals "The Challenge of Peace" and "Economic Justice for All"—and are devising and promoting programs addressing challenges such as hunger, civil rights, militarism and others. Concern for community building and discipleship often goes hand in hand with sociopolitical awareness and action as in the case of creative ecumenical Christian minorities, including special witnesses such as the sanctuary movement. In short, the call for the churches to become alternative "base" communities with a countercultural consciousness suggests the intersection of, among others, Anabaptist-believers' church and liberationist prophetic visions. That is a conviction that has stimulated our conversation as well as the work on this volume.

The main thesis of this project has been that by looking at liberation theology from an Anabaptist-believers' church perspective, a fruitful mutual assessment can take place. In this manner both strengths and contributions as well as weaknesses and shortcomings may become apparent, and meaningful questions are addressed from both perspectives in a critical, creative and illuminating fashion. A major assumption and conviction is that the reflection and dialogue elicited in such an endeavor is welcomed to the extent that the church's "faith seeking understanding" is thereby somehow encouraged or assisted for the sake of increasing freedom and nurturing discipleship.

In light of these considerations the purpose of this collection is twofold. First, we attempt to make a contribution to current theological discussion with this report on a conversation engaging two Christian traditions and movements. And the mutually enlightening interplay thus generated involves the inseparable facets of content and process in the theological task. The other directly related goal of this project is to spell out further foundational material for the ministry of the church. In fact, the participants in this dialogue would agree that the privileged public of theological reflection is the church rather than the wider society or the academy.[20] The idea is, more precisely, to suggest foundations for both building and equipping the ecclesial community and empowerment for mission, especially the witness of peace and justice in word and deed. A strong bias and indeed a kind of passion are detectable throughout this discussion, in the sense of a call to greater faithfulness in the direction of God's reign and in light of the contours and challenges of the present historical situation.

The design of this book emerged rather naturally in light of the thesis and the stated purpose. A number of representatives of the Anabaptist-Mennonite tradition were invited to write or revise recent essays dealing with several dimensions of liberation theology. The writing would be in itself an expression of ongoing conversations and reflections in terms of concrete involvements in diverse North and Latin American settings. The contributors in fact reflect theological viewpoints conditioned by their different ethnic, socio-cultural and denominational backgrounds as well as their vocational commitments. An effort was made to address specific hermeneutical, ecclesiological, christological, ethical and eschatological concerns. Some overlapping and repetition is unavoidable, but I hope not distracting, in this kind of project.

A distinctive feature of this collection, when compared with other collective appraisals of liberation theology,[21] is its *dialogical* character and the explicit encouragement of mutual illumination and reformulations. With that intention and spirit, several proponents of liberation theology readily accepted the invitation to respond to the eight essays that comprise the first part of the book. A major gap and limitation of this volume, however, is the absence of Catholic theologians among the writers, although a number of them have been involved in the conversations.[22] In any event the two final articles in the book register the challenges and possibilities of an ecumenical theological dialogue and point to further agenda for both reflection and action.

OVERVIEW OF THE COLLECTION

The discussion in this book is divided into two major parts. The first of these—"Perspectives on Liberation Theology"—consists of eight essays containing analyses, critical assessments, and comparative evaluations that engage liberation theology at various points and in different manners. In the second part—"Dialogical Interface and Implications"—six chapters reflect the ongoing conversation in a more dynamic and dialectical fashion. A brief reference to the content of the collection follows.

In chapter 2 C. Hugo Zorrilla presents a study of John 8:31-32 with a discussion of Jesus' praxis and teaching that addresses in detail the questions of freedom, liberating truth and radical discipleship in light of that biblical context. This is a fitting beginning for our collection given the converging emphases on an "epistemology of obedience" and "praxis knowing" which are deemed of crucial importance in the two Christian traditions in dialogue.[23] In the following essay (chapter 3) C. René Padilla explicates the methodological approach of liberation theology in terms of the priority of praxis, the historical situation as starting point of the theological task, the utilization of the social sciences, and the question of theology and ideology. In the second part of his essay Padilla offers a parallel fourfold critique culminating with a restatement of the dialectics of hermeneutical circulation involving historical situation and Scripture.

In chapter 4 LaVerne Rutschman presents the first discussion of areas of interaction and commonality between Latin American liberation theology and what he calls Radical Anabaptism. After providing background considerations, Rutschman refers to four areas of special interest: the source and nature of authority; the identification and role of the people of God in the liberation struggle; the place of christology in Christian thought and action; and the question of final goals or eschatology. Partially building upon that analysis, Willard M. Swartley (chapter 5) invites us to consider the mutual challenge between the hermeneutical contributions of the Anabaptist pacifist tradition and the hermeneutical contributions of liberation theology. Swartley also shows two forms of hermeneutic within sixteenth-century Anabaptism aiming to stimulate a better understanding of the two main alternatives under comparison in the essay. Finally, there is a normative statement of hermeneutical perception informed by both the liberationist and discipleship strands within biblical tradition. The essay by John H. Yoder (chapter 6) deals with the centrality of the Exodus story in the Old Testament. The study proposes several theses with an alternative critical interpretation of the foundational and paradigmatic character of the Exodus. Yoder claims that the authenticity and integrity of the language of liberation and hope depend on proper attention to the fuller imagery of elect peoplehood within the larger picture of the biblical records.

In chapter 7 Ronald J. Sider focuses on the most outstanding issue in liberation theology, namely, the question of God's attitude toward the poor and oppressed. He suggests the possibility of developing an Anabaptist theology of liberation by way of appropriating the mutual challenges presented by the two traditions in serious dialogue, together with a fresh look at the biblical message and actual congregational implementation of the *shalom* vision in contexts of human suffering. Then John Driver discusses the contemporary struggle for social justice in Latin America from the standpoint of radical Anabaptism and its vision of the church and society (chapter 8). After discussing prevailing alternatives, Driver outlines a strategy consistent with a radical Anabaptist vision which emphasizes the motifs of nonresistant suffering, servanthood and messianic community. In the following essay (chapter 9) C. Arnold Snyder ponders the question of the relevance of nonviolence in the context of a revolutionary process. He juxtaposes the discussion of sixteenth-century events in Europe such as the Peasants' War (1525) and the Anabaptist Schleitheim confession (1527) and the Nicaraguan Revolution of 1979 in light of the germane questions of the ethical meaning of the model of Jesus and how Christians assist in bringing justice to the world.

The second part of the book is more deliberately dialogical both in format and substance. Three proponents of liberation theology react to the eight previous essays, followed by another response from a peace/believers' church perspective. Further reflection and ramifications are indicated in the two final essays.

José Míguez Bonino (chapter 10) first affirms key analogies emanating from the "common ethos" that undergirds the integration of faith and life in both Christian traditions. He then proceeds to explore critically two related issues: the rejection of Christendom, and justice in the world. Míguez argues that the thorny, open and theological question of violence is one to be discerned in terms of the wider problem of power and politics. In chapter 11 George V. Pixley vindicates the priority of the "practical" dimension of the whole discussion—how to follow Jesus so as to maximize his promised freedom—as suggested in the subtitle of this book. From the perspective of his denominational and vocational identity, he then sharply confronts the questions of discipleship, nonviolence, and suffering for the sake of justice, and challenges the very ideal of the messianic community in terms of the dilemma engaging faithfulness and responsibility. In his response Richard Shaull (chapter 12) underscores the contributions of both movements for biblical, theological and ecclesial re-creation in an ecumenical scale. He also challenges present-day heirs of the Radical Reformation to greater faithfulness, not only in light of the subversive memories of sixteenth-century witness but, especially, the related eschatological vision embodied in the base ecclesial communities. Finally he proposes two conditions for critical fruitful interplay: sympathetic understanding and mutually reconstructive criticism.

John H. Yoder responds (chapter 13) with a restatement of the lingering threat of neo-Constantinianism impinging on ecclesiology, ethics and eschatology, and the pervasive issues of the church's distinctness from the world— "separation"—and political involvement (including the possibility of violence)—"responsibility." He critiques the framework of the project and the resulting discussion because of what he sees as a constricting reification of both "liberation theology" and "Anabaptist perspective." Yoder suggests that traditional dichotomies and polarizations must be transcended with a more critical and ecumenical methodology. In chapter 14 Gayle Gerber Koontz points to key dimensions of marginalization and bondage missing in this conversation so far. Especially she reminds us that God's liberation through Jesus Christ involves also the politics of women/men relations. From a feminist perspective the value of a threefold theological hermeneutics of suspicion, peoplehood and generosity, and the need to integrate prophetic and incarnational spiritualities are affirmed as essential for a wider reflection on, and engagement in struggles for liberation, peace and justice. In the final essay (chapter 15) LeRoy Friesen summarizes six sets of fundamental questions raised in and by this theological conversation and, lastly, his own statement on the church as harbinger of God's future. These formulations are aimed at both the revitalization of theological reflection in the tradition that Friesen represents as well as the continuation of an ecumenical dialogue that reflects and inspires our witness for peace and justice.

This book is presented as a deliberately inconclusive project. You are invited not only to become acquainted with the ongoing conversation but also to join the dialogue. Further discernment of issues and alternatives concerning freedom and discipleship is obviously called for far beyond the limited agenda discussed in this volume. Other theological perspectives and analyses are indeed indispensable. It is hoped that in some way that process of critical reflection will be stimulated by this work.

NOTES

1. Gustavo Gutiérrez, *A Theology of Liberation,* trans. Caridad Inda and John Eagleson (Maryknoll, N.Y.: Orbis Books, 1973), p. 13. The idea is that theologizing is a "second act," the first one being "faith that works through love" (Gal. 5:6) or, in liberationist perspective, solidarity with the poor and oppressed and involvement in historical liberation praxis. Gutiérrez also writes: "When we speak of 'first act' and 'second act'. . . (we) are talking life style—a way of living the faith. In the last analysis we are talking spirituality in the best and most authentic sense of the word. . . in liberation theology, our methodology is our spirituality—a life process in the way to

realization" Gustavo Gutiérrez, *The Power of the Poor in History,* trans. Robert R. Barr (Maryknoll, N.Y.: Orbis Books, 1983), pp. 103-4.

2. For a broad and critical overview of liberation theology from the unique vantage point of religious education, see Daniel S. Schipani, *Religious Education Encounters Liberation Theology* (Birmingham, Ala.: Religious Education Press, 1988). Several major liberation motifs are discussed in terms of an interdisciplinary approach: conscientization, liberation and creativity; a prophetic-utopian vision; a praxis way of knowing; critical interpretation and understanding for transformation; and the oppressed and the base community.

3. The question of the dialogical interplay engaging liberation theology from an Anabaptist perspective was previously raised in my work and research on the *conscientization* process and approach developed by Paulo Freire. See Daniel S. Schipani, *Conscientization and Creativity: Paulo Freire and Christian Education* (Lanham, Md.: University Press of America, 1984), especially chapters 3 and 4. This book includes the first thorough epistemological and theological reinterpretation of Freire's contribution through his work and thought, a contribution which suggested the key methodological principle for liberation theology in terms of the approach and philosophy of *conscientization*. Freire's pedagogical practice, together with his reflection and writing, provided a timely twofold impetus in Brazil and elsewhere; it further encouraged the church's involvement with the poor and oppressed and stimulated new insights on Christian "praxis" that became decisive in shaping the method of liberation theology. In articulating his own liberationist view, which affirms the primacy of commitment and praxis, Freire helped to lay the foundation for the method adopted by liberation theologians. No wonder, then, that several crucial issues of concern for Freire such as the question of ideologies to be exposed, the problem of political-economic domination, and the challenge to work for the humanization of all in the midst of history appear also in the liberationist theological agenda.

4. It can also be argued that other liberation theologies, such as black or feminist, share some basic analogous concerns and methodologies and provide similarly meaningful contributions in certain areas. The following works are helpful for an interpretive consideration of liberation theologies: Frederick Herzog, *Liberation Theology: Liberation in the Light of the Fourth Gospel* (New York: Seabury, 1972); Rosemary Radford Ruether, *Liberation Theology: Human Hope Confronts Christian History and American Power* (New York: Paulist Press, 1972); Letty M. Russell, *Human Liberation in a Feminist Perspective* (Philadelphia: Westminster Press, 1974); John C. Bennett, *The Radical Imperative: From Theology to Social Ethics* (Philadelphia: Westminster Press, 1975); James H. Cone, *God of the Oppressed* (New York: Seabury, 1975) and "From Geneva to Sao Paulo: A Dialogue Between Black Theology and Latin American Liberation Theology," in *The Challenge of Basic Christian Communities,* ed. Sergio Torres and John Eagleson (Maryknoll, N.Y.: Orbis Books, 1981), pp. 265-81, also *For My People: Black Theology and the Black Church* (Maryknoll, N.Y.: Orbis Books, 1984) ch. 3 and *My Soul Looks Back* (Maryknoll, N.Y.: Orbis Books, 1986) ch. 4, 5; Robert McAfee Brown, *Theology in a New Key: Responding to Liberation Themes* (Philadelphia: Westminster Press, 1978); Gerald H. Anderson and Thomas F. Stransky, ed., *Mission Trends No. 4: Liberation Theologies in North America and Europe* (New York: Paulist Press, 1979; Grand Rapids, Mich.: Eerdmans, 1979); Brian Mahan and L. Dale Richesin, ed., *The Challenge of Liberation Theology: A First World Response* (Maryknoll, N.Y.: Orbis Books, 1981); Harvey M. Conn, "Theologies of Liberation: An Overview" and "Theologies of Liberation: Toward a Common View," in *Tensions*

in *Contemporary Theology*, 2nd ed., ed. Stanley N. Gundry and Alan F. Johnson (Grand Rapids, Mich.: Baker Book House, 1983), pp. 325-434; Georges Casalis, *Correct Ideas Don't Fall From the Skies: Elements of an Inductive Theology*, trans. Jeanne Marie Lyons and Michael John (Maryknoll, N.Y.: Orbis Books, 1984); Roger Haight, *An Alternative Vision: An Interpretation of Liberation Theology* (New York: Paulist Press, 1985); Dean William Ferm, *Third World Liberation Theologies: An Introductory Survey* (Maryknoll, N.Y.: Orbis Books, 1986) and *Third World Liberation Theologies: A Reader* (Maryknoll, N.Y.: Orbis Books, 1986).

5. An alternative viewpoint can be found in Michael Novak, *Will It Liberate?: Questions About Liberation Theology* (Mahwah, N.J.: Paulist Press, 1986). Novak presents an unabashed defense of capitalism and the proposal of a so-called North American Liberation Theology supposedly embodied in the "liberal society."

6. Various critical assessments of traditional academic theologies from liberationist perspectives appear in the following books: Hugo Assmann, *Theology for a Nomad Church*, trans. Paul Burns (Maryknoll, N.Y.: Orbis Books, 1976), ch. 2,3; Leonardo Boff, *Jesus Christ Liberator: A Critical Christology for Our Time*, trans. Patrick Hughes (Maryknoll, N.Y.: Orbis Books, 1978), ch. 1, 2; Gutiérrez, *A Theology of Liberation*, ch. 1; José Míguez Bonino, *Doing Theology in a Revolutionary Situation* (Philadelphia: Fortress, 1975); Juan Luis Segundo, *The Liberation of Theology*, trans. John Drury (Maryknoll, N.Y.: Orbis Books, 1976), ch. 1; Samuel Silva Gotay, *El Pensamiento Cristiano Revolucionario en América Latina y el Caribe* (Salamanca: Sígueme, 1981), ch. 1 to 4; Jon Sobrino, *The True Church and the Poor*, trans. Matthew J. O'Connell (Maryknoll, N.Y.: Orbis Books, 1984), ch. 1.

7. There is an interesting and complex relationship between political theology and liberation theology, the latter affirming in principle the hermeneutical, prophetic and eschatological thrusts of the former. In fact many key theological themes discussed by leading European political theologians such as Johannes B. Metz, Jürgen Moltmann and Dorothee Söelle, have been taken up also by liberation theologians. However, underneath those similarities are profound differences stemming from the liberationists' methodological approach to doing theology, which is more grounded in concrete experience and praxis, more specific in analyzing socio-economic realities, and more committed to action and transformation. Further, the special nature of the Latin American setting, and the close connection with the church and with grassroots ecclesial communities particularly, account for the unique character and contribution of liberation theology. For a succinct presentation of the differences between these two theological movements see Francis P. Fiorenza, "Political Theology and Liberation Theology: An Inquiry into Their Fundamental Meaning," *Liberation, Revolution, and Freedom*, ed. Thomas M. McFadden, (New York: Seabury, 1975), pp. 3-29. Rebecca S. Chopp in *The Praxis of Suffering: An Interpretation of Liberation and Political Theologies* (Maryknoll, N.Y.: Orbis Books, 1986) includes helpful interpretive studies of Gustavo Gutiérrez, Johannes B. Metz, José Míguez Bonino and Jürgen Moltmann. She rightly affirms that a most significant area of both agreement and disagreement between German political theology and Latin American liberation theology is the vision of faith (and the church) acting in a critical relationship to the world and the germane question of the nature of theology as a political activity: "Locating the critical activity of the church through its political, educational, and social activity with the poor, Latin American liberation theology committed itself not only to interpreting critically the world, in the tradition of its German counterpart political theology, but also to transforming that world" (p. 20).

8. On grassroots Christian Communities in Latin America, see Alvaro Barreiro, *Basic Ecclesial Communities: The Evangelization of the Poor,* trans. Barbara Campbell (Maryknoll, N.Y.: Orbis Books, 1982); Sergio Torres and John Eagleson, ed., *The Challenge of Basic Christian Communities;* and especially Leonardo Boff, *Church, Charism and Power: Liberation Theology and the Institutional Church,* trans. John W. Dierksmeier (New York: Crossroads, 1985) and *Ecclesiogenesis: The Base Communities Reinvent the Church,* trans. Robert R. Barr (Maryknoll, N.Y.: Orbis Books, 1986). Also see Guillermo Cook, *The Expectation of the Poor: Latin American Ecclesial Communities in Protestant Perspective* (Maryknoll, N.Y.: Orbis Books, 1985).

9. The idea that the base Christian communities are in fact harbingers of a new Reformation is discussed by Harvey Cox in *Religion in the Secular City: Toward a Postmodern Theology* (New York: Simon & Shuster, 1984), ch. 11, 22; and by Richard Shaull in *Heralds of a New Reformation: The Poor of South and North America,* especially ch. 8. Johannes B. Metz also makes a strong case for a "second reformation" that will affect substantially, although in different ways, both Catholic and Protestant churches in *The Emergent Church: The Future of Christianity in a Post-Bourgeois World,* trans. Peter Mann (New York: Crossroads, 1981).

10. See the well-documented study by Guillermo Cook, *The Expectation of the Poor: Latin American Basic Ecclesial Communities in Protestant Perspective,* ch. 10, 11.

11. William Cook, "Base Ecclesial Communities in Central America," *Mennonite Quarterly Review* 58 (Supplement, August 1984): 410–412. The perspective of the sociology of knowledge is a helpful dimension in any such comparative study.

12. In this volume *Radical Reformation* and *Anabaptism* are used interchangeably. Only in this century have scholars begun to take seriously the Radical Reformation of the sixteenth century. Anabaptist studies have gained a place in the fields of church history and historical theology over the past two generations. See George H. Williams, *The Radical Reformation* (Philadelphia: Westminster Press, 1962). For a study of documents illustrative of the Radical Reformation see *Spiritual and Anabaptist Writers,* ed. George H. Williams and Angel M. Mergal (Philadelphia: Westminster Press, 1957) and the Herald Press series *Classics of the Radical Reformation,* ed., Cornelius J. Dyck, with Anabaptist and Free Church documents translated and annotated. This series includes works by and on Michael Sattler, Pilgram Marpeck and Conrad Grebel, as well as a collection of selected primary sources, *Anabaptism in Outline.* Works on Radical Reformers include Hans-Jürgen Goertz, ed., *Profiles of Radical Reformers* (Kitchener, Ont.: Herald Press, 1982); John Allen Moore, *Anabaptist Portraits* (Scottdale, Pa.: Herald Press, 1984); and studies of single figures such as C. Arnold Snyder, *The Life and Thought of Michael Sattler* (Scottdale, Pa.: Herald Press, 1984). Shorter and more popular discussions of Anabaptism include Walter Klaassen, *Anabaptism: Neither Catholic nor Protestant* (Waterloo, Ont.: Conrad Press, 1973); William R. Estep, *The Anabaptist Story* (Grand Rapids, Mich.: Eerdmans, 1975); and J. Denny Weaver, *Becoming Anabaptist* (Scottdale, Pa.: Herald Press, 1987).

13. Roland H. Bainton, "The Left Wing of the Reformation," in *Studies in the Reformation* (Boston: Beacon Press, 1963), pp. 119 ff.

14. Harold S. Bender, "The Anabaptist Vision," in *The Recovery of the Anabaptist Vision,* ed. Guy F. Hershberger (Scottdale, Pa.: Herald Press, 1957), p. 42.

15. Frank H. Littell, *The Free Church* (Boston: Starr King Press, 1957).

16. Donald F. Durnbaugh, *The Believers' Church: The History and Character of Radical Protestantism,* 2d. ed. (Scottdale, Pa.: Herald Press, 1985).

17. See Cornelius J. Dyck, ed., *An Introduction to Mennonite History* (Scottdale,

Pa.: Herald Press, 1967). The series *Studies in Anabaptist and Mennonite History*, published by Herald Press in cooperation with the Mennonite Historical Society, includes close to thirty volumes. See also, *One Lord, One Church, One Hope, and One God: Mennonite Confessions of Faith*, ed. Howard J. Loewen (Elkhart, Ind.: Institute of Mennonite Studies, 1985). For shorter discussions of Anabaptist-Mennonite faith see C. Norman Kraus, ed., *Evangelicalism and Anabaptism* (Scottdale, Pa.: Herald Press, 1979); and Paul M. Lederach, *A Third Way: Conversations About Anabaptist-Mennonite Faith* (Scottdale, Pa.: Herald Press, 1980).

18. Gregory Baum, "The Anabaptists: Teachers of the Churches," *The Mennonite Reporter* (August 4, 1975). Baum analyzes the forced marginalization and persecution of the Anabaptists as a regrettable and costly loss of the opportunity for mutual religious and theological enrichment. That loss was mainly due to the lack of disposition or of the established churches—both Catholic and Protestant—to listen to the faith of those oppressed and marginalized believers. The point Baum makes is that there is divine revelation in the encounter with the other, particularly with the marginal other. He reflects that the word of God is present in the human word, and that there is a significant transformation of our awareness-revelation in the other brother or sister in the faith. Baum concludes that "what we are discovering today . . . when we reflect on the history of the Anabaptists, is that there is even more divine revelation as we listen to the other oppressed . . . revelation which is so powerful that usually we can't accept it at all" (p. 5). This statement is significant not only for what it says about the Anabaptists, but mainly because it alludes to the so-called epistemological/hermeneutical privilege of the oppressed and marginal, a key liberationist motif (see Schipani, *Religious Education Encounters Liberation Theology*, ch. 5).

19. Any serious attempt to examine and assess the influence of Latin American liberation theology on recent theological reflection in the North American scene should take into account at least the following categories, with representative examples supplied: a) General interpretive appraisals such as McAfee Brown's *Theology in a New Key* and Roger Haight's *An Alternative Vision;* b) critical assessments such as Carl E. Amerding, ed., *Evangelicals and Liberation* (Nutley, N.J.: Presbyterian and Reformed Publishing House, 1977); Ronald H. Nash, ed., *Liberation Theology* (Milford, Mich.: Mott Media, 1984); Shubert M. Ogden, *Faith and Freedom: Toward a Theology of Liberation* (Nashville: Abingdon, 1979); Sacred Congregation for the Doctrine of the Faith, "Instruction on Certain Aspects of the 'Theology of Liberation,' " Appendix, in Roger Haight, *An Alternative Vision*. (For a comprehensive evaluation and response to the Vatican document see Juan L. Segundo, *Theology and the Church: A Response to Cardinal Ratzinger and a Warning to the Whole Church*, trans. John W. Diercksmeier [Minneapolis: Winston, 1985]. The subsequent Vatican's constructive document, "Instruction on Christian Freedom and Liberation," *National Catholic Reporter* [April 25, 1986], pp. 9-44, does not engage liberation theology explicitly. As an essay in Catholic social doctrine, it attempts to present an alternative approach.); c) Studies of a single theme or figure: Alfred T. Hennelly, *Theologies in Conflict: The Challenge of Juan Luis Segundo* (Maryknoll, N.Y.: Orbis Books, 1979); d) Evaluative comparisons between theological perspectives: Dennis P. McCann, *Christian Realism and Liberation Theology* (Maryknoll, N.Y.: Orbis Books, 1981); e) Partial adoption of the liberation perspective in the discussion of classical themes: Daniel L. Migliore, *Called to Freedom: Liberation Theology and the Future of Christian Doctrine* (Philadelphia: Westminster Press, 1980); f) Critico-constructive development of liberation theologies in the North American situation: Frederick Herzog, *Justice Church: The New Function of the*

Church in North American Christianity (Maryknoll, N.Y.: Orbis Books, 1981); Richard Shaull, *Heralds of a New Reformation: The Poor of South and North America* (Maryknoll, N.Y.: Orbis Books, 1984); g) Joint writing/publication projects on special areas: Norman K. Gottwald, ed., *The Bible and Liberation: Political and Social Hermeneutics* (Maryknoll, N.Y.: Orbis Books, 1983); Sergio Torres and John Eagleson, ed., *The Challenge of Basic Christian Communities;* h) Significant appropriation of liberation thought in reshaping certain theological traditions: Nicholas Wolterstorff, *Until Justice and Peace Embrace* (Grand Rapids, Mich.: Eerdmans, 1983).

20. In *The Analogical Imagination* (New York: Seabury, 1981), David Tracy analyzes the public nature of theology and the public roles and functions of theologians. He contends that the three publics of academy, church and society are part of the legitimation for three distinct theological disciplines: fundamental theology, systematic theology and practical theology. Our use of "public" is obviously less rigorous than Tracy's.

21. See, for example, *Evangelicals and Liberation,* ed. Carl E. Armerding, and *Liberation Theology,* ed. Ronald H. Nash. A more dialogical discussion, both in substance and format, is included in *The Challenge of Liberation Theology: A First World Response,* ed. Brian Mahan and L. Dale Richesin.

22. Two prominent Catholic theologians regretfully declined an invitation to write because of being already overcommitted.

23. Liberation theologians stress that *orthopraxis,* rather than orthodoxy, becomes the truth criterion for theology: obeying the Gospel rather than defining, prescribing or defending it. Interestingly enough, this reference to the theological task and mission is analogous to a sixteenth-century Radical Reformation emphasis on the matter, except for the exclusive normativeness of the biblical documents in the case of the Anabaptists. As put in the oft-quoted statement by Hans Denck: "No one may truly know Christ, except he follow him in life" *(mit dem Leben), Schriften, 2 Teil,* ed. Walter Friedmann (Gutersloh, 1956), p. 45. Cornelius J. Dyck has discussed the "epistemology of obedience" of the Anabaptists. See his "Hermeneutics and Discipleship," in *Essays on Biblical Interpretation,* ed. Willard M. Swartley (Elkhart, Ind.: Institute of Mennonite Studies, 1984), pp. 29–44. In the same volume see Ben C. Ollenburger, "The Hermeneutics of Obedience: Reflections on Anabaptist Hermeneutics," pp. 45–61. The clearest parallel statements on the part of liberation theologians are those of Jon Sobrino. In his *Christology at the Crossroads: A Latin American Approach,* trans. John Drury (Maryknoll, N.Y.: Orbis Books, 1978), p. xiii, he states: "The only way to get to know Jesus is to follow after him in one's real life; to try to identify oneself with his own historical concerns; and to try to fashion his kingdom in our midst. In other words, only through Christian praxis is it possible for us to draw close to Jesus. Following Jesus is the precondition for knowing Jesus." For Sobrino and others, theological method derives from the epistemological break consisting of the actual following of Jesus Christ: " 'Method' as road travelled is not found in critical reflection on the road travelled to reach understanding, but in the travelling itself. . . . It is the real following of Jesus that enables one to understand the reality of Jesus, even if this understanding must be explicated by using a plurality of methods, analyses, and hermeneutics. In its deepest meaning, method is understood as content" *(The True Church and the Poor,* p. 23). In other words, Latin American liberation theology conceives of theological method as a real journeying, a contextualized recapitulation of the praxis of Jesus, as it were, rather than merely thinking about that praxis. A number of dualisms are thus overcome such as the separation of process and content and, most important, the radical dualism between theory and praxis, between faith and history.

PART I

PERSPECTIVES ON LIBERATION THEOLOGY

2

The Obedient Disciple: Agent of Liberation (John 8:31-32)

C. HUGO ZORRILLA

INTRODUCTION

The Fourth Gospel presents us with a believing community's response based on the principle of obedient love, to a repressive situation. Understood within this context, "the truth shall set you free" is a statement that reveals participation in a reality that denounces oppression.

This study of John 8:31-32 arises from a concrete situation that emerges from the biblical text, but applies as well to the agonizing reality of millions of persons living in subhuman conditions in Africa, Asia and in Latin America. Liberation is a gift of God to these persons, made old before their time. In Christ Jesus the gift is liberation *from* something. This "something" is every manifestation of sin that denies men and women the right to a human existence. The unmasking of every kind of violence begins when Christ enters history. That is why it is necessary to desacralize the excessive wealth of a few; it is part of the overcoming of all evil.

We must emphasize that behind our text lie these questions: Free from what? and Free for what? After their encounter with Jesus, human beings leave situations of violence and, in obedience, adhere to a historical process that denounces evil as sin and slavery. In this way they become agents of liberation in the midst of conflicts, and their service becomes a sacrificial ministry.

Several steps are necessary to a study of John 8:31-32. The living and contextual dimension of the text must be established, followed by an analysis

Translated by C. Arnold Snyder

of the passage in its constitutive parts, and concluding with a reflection on the pastoral and practical dimension of the biblical text. Three propositions are basic as background to our reflection: 1) In the Gospel of John, Jesus' activity in both word and deed produces life, that is, freedom for the marginalized. 2) The theme of life is essential to an understanding of the kingdom of God; this kingdom comes with Jesus, the absolute Truth who liberates. 3) Following Jesus affects the personal and collective relationships of the disciple. Following Jesus makes the disciple an agent of liberation as Jesus' radical manner of being is incarnated in practice and in lifestyle.

I. CONTEXTUAL DIMENSION

We begin the study of John 8:31-32 by taking into account the living context, which sheds light on the text and its liberating force. This contextual dimension will help outline the limits of the freedom Jesus offers.

A. The Living Context

The text we are considering is located within Jesus' statements during the Feast of Tabernacles and forms part of the aggressive conflict between the Jews and Jesus. The Feast of Tabernacles has its roots in the agricultural era, during which Israel passed from a semi-nomadic phase to a sedentary stage.[1] This feast originated after the liberating experience of the Exodus. It became, together with Passover and Pentecost, one of the three annual pilgrimage feasts for the people of Israel. Its celebration carried a profound mnemonic weight, for it was to help the people remember their time of slavery in Egypt (Deut. 16:12). The feast is associated with living in tents, or with the pilgrimage through the desert for forty years (Lev. 23:39-43). In this way the Exodus is seen as the key to the pilgrimage.

The Feast of Tabernacles, with its symbolism and its liturgy, is the dramatization of Yahweh's historic acts performed for the people. Above all it is liberation that is relived in this feast. The symbolism of this feast of liberation causes one to think theologically of the tents as a prophetic denunciation. Amos, the prophet of justice, denounced the cultic corruptions of Israel, which profaned the name of Yahweh during the autumn festivals just as the idolatrous nations did. In the same way he announced God's judgment for the atrocities committed against the just, the poor and the helpless (2:1-16). Many years later Philo, making reference to the Feast of Tabernacles, said, among other things, that the booths were constructed to signify the precarious nature of life, to recall the pilgrimage in the desert and also so that the rich would remember the poor.[2]

Isaiah alludes to the joy of salvation in an eschatological sense. Yahweh brings salvation, as opposed to those who pillage and act treacherously (33:1), and Isaiah illustrates this in vivid fashion with the figure of the solemn feasts held in the midst of tents that will never be taken down (33:20-24). A very important element, which ties the Feast of the Tabernacles to the coming of the Messiah as liberator, is the fact that the year of Jubilee took place during the Feast of Tabernacles. If we accept the conclusions of Aileen Guilding[3] that Isaiah 61 was read during the Feast of Tabernacles in the year of Jubilee, then Luke 4:16-19 participates in this dual festive event: the Feast of Tabernacles and the year of Jubilee.

Given the profound meaning of liberation these texts carry, we can see that they provide the faithful and inclusive context for John 8:31-32 in the Feast of Tabernacles. Moreover it is no exaggeration, nor do we distort the Johannine text, when we read "liberty for the captives and sight to the blind" (Luke 4:18) in resonance with the great day of the Feast, when the children are freed and the blind man is cured (9:1). The messianic character of these texts indicates that this word has been fulfilled in Jesus, and that as a consequence this affects the social conscience of human beings. It affects the relationships and the manner of life of those who have found their liberty in Jesus.

It is evident that for the Johannine community Jesus is identified with the spirit of the Tabernacles. He "tabernacles" with them (John 1:14), opposing himself to the Temple and to the repression that the Temple represents. He is the living water, the light, the lamb, the liberty. The liturgical tradition of the feast, and above all the great day of the feast (7:37), provide the atmosphere or context for understanding the text in question.

The essential context for John 8:31-32 is permeated by freedom, with all its implications and exigencies. Not only is the year of Jubilee present, but also present is the ideological context of the Exodus, which etymologically refers to "the going out" of a people from an oppressive environment. Semantically "Exodus" is read as synonymous with "liberation." Even more, theologically speaking, the Exodus is seen as representing an "abiding" in the covenant with Yahweh, over and above any service to idols or lords such as Pharaoh.

Another element that forms part of the living and vital background to the text, and which we must take into account in order to understand John 8:31-32, is the dense atmosphere of repression palpable in the Fourth Gospel. This appears at two levels: first, in the public life of Jesus himself; and second, in the life and the actions of his followers, who were no strangers to Judaic persecution. The rupture between the synagogue and the church, in fact, was a key element in the social and theological formation of the Johannine community.[4]

Throughout the Gospel of John there are two parallel and antagonistic thematic lines, one which accepts, the other which rejects Jesus' message in what is a violent and repressive environment (from 1:11 to 20:31). These thematic lines can be synthesized as follows:

Life	=	Peace	=	Light	=	Liberty
Death	=	Violence	=	Darkness	=	Slavery

From the very start (John 1:19) the repressive system of the Jews directed against Jesus also reached his followers. Given the violent atmosphere in which John 8:31-32 is inserted, it is easy to see Jesus' promotion of life, light, peace and freedom, and at the same time to see the antagonism of the Jews, acting as agents of death. With no exaggeration we can see that the antagonism of the Jews reflects the violent position of those who hold the power in their hands.

In this sense we cannot truly understand "the truth shall make you free" without understanding the broad context within which Jesus' disciples incarnated this truth. It is worth noting here the various ways in which institutionalized violence is worked out.

1. There is a clear knowledge of the crime against Jesus. The Jews try to kill him and silence him (5:16-18; 7:30, 32; 7:44ff; 8:40; 10:31, 39). This situation is of public knowledge (7:25, 26) and is even feared by his disciples (11:8, 16).

2. Clearly, all such violence must be legal in order to justify a death. The Jews also do everything according to the law, to the gain of the Temple and taking the empire into account (7:45ff; 11:47; 18:19). There is even a public declaration of submission to the empire (19:12-15).

3. On the other hand, the atmosphere of repression intensifies for Jesus' followers and friends. They are to "abide in his word" (8:31) and, faced with this situation, some who have believed in him experience a crisis (8:30). Others, like Nicodemus, prefer to seek him out in secret (3:1; 7:50; 12:42). Given this perspective we can better understand the meaning of the phrases "in secret" or "for fear of the Jews" (7:13; 9:22, 28, 34; 12:10-11; 12:42-43; 14:27; 15:18-19; 16:1ff.; 19:38). Furthermore, it is quite clear that the Jews play an instigating and intimidating role in seeking out Jesus' disciples (7:47, 52; 18:19).

Jesus' approach, on the other hand, includes a strategy that produces life and complete liberty for those who follow him. What kind of strategy does Jesus employ? Is it a resistance without defense? Is it a secret resistance, or a subversive one? In this Gospel the following points are clear:

1. Jesus denounces the center and chooses the periphery. He is incarnated into the historical reality of the despised. The Jews seek him out, but he chooses the Galileans (the accursed) and the Samaritans (heretics and children of fornication). Whenever they try to kill him he finds refuge, he "seeks asylum" in the lands of the periphery (7:3-4, 10;8:59; 10:40ff.; 11:53, 54).

2. The authorities in Jerusalem, the center of the official religion, with its repressive system and with all the advantage of its ideological and physical resources, will not accept the messiahship of Jesus because he disturbs their consciences (1:11; 10:24). Nevertheless, the heretics (Samaritans) discover his messiahship; they see that the Messiah has been incarnated, that he is one of them, and they accept him (4:40-45). He performs works that generate life, signs that make clear the glory of God. God himself is with the undesirable, the sick, the Samaritans, the paralytics—those whom the dominant ideology has marginalized. He offers them human integrity as the concrete sign of the freedom to which they are entitled as children of God. Jesus' expressions, actions and words indicate denunciation and judgment, but without clear

suggestions of violence. Faced with the violent aggression of the authorities, Jesus does not appeal for the right his servants might have to fight for him. Nevertheless, he does not offer the gift of freedom as an escapist or alienating route, but rather as a reality that affects the daily life of his followers.

Faced with institutionalized violence on one side and revolutionary violence on the other, Jesus refuses to choose. Where would Jesus be placed in the theological world of today? Some believe that he would collaborate with oppression; others that he would be in the reformist camp. For some he would be a conformist and supporter of the status quo; others would say that he was a revolutionary zealot, or a resigned pessimist. Perhaps it is more appropriate to say that he was convinced that the kingdom had to be incarnated as the fullness of life. Jesus formulated an alternative that is still valid today: the concrete practice of incarnate love, a life of service as evidence of the kingdom.

Our people today suffer many forms of violence that amount to slavery. To this Jesus offers life and freedom through the incarnational and sacrificial work of the church. This can be seen throughout the Gospel of John.

1. Faced with the violence of discrimination, Jesus offers his incarnate deeds (chapter 4).

2. Faced with the violence of hunger, Jesus offers bread and the bread of life (chapter 6).

3. Faced with the violence of illiteracy, he offers the teachings of his Father (chapter 7).

4. Faced with the absolutist violence of orthodoxy, he offers his own person as the truth which liberates (chapter 8).

5. Faced with religious violence, he humanizes all persons with messianic signs (chapter 9).

6. Faced with verbal violence, he proclaims the beginning of the judgment of God (chapter 9).

7. Faced with repressive violence, he offers his resistance without defending himself (chapter 10).

8. Faced with inhuman violence, he offers his life (chapter 10).

9. Faced with the abuse of wealth, he offers himself as a servant (chapter 13).

10. Faced with terrorist violence, Jesus gives his peace and his Spirit (chapter 14).

11. Faced with political violence, he announces his absolute reign (chapter 18).

12. Faced with the powers of death, he offers *libertas Dei* as the style of life for living human beings (chapter 8).

B. Narrative Scope

On a structural level we can see that John 8:31-32 belongs to the whole section composed of 7:1 to 10:21, within the narrative of the Feast of Tabernacles where Jesus reveals himself as the liberating Messiah. Seen at less distance, the text belongs to the fourth festive sequence, after the great day of the feast

(8:12-10:21). Looking even closer, we see that the proclamation of liberation is the element that generates the most conflict between Jesus and the Jews (8:31-38).

The evangelist organizes the section "following the great day of the feast" around six small narrative sequences (8:12-20; 21-30; 31-38; 39-47; 48-59; 10:1-21) and he includes two accounts that illustrate the liberating meaning of the christophany within the feast, the revelation of Jesus as giver of life, light and freedom (8:1-11; 9:1ff). The narrator allows the characters to participate, reserving, however, the protagonist's role for Jesus. In this sequence the multitude is absent, and the Jews emerge as more aggressive. There is no doubt that the narrator reinforces his anti-Jewish ideology when he reminds his hearers, in an ample gloss, of the risks Jesus was taking (8:20).

In the former context it has been established that following Jesus produces life, a following the Jews cannot undertake because they do not know Jesus. They belong to the world of death, to a world that seeks to kill Jesus and which creates oppression and darkness, the opposite of Jesus' world of life and freedom. From this it follows that 8:12 is consonant with 8:31-32 and 7:37-38. Within the context of the feast of liberation, light and truth all point to the same reality: God is liberator in the person of Jesus. On the other hand, coming to Jesus, following him and knowing him, all describe the committed attitude of one who, wishing to be Jesus' disciple, remains in his word, which is Jesus himself made flesh, in whom is seen the glory of God.

Furthermore we can see that the person of Abraham is deeply significant, since this is the only time that Abraham is mentioned, and especially because he is mentioned in order to testify to the messianic excellence of Jesus. In this way 8:31-36 demonstrates how to become free and how to become children; 8:37-47 makes the point that the Jews are not true children of Abraham; and 8:48-59 asserts that Jesus predates Abraham.

In this section the narrator allows the Jews and Jesus to characterize their attitudes in a direct discourse. Jesus denounces the murderous aggression of the Jews. In the midst of mounting tension they defend their religious, social, political and racial privileges. The climax of the aggression is reached when Abrahamic legitimacy is defended over against Jesus' decision to be on the side of those who follow him and who accept his offer of freedom. This is why the Jews call him a Samaritan (8:48), not only as a great offense, but also as a tactic meant to discredit his messianic practice of liberation for the poor of the earth *(am-ha'aretz)*.[5] Once Jesus accepts the destiny of the marginalized and despised, he too is marginalized by those who have power, and they seek to kill him (8:37, 40). Jesus' defense is direct and cutting in favor of the poor of the earth. He unmasks those who take their refuge in God in order to repress, and he denounces their idolatry and their murderous slavery (8:42-47).

The elements of the context that follow are organized in chiasmatic fashion, forming a whole which is held together by the central theme of liberation. The structure of John 8:31-36 begins, continues and concludes with this theme.[6] We may note that the liberating proclamation has its counterpart in the denunciation of slavery following the generative question in verse 33c.

A—If you abide in my word then you are truly disciples of mine and you shall know the truth and the truth shall make you free (3lb, 32).
    B—We are Abraham's offspring (33a)
        C—And have never been enslaved to anyone (33b)
            D—How is it that you say: you shall become free? (33c)
        C'—Everyone who commits sin is a slave to sin (34).
    B'—The slave does not remain in the house forever; the son remains forever (35).
A'—If the Son shall make you free, you shall be free indeed (36).

Sections A and A' correspond directly not only because the conditioning conjunction "if" introduces both verses, but also because each has the theme of freedom. The disciple is a free person because of the gracious act of Jesus in response to the disciple's constant fidelity to his word. This parallelism ties the entire section together. Freedom is the basic reality, the point of departure, and the arrival, in the concrete destiny of Jesus.

8:31 A—If you abide in my word
        B—you are truly my disciples
8:36 A'—If the Son shall make you free
        B'—you shall be free indeed

Section B and B' also correspond to each other. The ethnic-nationalist element corresponds by means of the Abrahamic story of the slave and the free woman (Gal. 4:21 ff.). In the same way verses 33a and 35 are held together by the theme of who are authentic children and who illegitimate, who are descendants and who are property. Jesus' words invert the values of those who, like the Jews, consider themselves privileged and with the power to decide the historic relationship of human beings. Those who believe themselves to be free are, from Jesus' point of view, slaves. This inversion of realities can be seen as a dialectical opposition:

Jesus =	in the Abrahamic family	=	permanence	=	free	=	(Isaac)
Jews =	outside the family	=	no permanence	=	slaves	=	(Ishmael)

Concerning sections C and C', the relationship between the Jewish announcement and the denunciation of Jesus revolves around slavery as the chain of sin. The ethnic-nationalist self-sufficiency of the Jews is a collective sin. The text makes no explicit mention of an abstract and ahistorical liberation from sin. On the contrary, both individual and collective sin are mentioned in a context of liberation that affects human beings as persons and as community.

The pivotal verse 33c, in which both parts of the chiasma converge, reveals an ironic nuance that demonstrates stylistically the historical rejection of Jesus. That is to say, it is possible that the Jews do not understand the liberating words and deeds of Jesus. In fact, chapter 8 is a series of misunderstandings. Jesus says something, and the Jews understand it in accordance with their interests and their program of power (8:21, 22, 31, 41, 51-53, 56-58). In this stylistic context, John presents Jesus' words (8:31, 32), which are misunderstood (8:33) and which require Jesus to clarify their meaning (8:34–36).[7]

II. TEXTUAL DIMENSION

A. Redactional Analysis

After having outlined the various hues that color the liberating message of Jesus in the festive and editorial contexts, we now pass to a close examination of the specific text of John 8:31–32.

The perfect tense of the verb "believe" in the 8:31a gloss demonstrates that these Jews had not totally accepted Jesus, and therefore they did not commit themselves to his project of human liberation. We can note a qualitative difference in the manner of believing: one either stands by Jesus or merely promises to.[8] Perhaps this is how we can understand questions such as Who were these Jews? Had they really believed in Jesus? If they had believed in him, why are they now seeking to kill him? Jesus' words show that they were not really his disciples, but rather disciples of Moses, followers of an enslaving order. They had not come to Jesus in order to follow him in all things.

Furthermore, we see the process by which the believing community came to be composed of both his own and the non-disciples, the crypto-Jews and Judaizing leaders. These Jews were not ready to stand in solidarity with the ones with whom Jesus stood in solidarity; that is, they were not ready to stand with the Samaritans and the Galileans, the poor of the earth. Jesus had no intention of seeking members of mere good will, nor was he interested in hearing "That is very interesting" or "I will follow you later." Jesus sought commitment and a sacrificial following, not populist membership.

The perfect participle *pepisteukotas* with its negative nuance helps us understand the immense semantic value of "abide" for the rest of verse 31. Between verses 30 and 31 there is an atmosphere of inconsistency, instability and convenience, all of which contrasts deeply with the liberating weight of an obedient discipleship. Those who believe deeply in Jesus will not be scandalized by his words nor will they turn back (6:66). Others will become fearful at the signs Jesus makes in favor of the poor and will not even dare to walk with him for fear of repression. They prefer the praise of the powerful and the privileges of the system. They remain hidden "for fear of the authorities" or "so that they not be expelled from the synagogue"(12:42-43). It is because of this that Jesus' question, "Do you also want to go away?" (6:67), is such an intense challenge to commitment today as well as in the past. All disciples of Jesus have to decide between obedience or infidelity, permanence or inconstancy, a costly discipleship or a religion of privileges; between a commitment that creates life and the surrender of sacrificial love, or a murderous complicity and a cowardly silence in the face of human injustice.

We can now structure Jesus' words, following the Semitic style, in parallel fashion.

A—If you abide in my word
    B—you are truly disciples of mine
A'—you will know the truth
    B'—and the truth shall make you free.

Rather than individuals satisfied with their own individual religiosity, John presents a group that needs to define itself in terms of its following of Jesus. Sections A and A' correspond to each other in the same way as do B and B': The force of the phrase is carried by the conditional conjunction "if," as is also the case in the chiasma found in 8:37b, 38a. This parallelism forms a complete relationship against a background of obedience, within a context of liberation.

The protasis in the conditional clause puts the emphasis on the prepositional phrase "in me," which is at the same time in clear contrast to the pronoun "you." On the other hand, the apodosis points to the attainable reality of a continual discipleship based on permanence. The adverb "truly" establishes, at the same time, an intimate and complete relationship between the subject and the predicate. The logical implication is that abiding in Jesus means being a disciple. This can be seen clearly in the pronouns *emó* (my) and *mú* (my). Both refer the followers back to Jesus.

The correspondence between A and A' is symmetrical in the sense that the subject of both clauses is the same and the predicates reinforce each other, based on the idea of the word of Jesus and his truth. The conjunction "and" can also function adverbially, thus giving a resultant continuity ("and then") to abiding in the word of Jesus. This knowing is given only to those who already are, and who continue to be, his disciples.

The relationship between A' and B' is a simple one, given its paratactic editing. But there is an interchange in the function of the parts of the clause, held together by the conjunction "and." The subject of A' becomes the predicate of B' and the predicate of A' becomes the subject of B'.

The background, which gives meaning and cohesion to the message of Jesus, is the liberation acquired on the basis of the truth that is appropriated, known and lived by those who have passed from mere recognition to adherence to the word that has transformed them into disciples. This intimate and transforming experience results in their recognition of the reality to be known. Even more, this knowledge will not be attained by those who do not abide in his word. Furthermore, there is no complete freedom without knowledge of the truth in Jesus. And, as has already been seen, since the disciples are free, they become legitimate sons, participating in this way in the messianic promises of the Father. Let it be observed that the message condensed in this parallelism refers back to the subject. *Hymeis* (you) opens the parallelism and *hymas* (to you) closes it. As a result, Jesus' entire action refers back to the disciple.

B. Radical Obedience

Throughout the entire Gospel a separation as clear and open as the sea is maintained: on the one hand stands Jesus' program of liberation, which in itself creates life in abundance; on the other, the repressive program of the Jewish authorities and all that they represent in the world. We face questions such as, What is Jesus seeking from human beings? What response does he expect from those who hear his message? Were not his demands so radical in and of themselves that they already outlined the essence of a radical discipleship? We will examine his motives more closely.

1. ABIDING IN HIS WORK. From the start of the text Jesus is looking for faithful fulfillment on the part of his disciples. The commitment that he expects rests in his word. This abiding is what will lead his disciples from anonymity and a life of hiding to public life and persecution. Jesus himself knows that the world hates him (John 7:7; note the role of the authorities and the Jewish world in John), and that it will also persecute and hate his disciples (16:1-4).

The theme of abiding is central to the Fourth Gospel (it is mentioned forty times in John) and is fundamental for the understanding of radical discipleship. Abiding is not only the motive force behind personal faith in Jesus Christ, but also behind the personal commitment with those who already obey Jesus in the practice of "good works," as opposed to "evil works." These evil works are signs of the hatred and the murderous attempts to which Jesus has been submitted (7:7). As a result, those who abide in him and who walk with him in the light (8:12) do not belong to the world and, it is clear, do not do the works of the world, which generate death. For this reason the world also hates them, with a murderous hatred (15:18, 19; 17:14, 15).

Those who are disciples, as had been said, are free and are children. This is a present reality that has eschatological implications; it stands against the children of the devil (18:34, 44). Abiding requires action in favor of the other, the neighbor. In the same way it defines the diabolical action of those belonging to the evil one. Along this line Ignacio de la Potterie notes a parallelism between 1 John 3:4-9 and John 8:31-47, where Jesus' line of action is clear[9] and where abiding in radical obedience connotes victory over evil and murderous practice (1 John 2:14).

In this way abiding takes on an element synonymous with hearing and living. One who does not abide does not hear, or keep, or live in his word (5:38; 8:51, 55). These realities identify those who are not ready to be disciples. Those who understand the radicality of Jesus' message also receive his words and keep them, not so much as a treasure to be hidden, but rather as a life which becomes liberating practice in love (12:47-48; 14:15).

This abiding, clearly, is reciprocal for Jesus; that is, when we abide in Jesus or in his word, he likewise abides in us (6:56; 15:4). But on the other hand, this reciprocity only clarifies further the opposition of an aggressive world, the world as the sphere of the evil one, the world of those who, since they refuse to believe in him, remain in darkness (8:44; 9:41; 12:46). The requirement of abiding in radical obedience to the directives of Jesus' words creates a direct antagonism for the Jewish disciples. They obey, rather, a brutal and fratricidal project that creates hate, affliction and death (16:2,33). To the contrary, "abiding in my word" has its synonymous counterpart in "abide in my love" (15:9-10) and "abide in me" (15:4-5,7).

Likewise an intimate and interchangeable relationship is established between "my word" and "my commandment" (15:10,12) in the rule of obedient and sacrificial love. José Miranda observes this relationship in John 14:15 and 23 from the perspective of the neighbor, in whom all of Jesus' commandments are synthesized into one.[10] Nevertheless, in a different stratum of Johannine theology it is obvious that Jesus' words constitute an exegesis, an explanation of the love of the Father (1:18). Therefore, abiding in his word requires a radical choosing of all that the Father has planned for the good of humankind. In fact, Jesus himself is the word who manifested, concretely and historically, the glory of God as in the liberating expeditions of the Exodus: God traveled with his people by day in a cloud and by night in a column of fire. To abide does not mean to be static, neutral or immobile; on the contrary, to abide means to assume the radicality of the liberating project of God in favor of an obedient and pilgrimaging people, who continue on until their liberation is consummated.

The lack of commitment to Jesus leads the quasi-disciple to be happy with a casuistic theology that ideologically legitimates any repressive and brutal system. Jewish legalism falsified the commitment to the poor and the marginalized. For the Jews it was more important, it was a matter of life and death, to maintain a calculated system of power and privilege. Healing a blind man, forgiving an adulteress, and denouncing crimes are the "good works" shown by Jesus (10:32). They demonstrate that his Father is the God of the living. The father of those who defend an orthodoxy complicit with repression is a father who does "evil works" or dark signs that manipulate and dehumanize persons, that hijack the Gospel of the kingdom. Consequently, this truth remains hidden and in darkness for those who do not commit themselves to Jesus, for those who prefer to obey the gods of death, bloody idols that falsify the radicality of obedience with the masks of a false morality. Therefore, for those who abide, obedience and faithfulness to the Gospel require a following in announcing and in the unmasking of falsity.

2. TRULY DISCIPLES. We have already seen how closely the adverb relates the predicate to the subject. The disciples are, in actuality, those who follow Jesus' project. Jesus is discovered to be a true prophet because of his works (6:14; 7:40). Those who oppose him side with falsity, unreality, dishonesty. The connection between Jesus and his disciples establishes a genuine quality of following. Furthermore, the continuous reality of being Jesus' disciples directly fulfills the prior condition. The revealing and confronting manifestation of Jesus is seen, from the beginning of the Gospel, as the glory of God, the light in the world that must be followed.

This glorious light is different, in fact it is superior to that of Moses (Ex. 34:29ff.). The works of Jesus are also greater than those of Moses. When Jesus speaks to the Jews, the law of Moses is "your" law. In the same way Jesus' disciples assume a common liberating destiny with their Master, quite opposed and antagonistic to that of the disciples of Moses (9:28). The field of battle shifts from the personal to that of communities with divergent tasks and projects, according to whether Jesus is followed or rejected.

The question then arises, Did Jesus, as a condition of faithful following, demand that one group be opposed to all others? It is very possible. John the Baptist had his disciples, the Jews believed themselves to be disciples of Moses, and Jesus had his disciples. They are the true disciples because they abide in his love, his word and in truth. The context described in 8:31-32 radically colors the concept of discipleship as being not only liberating, but also liberated. It is a discipleship that assumes a pilgrimage of following Jesus and the renunciation of other masters. Jesus cares very much that his followers be true followers, not just because of what awaits them in the world but also because of what has been Jesus' own experience in a hostile and aggressive society.

We do well to observe that, faced with the requirements of a true discipleship, there are those who did not live the Gospel with all its announcing and denouncing. Many of the disciples turned back and no longer believed in Jesus (6:64, 66). Others practiced their discipleship secretly, without risks and without losing their privileges (19:38, 39). It was clear to Jesus that those who committed themselves to him were his friends, his little children, his own sheep. In this sense there is a process of selection or election (15:16) with the aim that they not only abide as his disciples, following his plan, but also that this abiding bring forth permanent works. Thus the Johannine understanding of discipleship indicates that belonging to Jesus means more than a closed set of beliefs; it means to "believe *in*."

Following Jesus is not proposed as a route of escape, but rather as a commitment. This is not an aimless or blind following, but rather a following with the Christian aim to create a permanent life. A discipleship that reflects commitment will demonstrate an intimate and living bond between the disciples and their Master. This cannot be an experience for mere spectators, but rather a discipleship for servants carrying out a labor of pilgrimage in a new Exodus.

In the context of the Feast of Tabernacles this following of disciples indicates a walking in the light. That is, it indicates a behavior, an ethic, a style of light that generates life in an Exodus now led by Jesus, one greater than Moses. The true disciples are also the sheep, whom the good shepherd draws out. They hear his voice and they follow him (10:1ff.). These sheep are the disciples of a new Exodus, followers of liberation. They are not the same as the disciples of Moses. Those are the salaried ones, attackers, robbers. They steal, kill and destroy (10:10). But those who belong to Jesus, we can conclude (since he is life and the giver of life), are also subjects of a creative practice of life and justice, because life is what matters to them. In this sense Jesus and his followers struggled against the idols of death.[11]

3. LIBERATING TRUTH. Knowing the truth is not the result of some academic exercise. Particularly in the compass of our text, and in Johannine theology in general, the truth responds to the practice of service. This practice incarnates the demands of Jesus in favor of those who have been dehumanized. Without a doubt the statement "the truth shall make you free" (8:32) is an attractive one to any ideology with demagogic ends. But recalling the living context in which the text is found, we cannot see any programmatic confusion on Jesus' part concerning what liberation requires. That is, beyond a mere "abiding," the obedient disciple will live out the truth of the liberating life of Jesus. It is very possible that it was impossible for Pilate to discover what Jesus meant by the truth.

It is more than superficial suspicion—there is clear verification in the exegetical history of the text—that leads us to note how the Hellenistic tendency has found support in the interpretation of "the truth shall make you free." We see this above all in the "official" theologies which, lacking any evangelical practice against injustice, have placed a Christian mask over structures that create injustice. How many crimes today are committed against human beings in the name of truth by means of repressive projects camouflaged by a manipulated "freedom"? That is why within the believing community the truth becomes a space where the cry of anguish is listened to. Even more, the God who acts in history to liberate the poor threatens the unjust idols and systems because the marginalized unmask them in the truth of Jesus. In their announcing they become the interpreters of inhuman reality; their cries become a subversive denunciation, because they are seen to be true.

In the context of John, we understand truth as colored by the surrounding Jewish world. Nevertheless, it is clear that the dualism truth/falsity is not exhausted by a gnostic understanding. The gnostic tendency has been to say that liberation is achieved by knowledge conceived as a spiritual experience. This is a clear rejection of the body, and assumes that the world is something bad, like a jail for humankind.[12]

The truth for John is Jesus himself, and all that he represents as the one sent by the Father. He brings grace and truth in opposition to Moses (1:14–17). In the context of John, the truth for Jesus' disciples is the reason for freedom. On the other hand, the disciples of Moses are the cause of anti-liberation because of their legalism. If Jesus is the liberating truth of the Father, this is understood as the historic revelation and manifestation of the salvific will and testament of God with the living.[13] This underlines, logically, the liberating function of the kingdom of God.

Another perspective for seeing this truth, again through John's eyes, is the concreteness that Jesus gives to truth "from below," from the history of his incarnation among human beings, and not from an ahistorical and absolute divine perspective, as hegemonic ideologies would have it. God enters history through a people on pilgrimage. Jesus seeks obedient disciples who will be subjects of his salvific history. This experience relativizes all that the world, with its "evil works," believes to be absolute. At the same time it absolutizes the life of oppressed human beings. From the time of their encounter with Jesus, the merciful and faithful one, the disciples commit themselves to promote a plan of liberation with concrete acts of love in favor of the poor and marginalized.

III. THE PASTORAL DIMENSION

The process initiated by the transforming encounter with Jesus leads to a radical discipleship which, in turn, passes through a commitment and a living together in the truth, following the demands of the kingdom. This process takes place without hesitation, and in a liberating way, when the truth is not merely said, but also lived. The truth which liberates is fulfilled in Christian practice.

Truth and justice take on a pastoral dimension among the poor in their many contexts. The aim is not the use of persons, but rather the development of a pastoral dynamic of free human beings who, in obedience to God, make their own history. The gift the believer as disciple receives from Christ results in a discipleship made concrete in works of love. These are the signs of life, proof that one does not belong to the world. If he or she does not belong to this world, the disciple is sanctified in that truth of Christ (17:17).

This leads us to assert that, for John, liberation enters history with the taking on of the pastoral task presented by the poor of the world. The position of the obedient disciple is clear. His practice does not aim at wordiness, or metahistorical or metaphysical investigations. Neither does the disciple pursue an interiorization, which distances and estranges him from the neighbor. The spirituality inherent in the work of the disciple results in his ethic being Jesus' ethic, in his works being Jesus' works. In the same way that Jesus became "kind faithfulness" and performed works of truth, the disciple also practices the truth (3:21). In this way we know the criterion for identifying the true disciple, the one who walks in the truth, the one who gives his life for his friends, the one who is not a slave to sin, the one who is a free child. The criterion is the practice of justice (1 John 2:29) in concrete situations of abundance, opulence and murderous hatred (1 John 3:7ff.; 17-18).[14]

This is not a matter of some isolated acts performed as publicity "hooks" or "come-ons." It is clear that there is a plan with a communitarian direction and manner within the demands of the kingdom of God. Egoism and individualism are for those who wish to walk in darkness. This communitarian pastoral is also a solid and distinctive Anabaptist inheritance.[15]

Obedient discipleship should also become a missionary task of the underprivileged, directed from the poor of the earth toward the Christianity of the wealthy countries, which serves as ideology for those who have discovered how to coldly systematize the misery of human persons. Many Christians are so hypnotized by a faith of prosperity and success that they cannot discover their own complicity with unjust social structures. In this sense, as Ronald Sider put it, "social evil is just as displeasing to God as personal evil. And it affects more people and is more subtle."[16]

As is true in any Babylon—it is only right that we recognize this—the context of opulence and waste has numbed the consciences of many people who do not want to risk their comfortable faith. They no longer *do* the truth, but rather enjoy the privileges of power.[17] With their silence they become accomplices of a genocidal state. They simplify the Gospel and reduce the Christian faith so that it legitimizes as absolutes the sovereignty of the state, institutionalized violence, free trade and prosperity, with little regard for human life.

Within a radical discipleship the necessity of a ministry that favors the majorities leads to a way of "seeing" and "reading" the Gospel of the kingdom in a different way than the traditional idealism. This new hermeneutic of obedience becomes concrete within a practice or a theology of the road, within an Abrahamic community. In this same way God is evangelizing the world through the oppressed community, to establish a theology of liberation; God's word is "read" with the depth of the liberating practice of a faithful people who follow freely, with hope.[18]

The many contexts in which a ministry of faithful disciples enters history leads to ministries full of possibilities for service, which in turn demonstrate their liberating and eschatological character. Only the disciple can know the true repercussions of his or her Christian practice. The disciple surrenders to the truth of Christ, enthralled by the future promise of liberation. That is why what is realized today is outlined on the horizon of hope.

CONCLUSION

The truth is realized and put into practice in obedience and love. Liberation and becoming children are the consequences of an obedient faith and a sacrificial love. The truth of Christ concretized in his kingdom is absolute. Disciples, in this perspective, discover that the historicity of Jesus helps them to discern the truth of God in the truths of the world, and to relativize the actions of those who, from their position of power and comforted by what they take to be the truth, massacre the marginalized peoples. We have here a distorted vision of the world, treated as if it were an absolute. The "small truths" of the oppressors lead to evil works. Even more, the impudent masking has reached such a point that "the world" absolutizes a genocidal and oppressive ideology. This is the logical consequence of a manipulation of faith. Today this manipulation has become so severe that peace, life and humankind itself seem to be gifts given by those who dominate rather than gifts of God and of life. Unjust systems today repress many millions of human beings, and at the same time believe that they are doing God a favor. Such is their "truth," their inhuman ideology, that they give the impression that God must be well pleased with them—just as the Jews sought Jesus and the Christians to kill them, thinking that they would be doing God a service thereby (John 16:2).

Those who serve other gods, idols and murderous structures have no future because they are slaves; they have no history because their past has been manipulated by the agents of oppression. In the face of a modern society, which at the close of a century is losing its sense of the future; in the face of a technical society, which every day discovers more brutal forms of repression; in the face of ideologies, which, like sirens' songs create false hopes, the words of Jesus still apply: "The truth shall make you free." But behind these words lies the challenge of making Jesus' commandment concrete by means of an obedient discipleship.

NOTES

1. Many of my affirmations regarding this are treated in C. Hugo Zorrilla, *La fiesta de los oprimidos: Relectura de Jn. 7. 1-10.21* (San José: SEBILA, 1981).

2. Philo, *De Specialibus Legibus,* 33, 2, pp. 208-9.

3. Aileen Guilding, *The Fourth Gospel and Jewish Worship, A Study of the Relation of St. John's Gospel to the Ancient Jewish Lectionary* (Oxford: Clarendon Press, 1960), p. 110. In a creative way Thomas Hanks does a study of the year of Jubilee: "Isaiah 58, The Jubilee Year and Our Central American Colonies," *God So Loved the Third World: The Biblical Vocabulary of Oppression, Part 3* (Maryknoll, NY: Orbis Books, 1983).

4. Louis Martyn, "Glimpses into the History of the Johannine Community," in M. de Jonge, *L'Evangile de Jean, Bibliotheca Ephemeridum Theolgicanum Lovainiensium* 49 (1975), p. 168. Along this line Raymond E. Brown establishes that a more developed christology lends itself to the violent expulsion of the Johannine Christians from the synagogue *(The Community of the Beloved Disciple* [New York: Paulist Press, 1979], pp. 40ff). Also see Zorrilla, p. 147ff.

5. Zorrilla, pp. 140ff.

6. M. E. Boismard A. Lamouille, *L'Evangile de Jean* (Paris: Les Editions du Cerf, 1977), p. 233; J. Tuñi, *La verdad os hará libres: Jn. 8:32* (Barcelona: Herder, 1973), p. 126; H. Zorrilla, p. 175.

7. Alan Culpepper, *Anatomy of the Fourth Gospel* (Philadelphia: Fortress Press, 1983). The detailed study of this stylistic aspect where the dialogue separates into a misunderstanding is pursued on pages 161ff.

8. The difference in meaning of the text between to believe in Jesus (v. 31) with dative and to believe in Jesus (v. 30) with accusative should not be insisted upon. Both expressions can be used interchangeably. See R. E. Brown, *The Gospel According To John* (Garden City, NY: Doubleday, 1978), 1, p. 354; J. H. Bernard, *Gospel According to St. John* (Edinburgh: T & T Clark, 1976), 2, p. 30; R. Bultmann, *The Gospel of John* (Philadephia: The Westminster Press, 1976), p. 433; B. Lindars, *The Gospel of John* (Grand Rapids, Mich.:Eerdmans, 1972), p. 323.

9. Ignacio de la Potterie, *La verdad de Jesús* (Madrid: BAC, 1979), p. 31.

10. José Miranda, *El ser y El Mesías* (Salamanca: Sígueme, 1973 [English trans.: *Being and the Messiah* (Maryknoll, N.Y.: Orbis Books, 1977)]). Here I follow the original Spanish version, pages 130, 131. R. E. Brown, *The Gospel According to John,* p. 765.

11. Jon Sobrino, "The Epiphany of the God of Life in Jesus of Nazareth," in Pablo Richard *et al., The Idols of Death and the God of Life: A Theology* (Maryknoll, NY: Orbis Books, 1983), p.68.

12. Tuñi, pp. 32ff. C. H. Dodd indicates the tendency of platonic philosophy which sees truth as synonymous with reality in *The Interpretation of the Fourth Gospel,* 2 (Cambridge: University Press, 1968).

13. De la Potterie, p. 19.

14. John H. Yoder, *The Politics of Jesus* (Grand Rapids, Mich: Eerdmans, 1972), pp. 115ff.

15. Walter Klaassen, "The Meaning of Anabaptism," *Mennonite Brethren Herald* (Jan. 24, 1975), p. 7.

16. Ronald J. Sider, *Rich Christians in an Age of Hunger* (Downers Grove: InterVarsity Press, 1977), p. 137.

17. Walter Klaassen, "The Meaning of Anabaptism," *The Christian Leader* (March 4, 1975), p. 4.

18. Ben Ollenburger, "The Hermeneutics of Obedience," in *Essays on Biblical Interpretation: Anabaptist-Mennonite Perspectives,* ed. Willard Swartley (Elkhart: Institute of Mennonite Studies, 1984), p. 59; Julio De Santa Ana, *Towards A Church of the Poor* (Maryknoll, NY: Orbis Books, 1979), p. 165.

3

Liberation Theology: An Appraisal

C. RENÉ PADILLA

The task of defining and evaluating liberation theology is an impossible one. This is so not only because of the obvious limitations of a paper, but also because strictly speaking liberation theology does not exist. The term is useful in referring briefly to a wide variety of theologies sharing common characteristics, but the heterogeneity of theological positions associated with the term must not be overlooked.

One possible approach to our subject would be to describe the emphasis that liberation theologies have in common. We have, however, preferred to concentrate on what may be regarded as the distinctive mark of all liberation theologies, namely, their understanding of theology as a reflection upon that which is *done* rather than merely *believed*.

Already in the early seventies Gustavo Gutiérrez, one of the foremost liberation theologians in Latin America, claimed that liberation theology proposes "not so much a new topic for reflection as a *new way* of doing theology"[1] that takes as its starting point a "historical praxis" through which the world is to be transformed into a new society. At the end of the same decade Andrew Kirk affirmed that "the real novelty of the theology of liberation lies in its methodological approach."[2]

The agreement between the two authors, one an advocate and the other a critic of liberation theology, goes a long way to explain our own effort to view this theology from the perspective of its emphasis on praxis as the first theological reference point. We shall first endeavor to understand this "methodological approach" (Part I) and will then proceed to make a critical evaluation of it from our own perspective (Part II).

I. "A NEW WAY OF DOING THEOLOGY"

According to Gustavo Gutiérrez, theology has traditionally had two tasks. In the early church, theology was seen as *wisdom* and consisted primarily in a

Bible meditation for the sake of spiritual progress. Later on, beginning in the twelfth century, it was seen as *rational knowledge,* a science. Both views, claims Gutiérrez, point to permanent tasks of theology.[3] Today, however, they have been superseded by the view of theology as *critical reflection on praxis.* To be sure, such an understanding of theology is not totally new—Augustine's *The City of God,* for instance, begins with an analysis of the signs of the times and moves on to a consideration of their implications for the Christian community. Today, however, there is a rediscovery of the centrality of "historical praxis," and this has in turn resulted in a rediscovery of the role of theology as critical reflection on historical praxis. Theology thus becomes

> . . . necessarily, a critique of society and the church, inasmuch as they are summoned and questioned by the word of God; a critical theory, in the light of the word accepted by faith, with a practical intention in view and, consequently, indissoluably united to a historical praxis.[4]

The implications of this approach to theology may be summarized in the following points: 1) A "historical praxis" is a *conditio sine qua non* for doing theology; 2) the "historical situation" is the starting point for theological reflection; 3) the understanding of present historical reality with the help of the social sciences is an essential aspect of the theological task; and 4) theological reflection inevitably takes on ideological forms. We shall briefly examine each of these tenets, making an effort to let liberation theologians speak for themselves.

A. *The Priority of Praxis*

A basic assumption of liberation theology is that the true knowledge of God is equivalent to the doing of God's will. According to Míguez Bonino, two blocks of biblical material confirm this approach, namely, the prophetic literature in the Old Testament and the Johannine writings in the New Testament. For both of them, says Míguez, the knowledge of God is not theoretical or abstract knowledge but active obedience to God's concrete demands.[5] Obedience is our knowledge of God. "We do not know God in the abstract and then deduce from his essence some consequences. We know God in the synthetic act of responding to his demands."[6] From this perspective historical praxis always takes priority over theologizing. As Gutiérrez puts it, "Theology comes *afterward,* it is the second act."[7] Consequently, a theological position is not to be validated in terms of agreement with timeless truths, but in terms of its efficacy in relation to a concrete historical project. "In the end, in fact, the true interpretation of the meaning uncovered by theology is shown in the historical praxis."[8] Historical verification is thus seen as the only possible verification for theology.

What, then, is the purpose of theology? As the *critical* reflection on historical praxis, theology is the handmaid of pastoral action. By taking up the questions raised in the world, it fulfills a critical function in relation to the church; by going back to the sources of revelation it prevents pastoral action from falling into activism; by interpreting the "signs of the times" and proclaiming their meaning it performs a prophetic role and makes the liberating involvement of Christians more radical and more lucid. It thus points to the future with the view to transforming the present.[9]

B. The Historical Situation as the Starting Point

Where does theological reflection begin? If theology is the critical reflection on historical praxis, it has to begin with the concrete situation where faith is to be lived out in terms of action. The historical situation is, therefore, the starting point. As Hugo Assmann has put it,

> The "text" . . . is our situation. This is the "first theological reference point." The other reference points ("loci theologici," Bible, tradition, magisterium, history of the doctrines), even though all of them require an ever actualized praxis, are not the first reference pole of a "sphere of truths in itself" unconnected to the historical "now" of truth-praxis.[10]

In Latin America, as in the rest of the Third World, the situation is marked by the overwhelming presence of the poor, who are perceived as "nonpersons." If theology is to respond to questions that people raise within their own context, it cannot avoid the questions posed by these "nonpersons." According to Gutiérrez, the problem for theology in this situation is not, "How can God be proclaimed in a world which has become adult?" but rather, "How can God be proclaimed as Father in an inhuman world? What does it mean to tell the nonperson that he is a son of God?"[11] A call to resignation in the face of oppression and exploitation is totally inadequate; theology must never be used as a mere camouflage to cover up injustice. The task of theology is, rather, to help Christians in their struggle to create a new society characterized by justice and freedom.

The fulfillment of this task, however, requires both a "reading" of our situation with its social, political, economic and cultural dimensions, and a reading of the Bible from the perspective of solidarity with the poor. In other words it requires a "hermeneutic of liberation" in which the Bible is read, in Raúl Vidales' words, "from that 'other' Bible, namely, history,"[12] and its revolutionary power is released into our situation. Liberation theology thus proposes a "hermeneutical circulation" between two "texts" in dynamic interplay. When this circulation is appropriate, says Severino Croatto, the question as to whether theological reflection should go from the text to the historical situation or from the historical situation to the text becomes irrelevant, for the two itineraries are then simultaneous:

> What allows us to "enter" into the meaning of the text is the present event; therefore, even when one begins with the biblical text, he is "preunderstanding" it from his own existential situation, which we Latin Americans know what it is.[13]

C. The Use of Social Sciences

As already has been suggested, in this "new way of doing theology" the "reading" of the historical situation plays an important role. The use of the social sciences is therefore incorporated into the hermeneutical task. Juan Luis Segundo detects at this point "the fundamental difference" between an academic theologian and a liberation theologian, for

> the liberation theologian is compelled at each step to put the disciplines which open up the past together with the disciplines which open up the present, and to do that in the elaboration of theology, that is, in his attempt to interpret the word of God addressed to us, here and now.[14]

Hugo Assmann goes even further and claims that theology is not only "the second act," which follows the first act of praxis, but also "the second word," which follows the first word of the social sciences.[15]

The rationale behind the use of the social sciences is mainly that if theology is to be liberating, it cannot be limited to the study of the sources of revelation (which, at any rate, is historically conditioned); it requires rational criteria to judge the validity of praxis. The day is past when Christians could be satisfied with an idealistic love; we now have the tools to analyze social reality and to make love efficacious through political action.

It is at this point that the tools of Marxist socio-economic analysis become important for liberation theology. In contrast with functionalist sociology Marxist sociology provides a global diagnosis of historical reality; it shows the dynamics that operate within the social structures and throws into relief the *causes* (not just the phenomenon) of poverty in the Latin America context. Thus, with the help of Marxism, it becomes clear that the existence of the poor is not due to fate, but the result of a system of injustice. In Gutiérrez's words, "the poor is the oppressed, the exploited, the proletarian, the one deprived of the fruit of his labor, the one whose humanity has been despoiled."[16] And once that is seen, the conclusion is unavoidable that what is needed is not economic development but a totally new social order. If oppression-dependency is the real problem, the answer is not development but liberation. Unless the system is changed, development will only benefit the oppressors. Only revolution will bring in a different society where a more authentic human existence will be possible.

The "theory of dependence," according to which the underdevelopment of the poor nations is "the historical product of the development of other nations,"[17] is accepted by liberation theology as a scientific key essential to the understanding of Latin American reality. Its advocates will of course admit that, like any other analysis of social, economic and political reality, it is subject to correction or revision. They would insist, however, that at present it is the best available instrument to analyze the situation. In Oliveros's words, "Up to now the theory of dependence provides the widest and most global interpretation of the heavy weight afflicting our nations."[18]

The liberation theologians claim that in its analysis of social reality Marxist sociology provides a rational way to make love historically efficacious. Love, if it is not accompanied by an adequate understanding of the real dynamics of society, can easily fall prey to the interest of the oppressors. In order for love to be operative on the historical plane—a plane where humankind is summoned to act as free agent, the master of its own destiny—love needs a historical mediation as objective and concrete as possible. Since we live in today's world, we cannot simply reproduce biblical models. We must therefore make use of that sociology which will enable us to articulate love historically.

D. *Theology and Ideology*

According to the Marxist socio-economic analysis, the poor are poor because the rich exploit them. Society is thus marked by a polarity between the social class of the oppressed and the social class of the oppressors. There is a *class struggle*. It follows that one cannot side with the poor without siding *for* one social class and *against* another. Neutrality at this point is impossible; social conflict is a fact and "there is nothing more solid than a fact."[19] The attempt not to take sides is in fact a decision to leave the situation unchanged, which means siding with the oppressors. "Forging a just society today necessarily involves a conscious and active participation in the class struggle which is taking place before our eyes."[20]

Looking at the problem of social conflict from a global perspective, siding with the poor today concretely means, according to liberation theology, siding for socialism and against capitalism.[21] Should anyone object to the option between capitalism and socialism being imposed on theology, the answer is that if faith cannot enable us to choose a desirable socio-political system—if faith cannot be historically verified—it is useless. The effort to relate the word of God to political events, says Juan Luis Segundo, goes back to the prophets as well as to Jesus. So any theology that fails to do that, with the claim that socialism gives no assurance of a better future, clearly abandons its prophetic function and is out of line with Jesus' "historical sensitivity" toward "the signs of the times." In today's world the option between capitalism and socialism is a *crux theologica,* and theology cannot remain neutral as if the left and the right were simply two sources of social projects to be judged by a reason exactly located at an equal distance between the two. Because of its openness to the future, leftist historical sensitivity is "an intrinsic element of an authentic theology" and it should be "a necessary form of reflection in which historical sensitivity has become a key."[22]

The liberation theologians are certainly aware that in taking sides with the oppressed they leave themselves open to the accusation of partiality. They respond that their partiality has been consciously accepted on the basis of human criteria for the sake of "the obedience of faith" in a concrete historical situation. If theology is *fides quaerens intellectum*—faith seeking understanding—for the purpose of historical praxis, it cannot avoid taking sides. A faith without an ideological mediation is dead because it is historically irrelevant. In Segundo's words, "Faith is not an ideology, that is true, but it only makes sense as a founder of ideologies."[23] If theology does not consciously accept its partiality, liberation theologians add, it should be "unmasked" as an ideological expression of the self-interest of the bourgeoisie.

Here again, the need of a hermeneutic that integrates the use of sociological analysis becomes obvious. Accordingly, Juan Luis Segundo has proposed a "hermeneutical circle" in which four elements are taken into account: 1) our way of experiencing reality, which leads us to ideological suspicion; 2) the application of this suspicion to the "ideological superstructure" in general and to theology in particular; 3) a new way of experiencing theological reality, which leads us to "exegetical suspicion," that is, the suspicion that the usual biblical interpretation does not take into account important data; and 4) a new hermeneutic, that is, a new way to interpret Scripture, which includes all the new elements gained in the process.[24] The point of the circle is not the formulation of theology *per se* but the articulation of a liberating theology, a theology which will necessarily be *partial,* for in it the word of God will be "that part of revelation which today, in view of our concrete historical situation, is more useful for the liberation to which God is calling us and pushing us."[25] If we understand the hermeneutical circle, adds Segundo, we will also understand that Latin American liberation theology is partial precisely because "it is faithful to Christian tradition and not to Greek thought"; and that those who attack it because of its partiality are even more partial, without knowing it, for "they make of a part of Scripture not only the word of God for that time or other similar times, but for all times, thereby by their partiality choking the word of God."[26]

II. A CRITICAL EVALUATION

I can hardly attempt an evaluation of liberation theology without the feeling of standing face to face with a passionate prophet-theologian who right at the outset confronts me with a saying of Jesus: "Anyone who is not for me is really against me; anyone who does not help me gather is really scattering" (Matt. 12:30). Quite clearly the theological discourse with which I am confronted is not an academic dissertation but a prophetic message. The purpose is not to inform me or to propound theories that I may freely accept or reject but to shake me out of complacency and to call me to repentance. I am not invited to consider a new and interesting theological theory but challenged to come to terms with my need of making the faith relevant to my historical context.

As a person trained in the ways of doing theology in North America and Europe, I could easily take refuge in that set of arguments with which Anglo-Saxon theologians and others have assailed liberation theology: that it has Marxist leanings; that it espouses violence; that it reduces the Gospel to sociology, economics or politics; that its use of the Bible is too selective; that it is partisan and therefore destroys the universality of the Gospel; or that it is too contextually conditioned.[27] I will not use these arguments too quickly, however, lest I fail to face the challenge not only of liberation theology, but also, and primarily, of the poor with whom liberation theology has sided. The question for me is not, How do I *respond* to liberation theology, so as to show its flaws and incongruities? but rather, How do I articulate my faith in the same context of poverty, repression and hopelessness out of which liberation theology has emerged?

Because of my own family background as well as because of my confession of Jesus Christ as my Lord and Savior, I cannot be satisfied with the use of arguments that will get me off the hook. Fully accepting the challenge of people committed to "the view from below," I now offer the following critical evaluation of their theological methodology as an honest attempt to see the implications of liberation theology for my own life and ministry.

A. Liberation Theology Rightly Emphasizes the Importance of Obedience (Praxis) for the Understanding of Truth, but Is in Danger of Pragmatism

Theology in Europe and North America has been, by and large, an academic exercise. It has assumed the possibility of a "pure theology" that is derived from Scripture (and perhaps Tradition) and "systematized" or "applied" to practical, ethical problems. In other words it has assumed the possibility of a knowledge of truth separated from the *practice* of truth. As a result revelation has been reduced to the communication of divine truths and faith has been intellectualized.

Liberation theology is undoubtedly correct in criticizing this rationalistic approach to theology. From a biblical perspective, God's *logos* has become a historical person and the knowledge of this *logos*, therefore, is not merely an intellectual knowledge of ideas, but commitment, fellowship and participation in a new way of life. Gospel truth is always truth to be lived out, not merely truth to be intellectually known. "A correct knowledge depends on a correct action. Better, knowledge is manifest in the doing."[28] Accordingly the theological task, which is in essence a hermeneutical task, from beginning to end has as its purpose "the obedience of faith."[29] If Scripture is inspired by God and useful for teaching, rebuking, correcting and training in righteousness, "so that the person who serves God may be fully qualified and equipped to do every kind of good deed"(2 Tim. 3:16), the purpose of theology can never be any less practical than that. Theology should therefore be liberated from its rationalistic framework and become a servant to the word of God.

This emphasis on the existential dimension of truth, however, should not blind us to the pitfall of pragmatism. If there is no possibility of evaluating praxis on the basis of a norm outside praxis itself, the way is open for the justification of any praxis as long as it works; the end justifies the means. The answer could be that from the point of view of liberation theology the reflection on praxis is "in the light of faith." Assmann, in fact, maintains that "for a critical reflection on praxis to be theology, there must be the distinctive mark of the reference to faith and to the historical mediation of this faith (the Bible and the history of Christianity).[30]

But, then, how is faith to serve as a criterion to evaluate praxis, unless there is in it a cognitive content outside praxis itself? If theology is a reflection on praxis in the light of faith, but faith is, as Assmann claims, "historical liberating praxis,"[31] then theology is reflection on praxis in the light of praxis. Juan Luis Segundo recognizes the problem when he writes:

> If the Christian contribution is hung, as it were, from a prior revolutionary commitment, this latter appears hung, as it were, from a correct, non-deviationary, evaluation of socio-political praxis. One preunderstanding presupposes another. Do they not, then, enter into a circle?[32]

Again, if political relevance is the only criterion for the verification of theology, what is the truth content of a liberation theology that in a context of military repression (to mention only one historical limitation) is rendered totally unable to bring about the liberation of the poor and the oppressed? Granted that the historical verification of Christianity is not merely a question of apologetics, since "the meaning of Christianity cannot be abstracted from its historical impact—for good or evil,"[33] does that mean that biblical revelation has nothing to offer in terms of criteria to test our historical praxis? If so, there is no way for one as a Christian to discern whether one is a faithful disciple committed to Jesus Christ as Lord, or merely the upholder of a new law, committed to a particular political program.

Furthermore, the "praxeological" approach to theology implies the view that since Christian commitment, related to biblical revelation, plays no part in the Christian's understanding of reality, one's historical praxis depends entirely on a "scientific analysis" and science is the domain of a human reason autonomous from faith. Such a view, however, presupposes an *objectivistic concept of science,* according to which the scientific enterprise is conceived as dealing with facts and yielding pure, objective, impersonal knowledge, and a *subjectivistic concept of revelation,* according to which the knowledge of God is seen exclusively in terms of an existential encounter. It needs to be corrected by a recognition of two facts: 1) that there is no science without presuppositions (and, therefore, no self-authenticating analysis of reality);[34] and 2) that the knowledge of God has a belief-content, although it cannot be identified with believing certain things.[35] Unless these two facts are acknowledged, there is no possibility of evaluating one's praxis without entering into a vicious circle and, consequently, no possibility of theology as a reflection on praxis "in the light of faith." That the Christian cannot avoid evaluating praxis on the basis of criteria derived from biblical revelation is conceded by Míguez Bonino when he writes that

> Christian obedience, certainly understood as historical praxis and therefore incarnate in a historical mediation (rational, concrete) embodies,

however, a dimension which, to use christological language, cannot be separated nor confused with it. In other words, how is the historical praxis of a Christian affected by the original (or, better said, "germinal") events of the faith, namely, God's acts in Israel, the birth, life, death and resurrection of Jesus Christ, the hope of the Kingdom? If on this point we are condemned to remain silent, we are really resigning any attempt to speak of such a praxis as *Christian* obedience.[36]

If the "germinal events of the faith" are to affect praxis, reflection on Scripture is as essential to the theological task as reflection on praxis. Naturally, this reflection will have to take place in the context of a personal relationship with God, since its purpose is not merely the intellectual knowledge of revealed truth but the obedience of faith. Yet the facts of biblical revelation are also solid facts, and we ought to reflect on them in order to deepen our understanding of their significance for life here and now. We know in the extent to which we obey (and that is the existential side of truth), but we are better able to obey in the extent to which we know God's commandments, promises and judgments revealed in Scripture (and that is the cognitive side of truth).

God's *logos* is an incarnate *logos,* but he is also a *logos* who has spoken, and his words (his *rhemata*) are spirit and life (see John 6:63). One cannot understand Jesus' teaching unless one is willing to do God's will (see John 7:17); therefore, those who are not willing to hear—to obey—his message *(logos)* are not able to understand his words *(lalia)* (John 8:43). Thus, there is no understanding without commitment.

The fact remains, however, that there is a message (a *logos*) to be obeyed and understood. *Doing* the truth is not equivalent to *making* the truth through praxis, but to *practicing* the truth, which has been given us through revelation. Knowing the truth is not merely a question of exegesis, but since the *logos* has been historically given and inscripturated, the exegetical task is never optative. The obedience of faith—praxis—does not take place *despite* biblical texts but in dialogue with them in their concrete historicity. If theology is to serve praxis, and praxis is faith working through love, theology will have to be both a critical reflection on praxis *and* a critical reflection on the word of God which is addressed to faith *at the same time.* Theology reflects on praxis—the concrete, historical obedience of faith—and it reflects on the word of God—God's revelation which calls into being and nourishes faith. *Fides quaerens intellectum,* but the understanding that faith seeks results from the convergence between the knowledge of God's truth inscripturated in the Bible and the knowledge of God's truth incarnate in history. The Christian faith is not a *gnosis* but a "way of life"—yet not *any* way of life, but one informed by the word of God.

The conclusion is thus that, if theology is to be a critical reflection on praxis in the light of faith, the hermeneutical circulation between the past and the present—between Scripture and the historical situation—is unavoidable. The answer to both a rationalistic theology concerned with orthodoxy and a pragmatic theology concerned with orthopraxis is a contextual theology concerned with faithfulness to the word of God and relevance to the historical situation at the same time.

B. Liberation Theology Rightly Emphasizes the Importance of the Historical Situation, but Is in Danger of Historical Reductionism

Theology in Europe and North America has generally remained insulated from socio-political reality, indifferent to the needs and the suffering of the poor. Affected by the privatization of religion, which marks the West,[37] it has taken flight into a conceptual world where the cry of the people is never heard.

Liberation theology has rightly criticized this posture. Biblical revelation is a historical revelation; the Christian cannot avoid the question regarding the historical relevance of faith. As Gutiérrez has put it, "The proclamation of a God who loves all men without discrimination must become embodied in history, it must become history."[38] If God is relegated to the "spiritual" aspect of human life, and salvation is totally outside the historical realm, it is virtually the salvation of a spiritual monad. In contrast with this spiritualistic view, Scripture sees the person as a unitary human being in whom body and soul are inseparable. Nobody exists as a disembodied soul.

Furthermore, the God of the Bible is not merely a God who *acted* in history; God is the One who *continues to act* in history. If theology is to be faithful to Scripture, therefore, it cannot simply be "theology of the Word"; it has to be "theology of the Word *made flesh*." And in the context of poverty and oppression, theology, as well as preaching and education, must be liberating—it must be a denunciation of systemic evil and an annunciation of God's kingdom of justice and righteousness. In Gutiérrez's terms,

> It is not enough to say that God reveals himself in history and consequently the faith of Israel has a historical structure. It is necessary to take into account that the God of the Bible is not only a God who rules over history, but who orients history towards the establishment of justice and righteousness. He is more than a providential God; he is a God who sides with the poor and liberates them from slavery and oppression.[39]

When the situation is regarded as "the text," "the first theological reference point," however, the way is open for the subordination of the word of God to the human context. A "canon within the canon" is created and the kingdom of God is reduced in order to fit into history. As a result, Scripture is read selectively; it is thus allowed to speak only in relation to a concrete historical situation and a concrete historical project, a situation that has been interpreted and a project that has been conceived on the assumption that the word of God has nothing to contribute to these rational tasks. The concentration of hermeneutics on ethics and politics thus results in a theology that does an injustice to the totality of biblical revelation. Whatever is not in keeping with the interests of praxis is set aside as irrelevant.

It is not by accident that liberation theology is extremely inadequate when it comes to questions that have no immediate bearing on politics or point to the supra-historical and personal dimensions of the Gospel. It has nothing to say, for instance, on the question of the ultimate meaning of a person's life. The fact is that if the life of the individual person has meaning only in relation to the world of public, historical events, then it has no meaning beyond death. According to biblical teaching, however, the meaning of human existence is not exclusively found in relation to the historical process, but also in the ultimate destiny of the individual.

The point here is not to advocate an ahistorical, individualistic approach to the Christian faith. Such an approach is not only politically irrelevant but also unbiblical. Theology cannot avoid the question regarding the need of a concrete "historical project" in which faith is made visible. If it is true that "faith seeks understanding," it is also true that faith seeks a historical project. There must be, however, a better way to relate the public and the private, the social and the personal, life shared with others and the inner life of the individual person than the way suggested either by an ahistorical theology or by a theology bent toward historical reductionism.

Here again the answer is in a hermeneutical circulation between Scripture and the historical situation. If it is true that the historical situation poses questions to Scripture (How can God be proclaimed as Father in an inhuman world?), it is also true that Scripture poses questions to the historical situation (Where are you?). The great questions to the word of the Lord come from Christian practice,"[40] but also the great questions to Christian practice come from the word of the Lord. If theology is to be a reflection on praxis in the light of faith, it will have to read the situation in the light of Scripture and the Scripture in the light of the situation.

C. *Liberation Theology Has Rightly Emphasized the Importance of the Social Sciences but Is in Danger of Sociological Co-optation*

The Western tradition of theology has fairly consistently cast theology into philosophical molds. Under the influence of Greek rationalism, the concern of theology has been to relate faith to the contemporary thought patterns rather than to socio-economic and political problems. It has been conceived as "a form of intellectual service to the word of God,"[41] and it has therefore tended to disregard the life-and-death issues with which the large majority of people are faced in daily life.

Liberation theology, by contrast, has chosen the social sciences (especially sociology and economics) as partners for dialogue. It has correctly seen that, since the word of God is addressed to people, and people live, not in a world of ideas, but in a concrete, historical world, theological reflection must adopt an interdisciplinary approach, with sciences that interpret social reality. The social sciences thus become an essential aspect of the hermeneutical task.

The Marxist analysis offers a global interpretation of the Latin American situation in terms of the domination theory and the class struggle. The acceptance of the validity of its insights does not necessarily imply that one has become Marxist, and no honest Christian can deny the biblical overtones present in Marx's invectives against injustice. The question, however, is whether liberation theology has not, by and large, gone beyond an acceptance of Marxist insights warranted by biblical revelation and fallen into a sociological captivity.

To be sure, there are those who would claim that the Marxist analysis is a strictly "scientific analysis" of the historical situation, and that *as such* it is useful to theological reflection. Naturally, they add, the sociological analysis cannot be neutral—in order for it to be truly objective it needs a set of hypotheses with regard to the dynamics of history, which will point the direction for action—but the theology of liberation does not regard Marxism as an abstract, timeless theory with unchangeable dogmatic formulae. It views Marxism as a scientific theory, which needs to be "corrected, refined, broadened and supplemented," but which has proved to be "a useful instrument for projecting a historical praxis aimed at realizing the human possibilities in history."[42] The following questions would be relevant at this point.

In the first place, if Marxism is to be accepted as a scientific theory, what kind of precaution is taken so that the theory (with the philosophical premises that undergird it, which are part of a materialistic worldview) is kept under control by the belief-content of an authentic Christian commitment?[43] One need not be a reactionary to see that something is wrong if theology is asked to eschew objectivity in biblical interpretation and to be guided by the Marxist claim to scientific objectivity in the socio-economic analysis. As a human work, that analysis is not exempt from the relativities of the human situation any more than biblical interpretation; both the reading of the Bible and the reading of the historical situation are limited by social conditioning. The casting of a moral cause in the form of a scientific analysis will, of course, impregnate material ends with moral passion, but it will do little to clarify the real issues to be faced in the concrete situation.

In the second place, if Marxism is to be seen as a strictly scientific theory, on what basis is it regarded *also* as the historical project in which the Christian faith ought to be embodied in order to become historically relevant? When liberation theology finds in Marxism a political strategy to "build up the Kingdom of God,"[44] it has clearly fallen prey to a humanist illusion that is not in agreement with either the historical facts or biblical revelation. We are in the face of a sociological co-optation of theology.

The alternative is not a theology insulated from historical reality, unable to perceive the pains and aches of the poor and the oppressed. It is, rather, a theology engaged in dialogue with both Scripture and the concrete situation, concerned with the historical manifestation of the kingdom of God in terms of specific "signs" pointing to the kingdom that has already come and to the kingdom that is yet to come.

D. Liberation Theology Has Rightly Emphasized the Importance of Recognizing the Ideological Condition of Theology but Is in Danger of Reducing the Gospel to an Ideology

That theology in Western tradition is under "ideological captivity" is obvious to anyone fairly interested in studying the matter with critical eyes. The absence of an entry on "violence" in a major dictionary on Christian ethics,[45] the scarcity of comment on the biblical meaning of "poor" and "poverty" in a scholarly commentary on the Gospel of Luke,[46] and the transformation of the statement that "11 a.m. on Sunday is the most segregated hour in America" from "a millstone around Christian necks" into "a dynamic tool for assuring Christian growth"[47]—these are only random illustrations of the way in which ideology can distort biblical truth. And it is clear that as long as theology comes out of academic circles, it will be used to cover up the ideology of the status quo. Liberation theology is certainly right in claiming that no biblical interpretation is socially neutral. As Míguez Bonino has put it,

> All interpretation of texts which is submitted to us (whether as exegesis or as ethical or systematic interpretation) should be examined in relation to the praxis in which it has its origin. . . . Certainly, we cannot accept the interpretations coming from the "rich world" without suspecting and asking, therefore, as to what kind of praxis they reflect, support or validate.[48]

Once the relativity of exegesis is recognized, the attempt may be made to emphasize the scientific approach to Scripture, with a view to reduce the social conditioning. Exegesis is then turned into an academic discipline for the entertainment of a few members in "a very expensive and exclusivistic club,"[49] but biblical interpretation continues to reflect the historical situation of the interpreter. No theology, therefore, is free from ideological entanglements.

Is there a way out of the vicious circle in which ideology determines the historical praxis and this in turn determines theology? The answer given by liberation theology is that, since no neutrality is possible, the Bible ought to be read on the basis of the Marxist socio-political analysis so as to release its revolutionary power. Should anybody object to this partiality, the liberationist will answer that "in all hermeneutics there is a conscious or unconscious partiality. It is always produced from a partisan point of view, even if it pretends and believes that it is neutral." The important thing, therefore, is "that we elect well our own commitment and the partiality of our viewpoint."[50]

A deeper questioning, however, is here called for. If an objective reading of historical reality is believed to be possible, why is the possibility of an objective reading of Scripture rejected? Although absolute scientific objectivity is a myth and ideological suspicion is therefore essential to hermeneutics, biblical interpretation is condemned to failure if right from the beginning the possibility of an objective understanding of the biblical text is regarded as totally blocked. We must doubt our objectivity, but we must also hope to be able to understand the meaning of Scripture without our subjectivity preventing us from fulfilling our task of letting Scripture speak. What Peter Berger says with regards to social sciences is also applicable to the interpretation of Scripture: Objectivity is a necessary ideal for theoretical understanding and it means that one makes an effort to perceive reality apart from the consequences that one's interpretation may have for one's praxis; objectivity in the scientific approach, however, is not incompatible with a moral commitment and with actions emerging out of that commitment.[51]

Furthermore, can faith remain authentically biblical unless Scripture is allowed to judge freely one's ideological commitments? If it is not, the danger of turning the Gospel into an ideology is indeed real. The claim that all theology is class theology will then simultaneously serve to discredit "bourgeois" theology and to accredit liberation theology. The way will thus be open for a theological sanction of a political program leading up to a socio-political system that in actual practice may be just as oppressive as the one it is meant to replace.

A far better alternative is theology that reads the Bible on its own terms and refuses to force it into an ideological straitjacket, consequently imposing its own limitations on the word of God. The choice is not between a "pure" biblical theology and a theology that, paraphrasing Humpty-Dumpty, says, "When I use a text, it means just what I choose it to mean—neither more nor less." There is a third option namely, a theology that continually seeks the harmony between Scripture and present obedience through a "synthetic act" in which past and present—word and spirit—are brought together. As Míguez Bonino has correctly pointed out, the redemptive events, such as the death and resurrection of Jesus Christ, are not merely events of the past, but also present events; the biblical texts, are, therefore, bearers of a living word.

> These events, and consequently the kerygma in which they come to us, are present in our reading with all the weight of their concrete historicity as much as in the full efficacy of their power. For this reason, the theological hermeneutic cannot evade the effort to enter into the text by means of the historical, literary, traditional and linguistic instruments which the science of interpretation has created.[52]

Theology is the reflection on praxis in the light of faith for the sake of obedience to the whole counsel of God. It represents, therefore, a real merging of the horizons of the biblical text and the horizons of our historical context. Neither our understanding of Scripture nor our understanding of our concrete situation is adequate unless both of them constantly interact and are mutually corrected. Consequently the alternative to both the "theology of the word" and the "theology of praxis" is a hermeneutical circulation in which a richer and deeper understanding of Scripture leads to a greater understanding of historical context, and a deeper and richer understanding of the context leads to a greater comprehension of Scripture from within the concrete situation and under the leading of the Holy Spirit.

NOTES

1. Gustavo Gutiérrez, *Teología de la liberación-perspectivas* (Salamanca: Ediciones Sígueme, 1972), p. 40. [English trans.: *A Theology of Liberation* (Maryknoll, N.Y.: Orbis Books, 1973)]. According to Juan Luis Segundo, likewise, "the most progressive theology in Latin America is more interested in *being liberating* than in *speaking about liberation.* In other words, liberation belongs not so much to the content as to the method used to do theology in view of our reality" (*Liberación de la teología* [Buenos Aires: Ediciones Carlos Lohle, 1975], p. 13.). Unless otherwise noted, translations are by the author of this paper.

2. Andrew Kirk, *Liberation Theology: An Evangelical View from the Third World* (London: Marshall, Morgan & Scott, 1979), p. 206.

3. Gutiérrez, pp 22ff.

4. Gutiérrez, p. 34.

5. José Míguez Bonino, *Christians and Marxists: The Mutual Challenge to Revolution* (London: Hodder and Stoughton, 1976), pp. 31ff.

6. Míguez Bonino, p. 40. Cf, José Míguez Bonino, *La fe en busca de eficacia* (Salamanca: Ediciones Sígueme, 1978), pp. 114ff.

7. Gutiérrez, p. 35. Cf. Roberto Oliveros, *Liberación y Teología: génesis y crecimiento de una reflexión, 1966-77* (Lima: Centro de Estudios y Publicaciones, 1977), p. 109.

8. Gutiérrez, p. 38.

9. Gutiérrez pp. 34ff. et passim.

10. Hugo Assmann, *Opresión—Liberación: desafío a los cristianos* (Montevideo: Tierra Nueva, 1971), p. 141.

11. Gutiérrez, "Praxis de liberación: teología y anuncio," *Concilium* 96 (1974): 353-74.

12. Raúl Vidales, "Cuestiones en torno al método en la teología de la liberación," in *La nueva frontera de la teología en América Latina,* ed. Rosino Gibellini (Salamanca: Ediciones Sígueme, 1977), p. 46. [English trans.: *Frontiers of Theology in Latin America* (Maryknoll, N.Y.: Orbis Books, 1979).]

13. Severino Croatto, *Libertad y Liberación: pautas hermenéuticas* (Lima: Centro de Estudios y Publicaciones, 1978), p. 129.

14. Segundo, p. 12. In a similar vein Oliveros says that "the use of the rationality of the social sciences, besides philosophy, is the contribution of Latin America theology" *(Liberación y Teología,* p. 115).

15. Assmann, p. 65.

16. Gutiérrez, "Praxis de liberación y fe cristiana," in *La nueva frontera de la teología en America Latina,* p. 19.

17. Gutiérrez, *Teología de la liberación,* p. 118.

18. Oliveros, p. 320.

19. Gutiérrez, *Teología de la liberación,* p. 355.

20. Gutiérrez, *Teología de la liberación*, p. 355.
21. Segundo, "Capitalismo-socialismo, *crux theologica*," in *La nueva frontera de la teología en América Latina,* pp. 223 ff. Important for the understanding of Segundo's argument are his definitions of socialism and capitalism: "Here we call socialism the political regime in which the ownership of the means of production is taken from individuals and turned over to superior institutions inasmuch as they are concerned with the common good. As capitalism we understand a political regime in which the ownership of the means of production is left to economic competition" (p. 231).
22. Segundo, "Capitalismo-socialismo," p. 238.
23. Segundo, *Liberación de la Teología,* p. 124. [English trans.: *The Liberation of Theology* (Maryknoll, N.Y.: Orbis Books, 1976).]
24. Segundo, *Liberación de la Teología,* ch. 2.
25. Segundo, *Liberación de la Teología,* p. 45.
26. Segundo, *Liberación de la Teología,* p. 45
27. For a discussion of these and other arguments, see Oliveros, pp. 295ff; and Robert McAfee Brown, *Theology in a New Key* (Philadelphia: The Westminster Press, 1978), ch. 4.
28. Míguez Bonino, *La fe en busca de eficacia,* p. 116.
29. Cf. C. René Padilla, "Hermeneutics and Culture: A Theological Perspective," in *Gospel and Culture,* ed. John Stott and Robert T. Cook (Pasadena: William Corey Library, 1979), pp. 83ff.
30. Assmann, p. 67.
31. Assmann, p. 97.
32. Segundo, *Masas y minorías en la dialéctica divina de la liberación* (Buenos Aires: Editorial La Aurora, 1973), p. 94.
33. Míguez Bonino, *La fe en busca de eficacia,* p. 119.
34. See Malcolm A. Jeeves, *The Scientific Enterprise and the Christian Faith* (London: The Tyndale Press, 1969), pp. 35 ff.
35. Arthur Holmes, *Faith Seeks Understanding* (Grand Rapids, Mich.: Eerdmans, 1967).
36. Míguez Bonino, *La fe en busca de eficacia,* p. 124.
37. See Thomas Luckmann, *Invisible Religion: The Problem of Religion in Modern Society* (New York: Macmillan, 1967).
38. Gustavo Gutiérrez, *Revelación y anuncio de Dios en la historia* (Lima: Miec/Jeci, 1977), p. 21.
39. Gutiérrez, *Revelación y anuncio,* p. 8.
40. Gutiérrez, *Revelación y anuncio,* p. 5.
41. Willie D. Jonker, *Church and Theology in the Contemporary World* (Grand Rapids, Mich.: Reformed Ecumenical Synod, 1977), p. 8.
42. Míguez Bonino, *La fe en busca eficacia,* p. 121.
43. On the need for the belief-content of an authentic Christian commitment to function as control over the Christian's devising and weighing of theories, see Nicholas Wolterstorff, *Reason Within the Bounds of Religion* (Grand Rapids, Mich.: Eerdmans, 1976).
44. According to Juan Segundo, this is the "basic trait common to all liberation theologies: that men, both politically and individually, are building up the kingdom of God already in history" ("Capitalismo-socialismo, *crux theologica,*" p. 229).
45. See John Macquarrie, *A Dictionary of Christian Ethics* (London: SCM Press, 1967).

46. See I. Howard Marshall, *Commentary on Luke* (Grand Rapids, Mich.: Eerdmans, 1978).
47. See C. Peter Wagner, *Our Kind of People* (Atlanta: John Knox Press), 1979.
48. Míguez Bonino, *La fe en busca de eficacia,* p. 117.
49. Gutiérrez, *Revelación y anuncio,* p.4.
50. Segundo, *La liberación de la teología,* p. 341.
51. Peter L. Berger, *Pyramids of Sacrifice: Political Ethics and Social Change* (Garden City: Anchor Books, 1976), pp. 135ff.
52. Míguez Bonino, *La fe en busca de eficacia,* pp. 127ff.

4

Anabaptism and Liberation Theology

LAVERNE A. RUTSCHMAN

Latin America, despite its predominantly Christian population, has until recently contributed little to theological thought. Latin American church historians,[1] however, point to three creative periods in their theology. The first emerged in opposition to the conquest by Spain in the sixteenth century when a number of priests defended the rights of the Indians. This was in contrast to the position of leading Spanish theologians who justified the subjugation of the native population by appealing to the Old Testament paradigm of the holy war and the Augustinian concept of the just war. For the invaders the conquest of America became a new crusade against non-Christian powers not unlike the centuries-old struggle against the Moors of the Iberian Peninsula or the medieval efforts to take the Holy Land from the Turks. The basic motivation was, of course, political and economic, but then as now theologians were not lacking who would legitimate government action with a theology that provided an ideological cover-up.

Among the first prophetic voices that were raised in defense of the Indian was that of Antonio de Montesinos. It was through his preaching that the famous Bartolomé de las Casas was finally conscientized and converted after having participated in the oppression of the indigenous people of Cuba under the system of "encomiendas" in which Indian labor and resources were cruelly exploited for the benefit of the Spanish invader. Las Casas, through his active defense of the native people, became known as the "Protector of the Indians." Many others were also involved who believed in nonviolent evangelization and respect for the Indian language and culture; among them was the martyred Antonio de Valdivieso of Central America whose name now identifies a Christian center in Managua, Nicaragua. Despite strong opposition to their efforts, the situation of the Indians improved somewhat with the enactment of the New Laws of 1542. The prophetic influence of these men of the sixteenth century continues today in the struggle for the liberation of the oppressed.

For the following two and one-half centuries under Spanish and Portuguese colonialism there was little theological activity. The few dissenting voices were short-lived. The inquisition was effective. However, the stimulus of the emancipation struggle at the beginning of the last century gave birth to a second period of theological creativity in Latin America. Great numbers of seminary and university students along with their teachers abandoned the classroom to join the ranks of the rebels.

With the achievement of independence, however, theology soon lost its critical revolutionary function and quickly legitimated the political and economic position of the Creole oligarchies at the cost of the oppressed masses. (By Creole oligarchies we refer to the political leaders of pure European descent.) Certain Latin American liberal regimes, opposing the traditional power of the Catholic clergy, welcomed Protestant immigrants and even missionaries. These Protestants, with their imported theology, at first offered little to the development of a Latin American interpretation of the Christian faith. Today, Protestants in Latin America number in the millions and are now in a position to make their own contribution to Latin American Christian thought.

Unfortunately, freedom from the colonialism of Spain and Portugal did not end imperialistic exploitation. Great Britain soon became the dominant economic power in Latin America. The new form of imperialism was called neo-colonialism. Neo-colonial powers, despite their economic and political strength, accept even less responsibility for the victims of their exploitation than the system they replace. The need for abundant raw materials and cheap labor and the tendency to demand inflated prices for the product of their industry create greater injustice. With the decline of the British Empire as a neo-colonial power, other countries, especially the United States, have assumed this function. Latin America continues to be dependent.

In response to the injustice of neo-colonialism a new period of creative theological activity has emerged, the effect of which is felt throughout the world as Latin American Christians reflect upon the conditions of the poor in the light of the word. Returning to the sources of their faith and prompted by the tragedy of our times, they have made discoveries not unlike those of the radical Anabaptists of the Reformation period.

During the month of February 1985, under a program of regional leadership training sponsored by the Mennonite Churches of Panama, Central America and Mexico, I taught a course on the history of theology in Latin America. During this period we studied the history of both Catholic and Protestant thought in Latin America with major attention to the present period, in which theology has reached its most creative expression. We considered various areas of convergence between Latin American liberation theology and radical Anabaptism. Many young Latin American church leaders, loyal to Radical Reformation insights, have become impatient with certain traditional emphases and practices. They know that the Anabaptist theological heritage can be effective only as it is translated into their own situation as nonviolent Christians in a region of civil war and poverty. They are deeply interested in liberation theology as it reflects Anabaptist concerns, but they are also aware of important divergences between the two theologies. Many of these leaders minister in areas of constant danger where innocent victims are trapped between the forces of right and left. In the face of these conditions cheap grace is not enough. Ideological idols that conceal reality are destroyed. Discipleship becomes something more than merely following the example of Jesus or even taking an option for the poor. It means taking up the cross on behalf of the oppressed. It stirs up the enmity of those who are at ease in Zion and who insist that the Gospel must be apolitical, a posture that by its silence legitimates present oppressive regimes.

In order to study areas of interaction between Latin American liberation theology and radical Anabaptism, common concerns and interpretations as well as disagreements, it will be necessary to consider briefly certain characteristics of liberation thought.

LATIN AMERICAN LIBERATION THEOLOGY: WHY NOW?

Latin American liberation theology is a theology whose time has come. Although there are parallels in the sixteenth-century preaching of Montesinos and las Casas, only with the emergence of the social sciences following the desacralization of society and the slow demise of Christendom has it been possible to carry on the type of theological investigation that is giving birth to these new expressions of the Christian faith. Traditionally, the structures of society have been considered sacred, ordained by God and, therefore, not subject to scientific inquiry that might lead to change.

It is well to remember that liberation theology is not the only theology in Latin America, nor does it command the loyalty of the majority of church leaders. Within Catholicism traditional conservatism is strong among those related to agriculture, the landed gentry and those who work for them. Middle-class interests are expressed by a theology that still sees developmentalism as the key for the improvement of the lot of the poor. By contrast, liberation theology reflects the convictions of the emerging classes led by a growing number of Christian workers, both Catholic and Protestant. It expresses in part the convictions of the base ecclesial communities that meet for Bible study, worship and sharing. It is estimated that there are over 100,000 of these communities in Brazil alone.

Modern sociological studies point to the dependent status of Latin American people throughout their history. This dependence is political, economic, cultural and theological. As Latin American theology comes of age it carries a growing suspicion of imported North Atlantic emphases that respond to the needs of the developed nations but are hardly relevant in the Third World.

There are several possible approaches to the study of liberation theology.[2] It may be studied historically with its roots in Vatican II. It can also be approached from the standpoint of functional sociology, a study of how the church has related to social and political structures in its history. There is also the empirical approach, based upon the daily experience of the victims of institutional and overt violence. As we listen to the accounts of those who suffer and observe the results of oppression, supported by abundant statistical evidence, it is obvious that Christian theology must respond. Finally, there is the psychological approach, the deep need that Latin American Christians feel about developing their own nondependent interpretation of their faith in the light of conditions unique to their own situation. Centuries of colonialism have caused Latin Americans to underestimate their place in world affairs.

LATIN AMERICAN LIBERATION THEOLOGY: WHERE IS IT GOING?

Liberation theology can be described as a theology of the way, contextual rather than fully doctrinal. Liberation theologians share certain objectives and responsibilities, but this does not indicate full doctrinal homogeneity. However, people with broad differences are united in this movement. Confessional barriers tend to diminish on the level of praxis. The influence of liberation theology continues to spread as the recent struggle with the Vatican, fearful of the growing influence of liberation thought, suggests.

For liberation theologians theology is a second act, a reflection on praxis in the light of the word. The first act, usually described as praxis toward the liberation of the poor, is now defined by Gustavo Gutiérrez[3] as the Christian life itself with its mystical contemplation and its active involvement in solidarity with the poor. Only on this basis is a word of God possible. Theological reflection for the follower of Jesus is always grounded in contemplation and commitment. This presupposes a conversion experience that breaks the power of personal and social sin and the abandonment of selfish interests. It turns toward the oppressed neighbor, sharing his or her life.

Praxis, a term borrowed from Marxist literature, refers to the two-way traffic between theory and action. In liberation theology theory relates both to the analysis of the situation and the exegesis of the word, leading to action as suggested by Georges Casalís in what he calls hermeneutical circulation.[4] The diagram on page 55 illustrates the interplay between biblical exegesis and social science, the two basic tools for doing liberation theology.

Liberation theologians do not claim objectivity in the sense that one can approach the problems of Latin America with detachment. Theirs is a situated theology. Its context is the world of the poor, the "nonpersons." Impartiality is impossible for those whose option for the poor and whose discipleship demand both an ideological and a theological commitment that works for the transformation of society.

Liberation theology is world-affirming, since it is the world in which God is at work. Christians must join others who also seek the transformation of present unjust social structures. The church in itself is not the instrument of change in isolation from the world. Evangelism is not simply a periodic engagement with the enemy, carrying out raids in hostile territory to rescue the victims of sin and relocate them in the church as a place of isolated safety. The prophetic voice must be raised in the world and in the church wherever there is injustice. Christians must identify with the poor in their struggle and help to conscientize them of their condition and of the Gospel that promises a new life in a transformed world. This ministry is in continuity with that of the Old Testament prophets and of Jesus and his followers.

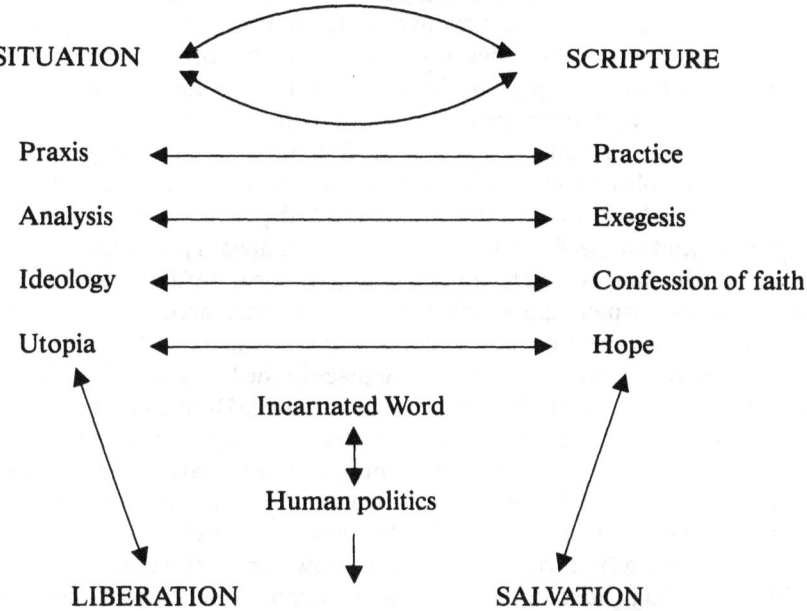

Another way to describe the process of conscientization and the development of liberation theology is to follow the sequence of the hermeneutical circle as projected by Juan Luis Segundo of Uruguay.[5] This circle takes the concerned Christian through a series of suspicions (ideological, theological and exegetical) toward a rereading and a rediscovery of the Scriptures unbound by traditional ideological, theological and exegetical cover-ups.

Parallel to the sequence of the circle is the study of the function of religion in society, especially in the light of the research carried out by Christian Lalive D'Espinay in Chile.[6] Following the functionalist-sociological approach of Henry Desroche, he pointed out three ways in which religion carries out its role. In the first place it may perform an *integrating* function in the legitimation of the structures of society. This is its traditional place in an integrated society in which religious pluralism is not present. As a legitimating force, conforming to the dominant ideology, it sacralizes the social structure, often at the cost of the kerygma. Religion may also protest from within the system, a *questioning* role in society. This is the reformist position. It does not threaten the system but it does seek change. Finally, religion may also protest from without as a society disintegrates, a *rebelling* role. This places religion on the side of revolution. Thus, according to Lalive D'Espinay, religion can conform, reform or rebel. It can legitimate, question from within, or question from without. The history of the church provides abundant material to support this typology. Today there are priests, pastors and lay people who work within the system, others who seek to reform it, and still others who struggle for structural change.

The Anabaptist experience suggests that religion can also function as a countercultural force. This may take the form of evasion, an escape from the world in isolated communities. It may also take the form of testimony. Countercultural groups may provide the nuclei for a new society, as light and leaven in a fallen world, that demonstrate God's intention for all humanity.

Both the hermeneutical circle and the functional study of religion in society point to the role of ideology in the expression of faith. In liberation theology the term *ideology* is used both negatively and positively. For some, such as Gutiérrez and Dussel following Mannheim, it is always pejorative, a system of concepts and images used to conceal reality for the benefit of the powerful who desire to perpetuate the existing order. However, according to Althusser, ideology is a "system of representations (images, myths, ideas and concepts) that has it own existence and historical place in the heart of a given society."[7]

No one can live in an ideological vacuum. André Dumas contends that faith cannot exist without ideology because ideologies represent human efforts to give meaning to life. He notes that it is not possible to leave our ideologies at the door of the temple when we enter to worship.[8] Juan Luis Segundo considers faith without ideology as dead. For Segundo faith transcends ideologies and functions critically in relation to them. However, faith cannot be expressed without ideology. Ideologies are necessary symbols, but they require vigilance lest they become idols.[9] As Paul Ricoeur noted, "We never reach an end of destroying idols in order to permit that symbols speak."[10]

Marxism is probably the most powerful political ideology of our times. As an ideological symbol it can be useful, but as an idol it conceals reality, becoming a rigid political system that threatens human existence. Capitalism is also a powerful ideology. As an idol it obscures reality while enjoying the legitimating support of great segments of the church.

North American Christians are often concerned by what seems to be a strong dependence upon Marxist thought in the development of liberation theology. Liberation theology does use Marxist sociology as a tool for its analysis of the situation in which the poor exist. But this does not mean that social science for most Latin American liberation theologians is synonymous with Marxist sociology. For example, the theory of dependence, so important for liberation thought as a tool for analyzing social reality, is not Marxist.

Christians can never accept an atheist ideology or a totalitarian version of history that denies human freedom. A Christian theologian, in contrast with a secular sociologist, knows that in the very heart of the unjust social reality in which we live there is sin. Sin separates us from God and from each other.

Gutiérrez insists that as Christians we must appeal to our own sources of faith.[11] However, there are those who, like Hugo Assmann, give greater importance to social analysis than to traditional authoritative Christian sources. For Assmann such an analysis is "the text," the first reference point for theology.[12]

It is obvious that most liberation theologians find certain Marxist insights useful for social analysis. Others would take the second step and accept Marxist strategy in what they consider the transition period toward the construction of the new order. This demands certain limitations of human freedom and a rejection of pluralism that under present conditions may function as a reactionary ideology, according to Dussel, creating division and making change impossible. Dussel sees the time when diversity will be necessary, but one should not destroy the baby before he or she is born.[13] Yet Dussel has deep doubts about the use of Marxist categories, questioning the possibility of being Marxist in economics and Christian in faith. He points out that in Marx there is a whole ontology underlying his economic theories.[14] But this does not mean that a Christian should not opt for social change. There can be no effective social change in Latin America without the participation of Christians in a continent in which religion is still *a priori*.

For many liberation theologians biblical exegesis is the primary tool for doing theology. Through the work of Paul Ricoeur, J. Severino Croatto [15] and many others, biblical studies have taken new forms that have enriched theological productivity in Latin America. The base ecclesial communities in Brazil and Peru as well as other areas of Latin America find in the Bible guidelines for their life in community. Expressions such as "rereading" *(relectura)*, "contextualization," "reservoir of meaning" *(reserva del sentido)* and "distancement" *(distanciamiento)* describe the new approach to Bible study. The text that is reread is the completed canon. Little interest is shown in the history of the text, although the work of critical scholars is accepted. The important element is the meaning of the canonical text in the present situation, a reservoir of meaning that by extending the original intent makes the text relevant today. The message of the text is enriched in proportion to its distance from the original source.

LATIN AMERICAN LIBERATION THEOLOGY AND RADICAL ANABAPTISM: WHAT DO THEY HAVE IN COMMON?

In our dialogue with liberation theology the Anabaptist vision of the sixteenth century provides an important frame of reference. Although the content of this vision has been investigated in many ways since it was first postulated by Harold Bender in 1943,[16] it is well to remember the three interrelated levels to which he referred: discipleship, the church of believers, and the ethic of love and nonresistance.

Discipleship for the early Anabaptists meant the transformation of life through suffering with Christ for both the individual and the community of believers. Faith in Jesus meant more than a mere intellectual assent or a spiritualization of the Christian message that denies the world. In contrast to

Luther's emphasis upon faith, the early Anabaptists were concerned about discipleship. The well-known words of Hans Denck, "to know Christ is to follow him in life," reflected the convictions of all true Anabaptists. For them faith and theology were not ends in themselves. Faith can only be expressed through following Jesus, made possible by God's grace through the forgiveness of sins and the creation of the new humanity.

Their concept of the church also differed from that of other reformers. Emphasis upon discipleship presupposes a mature decision that only believers can make. Infant baptism, so basic to the medieval pattern of Christendom, was rejected. This was a threat to the so-called Christian society.

Consistent with the call to discipleship and emphasis upon the church of believers is the ethic of nonviolence. Early Anabaptists accepted the suffering-servant model of redemptive love as the foundation for their life as disciples. The Christian takes up the cross in solidarity with Christ and the oppressed instead of the sword.

Although the sixteenth-century reformation movement occurred in a vastly different world, there are many parallels with conditions today in Latin America. Christendom, as a culture that unites church and state without religious dissent or division, dies hard in former Spanish and Portuguese colonies. Many people continue to view the obligatory political and religious unity of the past with nostalgia. Radical Anabaptism confronted the culture of Christendom in the sixteenth century in a way that makes pluralism possible today. Liberation theology, although hardly pluralistic in its stance, nevertheless represents a decisive break with Catholic traditionalism.

The remainder of this chapter will be devoted to a study of the interaction between liberation theology and Anabaptism in four areas: the source and nature of authority, the identification and role of the people of God in the liberation struggle, the place of christology in Christian thought and action, and the question of final goals or eschatology.

1. AUTHORITY: ITS SOURCE AND NATURE

Traditionally Catholicism has placed Scripture and Tradition on the same level of authority. In liberation theology, however, the scientific study of the social situation is also considered authoritative. Scripture and situation, as in the hermeneutical circulation of Casalís, are the two "texts" upon which theology is built. Protestantism carries on the tradition of the outer word of the Bible and the inner word of the Spirit in Christian experience. The Bible provides the basis for assessing the validity of the inner word. This relationship is usually described in terms of pure doctrine. The two words are reflected in early Anabaptism by the biblically-centered evangelicals and the experience-centered spiritualists.

As we have seen, liberation theologians utilize certain key concepts in their exegesis. The "rereading" of Scripture suggests that the original meaning of the text is not exhausted by the original intention of the author. There is a "reservoir of meaning," a richer dimension of the text, for each changing situation. This is not a new meaning since there is always continuity with the past. The meaning of the text is enriched by its distance from its initial appearance through accumulated interpretations, the fruit of centuries of study. But above all the text in all its significance is free to be applied in a new way in each changing situation. This is called *distanciamiento* ("distancement") in Spanish.

There is, however, no final consensus among liberation thinkers with relation to authority in theology. Hugo Assmann, as we have seen, describes the situation as "the text," the primary theological point of reference. Other points of reference such as the Bible, tradition, the magisterium and the history of dogma are not primary unless they are placed in connection with the praxis-truth of the situation.[17] Gustavo Gutiérrez, however, insists that theological authority must be based upon Christian sources.[18] Pablo Richard, on the other hand, commenting on the use of the Bible in the Latin American base ecclesial communities, notes that the Bible is never considered a fundamental reference in itself. The Bible itself points to its basic reference as the experience of God in the history of the oppressed. It provides criteria for discernment and is a means of communicating the Christian experience to others. For Richard the word is not so much the Bible in itself as the capacity of the Bible to enable us to discern and communicate the Christian experience.[19]

Although Anabaptism is based upon the authority of the word, there was no agreement in the sixteenth century with regard to the relation between the outer and the inner words. Hans Denck, a spiritualist and mystic, placed primary authority on the inner word of the Spirit.[20] Other Anabaptists such as Conrad Grebel, Menno Simons and Pilgram Marpeck reversed these roles. For them the New Testament was the new Torah. The rationalists of the Radical Reformation subjected both words to reason and conscience. As Williams suggests, for them worship became a period of study and the church a school of ethics.[21]

Early Anabaptists usually interpreted the New Testament quite literally, but the Old Testament was subjected to typological or even allegorical interpretations in continuity with pre-Reformation practices. With relation to the Apocrypha or Deuterocanonical books, the Anabaptists showed a more positive attitude than did the other reformers. There was as yet no consensus regarding the extension of the Old Testament canon.

Basic to the Radical Reformation was the role of the hermeneutical community. God's word is to be interpreted in the community in which the Spirit of Christ is present (Matt. 18:20).

Although many Latin American theologians formulate the question of biblical authority in a way that differs from most Anabaptists, and seem unconcerned about the most radical forms of biblical criticism, the Bible is still the basic source of authority for the majority. Traditionally, of course, the Roman Catholic Church has insisted on its exclusive right to interpret the Scriptures. This resulted in little exposure to the Bible on the part of the laity.

Why study the Bible if one cannot trust his or her own conclusions? However, since Vatican II the Bible is widely read.

In Segundo's hermeneutical circle the decisive point, following the series of suspicions, is the liberating rereading of the Scriptures. The early Anabaptists were also liberated through the study of the Bible that led them to reject the alienating social, political and ecclesiastical structures of their period. They found courage to defy church and state to the point of martyrdom because of their conviction that God was speaking to them in a new way through his word.

To reread the Bible in a new situation is to allow its message to contextualize itself in a way that parallels the festive celebrations of the Old Testament period. These feasts, contrary to popular opinion, were not basically commemorative, much less expressions of the eternal return, but rather actualizations of the great acts of God. God continues to act anew in each generation, but the form responds to ancient paradigms.

2. THE PEOPLE OF GOD

Another important area of interaction between Anabaptism and liberation theology relates to the concept of the people of God. Here the divergence between the two theologies is more marked. Although liberation thought has little in common with medieval Christendom, certain descriptions of the people of God in the new theology suggest the possibility of a new church-world synthesis. The special place given to the marginalized social classes and those who work for their liberation suggests the danger of a new people's church in which the baptism of poverty takes the place of infant baptism as found in traditional Christendom.

In liberation theology God's direct action in the world is often described without reference to the mediation of the church. The boundary between church and world is softened. However, for Gutiérrez the church as God's faithful people is responsible for announcing the good news of the kingdom of life. It is in the true church that the eucharist is celebrated in memory of the love and faithfulness of Jesus and in the ministry to the poor with whom Christians share both their sorrow and their resurrection joy. In general, however, the Anabaptist emphasis on continuity with the Abrahamic community in its call and mission demands a more sectarian view of the church as a body of believers that maintains its own identity yet is responsible for ministry in the world.

Liberation theology rejects all dualisms. History under God is one. The relation between the sacred and the profane or between the spiritual and the physical is dialectical, two dimensions of one reality. Radical Anabaptism in the sixteenth century, according to Walter Klaassen,[22] in the struggle with traditional Christendom also rejected these dualisms that tended to be alienating. However, the distinction between the church and the world was maintained much more sharply than in liberation theology today.

The basic Old Testament paradigm for liberation theology is the Exodus, the central saving act of God.[23] Around this nucleus other traditions are believed to have been added such as the creation accounts and the stories of the patriarchs. For Anabaptists the foundational paradigm is Abrahamic. This includes its historical trajectory throughout the Old Testament, which embraces the Exodus as well as the other great events in the history of Israel, especially the sequence that leads to the Suffering Servant of Isaiah fulfilled in Jesus and his church. The position of the base ecclesial communities in Latin America, so important for the formulation of liberation theology, also shows an affinity with the Anabaptist emphasis upon the Abrahamic Suffering-Servant model.

A few years ago in San José, Costa Rica I heard Leonardo Boff describe the origin of this community movement in Brazil. It was Christmas Eve in the decade of the fifties in a small Brazilian city when a group of Catholic Christians made their way after sunset to their parish church. Upon arriving they found the doors locked and the sanctuary unlighted. Returning home they walked by several Protestant churches that were brightly lighted and where Christians were joyfully singing their Christmas carols. They wondered why it was not possible for them to celebrate their faith in the absence of a priest as Protestants were doing. They contacted their bishop who gave them permission to hold meetings as lay people. The movement grew and now numbers hundreds of thousands of people among its adherents. In these meetings one who has suffered for the faith under government repression and has earned the right to be heard is often the leader. The Bible is read. Choruses are sung. There is a period of sharing in which community problems are considered. People refer to their conversion experiences, what they were before and what they are now, a new life that they have found in the community of believers.

This community concept of the people of God—a gathered disciplined sharing and discerning community of believers who feel responsible for each other but whose desire to serve extends to all—has much in common with early Anabaptism.

There is also the question of the responsibility of God's people for history in the two theologies. The kingdom of God is presented in Scripture as both gift and task. Anabaptists believe that grace, the gift, demands action, but that this action must not contradict the final goal of peace and justice. The nature of the struggle for the establishment of the kingdom differs for the two theologies. Anabaptists are convinced that Jesus, although sorely tempted to take the revolutionary Zealot route, rejected the use of violence. He also rejected the Zealot goals, in themselves reactionary, to reinstate the law and the former political and religious institutions. Few liberation theologians are pacifist, but they agree that although Jesus was possibly crucified as a Zealot, he did not belong to that movement. He was not interested in the restoration of the past. He looked forward to a new manifestation of the presence of God in the kingdom.

In the Abrahamic Suffering-Servant community the class struggle is resolved nonviolently in the sharing fellowship of disciples. Although sympathetic to this position, liberationists would not limit their efforts to the life and influence of a small community of Christians. Nonviolence is considered passive if not evasive. They are convinced that there are biblical bases to oppose injustice with physical force when other methods fail.

3. CHRISTOLOGY

For many years liberation theologians have lamented the limited christological studies carried on within their ranks. Christology, as other Christian doctrines, must be re-presented in each changing situation. The question of Matthew 16:15—"Who do you say that I am?"—must be answered in each generation. Major christological work has been done by Leonardo Boff[24] and, more recently, by Jon Sobrino[25] of El Salvador.

Sixteenth-century Anabaptists were often seriously divided in their understanding of Christ. Some, such as Melchior Hoffman, Menno Simons and Bernhard Rothmann were docetic in their efforts to maintain the purity of Jesus' human nature by denying the participation of Mary in his humanity. This was not unlike the ancient monophysite teaching or the Catholic doctrine of the immaculate conception of Mary that, although different, functions with the same objective. They failed to see that our hope as human beings depends upon what God can do with us as men and women. They emphasized the divine aspect of the regenerated person. Others, such as Hans Denck and Hans Hut, adhered to a Logos christology characteristic of Christian mysticism. This carried the danger of losing the historical dimension. The Swiss Brethren and Marpeck, however, maintained the orthodox formulations. All agreed that discipleship involves taking up the cross of Jesus, a sharing of his suffering and not merely following his example or suffering on his behalf. They understood their suffering to be *with* him, a redemptive act.

Liberation christology, as represented by Sobrino, takes the historical Jesus as the starting point. A renewal of faith always involves an encounter with the historical Jesus. Dogmatic historical statements have their place, but they represent the point of arrival of former generations. For us to begin with dogma is to start where former generations ended, with their conclusions, without the discipline of beginning where they began with the life of Jesus. This is deductive reasoning and bypasses the historical Jesus as the source of our faith.

Sobrino calls for the "dismanipulation" of christology.[26] Others, such as Bultmann, have engaged in demythologization without understanding that Christ is manipulated ideologically to conceal unjust structures. Nineteenth-century liberals sought to free Jesus from dogma by emphasizing the historical dimension of his life. They failed to see that their Jesus was identical with the ideal of the bourgeois image of a liberal Christian of their time. Sobrino notes that Christ has been manipulated through spiritualization in such a way that he is no longer relevant for the poor in traditional theology. Both liberation theology and Anabaptism find in Matthew 25 the call for action in favor of the oppressed in whom Christ is present.

At baptism Jesus accepted the servant role of the Isaianic songs. He proclaimed the New Covenant, declared himself to be the light of the nations and the one who offers life to the oppressed through his own death. At his baptism he was declared to be the Son of God with the language of the Servant of Isaiah 41:1. For Jesus the function of the liberating Messiah was carried out through suffering. The triumph was later and on a different level than that expected in the popular Jewish hope.

Jesus' actions were liberating on behalf of the poor rather than the nation. There is no liberation for a nation that maintains unjust social and religious structures. He did not meet the popular expectations of a rich military deliverer. The rich, with few exceptions, rejected Jesus. He died at their hands, but his death was liberating because he unmasked the oppressors and identified himself with their victims. He restored the law to its place as a liberating word, freeing it from its legalistic bondage. He fulfilled the Suffering-Servant role of redemptive suffering. His faith bore fruit in his resurrection, a historical event, the ultimate symbol of hope for all who are subject to the powers of death.

These statements demonstrate that which the two theologies hold in common with relation to the life and work of Christ. There are, as we have seen, however, obvious differences in the concept of discipleship. The disciple in liberation theology is called to make an option for the poor in their struggle. In Radical Anabaptism the follower of Jesus not only takes an option for the poor but is also called to share the suffering of Christ who is found in those who are helpless and defenseless (Matthew 25).

4. ESCHATOLOGY

Both liberation theology and Anabaptism look forward to the kingdom of God on earth, the new humanity in a just society. For Muntzer and the later Münsterites this vision was clear despite serious aberrations. However, we have been taught to spiritualize the kingdom, relegating it to heaven or, at best, to a very spiritualized millennial reign on earth. For Jesus and the Jewish people of his day the kingdom was very earthly and definable, but for Jesus it was not to be established by worldly methods or interpreted according to worldly values (John 18:36).

Biblical faith since the call of Abraham is the celebration of history in the trajectory of promise and fulfillment. There is confidence in the future under God. Biblical faith breaks with the traditional and almost universal myth of the eternal return. Because of God's promise it is possible to face the terror of history (Gen. 12:1-3).

For many Christians eschatology is an evasion of historical responsibility and of history itself. Anabaptists, facing persecution, have not been exempt from seeking to escape the world in the form of apocalyptic speculation. However, the temporal dimension has always been present and the struggle for a pure church, so important in early Anabaptism, is not unrelated to this hope.

Early Christianity was the faith of the oppressed. But with Constantine it became the religion of the rulers. The early Christians expected the return of

Christ and the establishment of his earthly kingdom. For the rulers the new age was established through Christendom. The early Christians demanded a pure church of committed disciples. The rulers made it possible to satisfy the conscience sacramentally. The early Christians were persecuted for their faith. After Constantine the enmity between church and state, with limited exceptions, disappeared and with it the Christian redemptive role of the suffering servant.

Anabaptism sought to return to the pattern of the early church. It rejected Christendom with its infant baptism and its accumulation of ecclesiastical baggage. Of course, it is impossible to forget fifteen hundred years of history. The early church can be actualized, but it cannot be restored. This is, essentially, what the early Anabaptism was able to do.

For liberation theology, as represented by Gutiérrez,[27] to hope is to grasp the future as a gift, opposing injustice and struggling for the establishment of peace and brotherhood, for the future begins now. Eschatology for liberation theology relates to the transformation of society and the establishment of God's kingdom on earth.

Anabaptism shares this hope but emphasizes its present manifestation in the gathered community of disciple-believers, the new humanity created by God through the work of Christ. In this community we can live today according to the norms of the coming kingdom.

NOTES

1. Cf. Enrique Dussel and Pablo Richard, eds. *Materiales para una historia de la teología en América Latina* (San José: DEI, 1981), pp. 401–52.

2. LaVerne A. Rutschman, *Anabautismo radical y teología latinoamericana de la liberación* (San José: SEBILA, 1982), pp. 35–38.

3. Gustavo Gutiérrez, "Teología y ciencias sociales," in *Teología de la liberación: Documentos sobre una polémica* (San José: DEI, 1984), pp. 71–93.

4. Georges Casalís, *Las buenas ideas no caen del cielo* (San José: DEI, 1979), p. 71 [English trans. *Correct Ideas Don't Fall from the Skies* (Maryknoll, N.Y.: Orbis, 1984)].

5. Juan Luis Segundo, *The Liberation of Theology,* trans. John Drury (Maryknoll, N.Y.: Orbis Books, 1976), ch. 1.

6. Christian Lalive D'Espinay, *Religión e ideología en una perspectiva sociológica* (Rio Piedras: Ediciones del Seminario Evangélico, 1973), pp. 47–62.

7. Louis Althusser, *La revolución teórica de Marx* (México: Siglo XXI, 1967), p. 191.

8. André Dumas, *Ideología y fe* (Montevideo: Tierra Nueva, 1970), p. 25.

9. Segundo, ch. 4, 5.

10. Quoted in Dumas, p. 30

11. Gutiérrez, pp. 76–82.

12. Hugo Assmann, *Theology for a Nomad Church,* trans. Paul Burns (Maryknoll, N.Y.: Orbis Books, 1976), pp. 104–5.

13. Enrique Dussel, "Sobre la historia de la teológia en América Latina," in *Lectura teológica del tiempo latinoamericano, ensayos en honor del Dr. Wilton M. Nelson* (San José: SBL, 1979), p. 160.

14. Enrique Dussel, *History and the Theology of Liberation* (Maryknoll, N.Y.: Orbis Books, 1976), pp. 133ff.

15. J. Severino Croatto, *Exodus, a Hermeneutics of Freedom,* trans. Salvator Attanasio (Maryknoll, N.Y.: Orbis Books, 1981).

16. Harold S. Bender, "The Anabaptist Vision" *The Mennonite Quarterly Review* 18:2 (April 1944), pp. 67-88.

17. Assmann, pp. 104-5.

18. Gutiérrez, pp. 72-76, 79-82.

19. Dussel and Richard, pp. 99-101.

20. Walter Klaassen, *Anabaptism: Neither Catholic nor Protestant* (Waterloo: Conrad Press, 1973), pp. 14-15.

21. George H. Williams, *The Radical Reformation* (Philadelphia: Westminster, 1962), p. 828.

22. Klaassen, pp. 14-15.

23. See Croatto.

24. Leonardo Boff, *Jesus Cristo Libertador. Ensaio de Cristologia Critica para o Nosso tempo* (Petropilis: Vozes, 1972).

25. Jon Sobrino, *Christology at the Crossroads,* trans. John Drury (Maryknoll, N.Y.: Orbis Books, 1978) and *Jesús en América Latina, su significado para la fe y la cristología.* (Salamanca: Sal Terrae, 1982). [English trans.: *Jesus in Latin America* (Maryknoll, N.Y.: Orbis Books, 1987).]

26. Sobrino, *Jesús en América Latina, su significado para la fe y la cristología,* p. 101.

27. Gustavo Gutiérrez, *Teología de la liberación* (Salamanca: Ediciones Sígueme, 1972), pp. 284-85.

5

Liberation Theology, Anabaptist Pacifism and Münsterite Violence: Hermeneutical Comparisons and Evaluation

WILLARD M. SWARTLEY

Although Anabaptist scholarship during the last several decades has shown that the Anabaptist movement was predominantly nonresistant and pacifist in its orientation, some analyses of Anabaptism (those focusing on the social class structure of the movement) and the Münsterite era of violence (1534-36) require us to look carefully at the ethical orientation of the Anabaptist movement as a whole.[1] Similarly, my hermeneutical descriptions of how theologies of revolution and liberation on the one hand, and nonresistant/pacifist adherents on the other hand, read the Bible have shown that both uses of Scripture are strong and convincing.

From a hermeneutical standpoint both readings of the text—that of liberation theology and that of nonresistance/pacifism—show selective use. My analysis identified five major hermeneutical emphases in liberation theology's appeal to Scripture. These are:
1. The Exodus, a decisive act of liberation from oppression, is central to God's action in the historical process.
2. The establishment of justice and righteousness within the social order is a major theme of both the Hebrew prophetic and Christian Scriptures.
3. Israel's messianic hopes were defined primarily in categories of liberation and justice.
4. Jesus' coming, the incarnation, means liberation, justice and humanization. Here the accent falls on Jesus' prophetic ministry, which judges the old oppressive order.
5. Jesus' death and resurrection provide a paradigm for radical change and revolution, personally and socio-economically.

The pacifist/nonresistant reading of the biblical text emphasizes the following:

1. Although war and violence appear often in the Hebrew Scripture, such is rooted in humanity's fall and is roundly criticized by the Hebrew Scripture itself, by over a dozen themes: in the paradigmatic act of the Exodus, God is the sole warrior and the people are "only to be still"; Israel's military battles resulted from the people's lack of faith in Yahweh's leadership, leading also to their request—against Yahweh's will—for human kingship; the writing prophets deplored Israel's amassing of chariots and horses and condemned military build-up; and throughout the Hebrew Scripture a pacifist universalist strand of teaching prevails, culminating in the theology of Isaiah 40–55 in which the servant finally gives his own life in the establishment of justice.
2. Jesus asks his followers to love their enemies, calling for a creative nonresistance that overcomes evil with good.
3. The nature of Jesus' kingdom proclamation and his messiahship show that he clearly rejected the revolutionary strategies of the Zealots and initiated a new "politics"; the founding of a new order through prophetic declaration, personal suffering and finally the giving of his own life.
4. The teachings of the early church concur with this portrait of the historical Jesus. Christ's atonement becomes a pattern for human discipleship and is understood as a final victory over evil, including the principalities and the powers. The atonement is the basis for justification before God and reconciliation with fellow humans.
5. The mission of the church is to witness to the peace of Christ's reconciled body. This peace is rooted in the eschatological hope that God will one day fully establish justice and righteousness, judging and destroying evil.[2]

These summaries of different readings of the biblical text, while essentially different, yet reflect converging insights and emphases. Both accent God's involvement in history and recognize that God's activity in the world not only participates in political realities but is essentially political, social and revolutionary. Both interpretations of the divine revelation remind readers that they should not spiritualize God's work, but see the divine activity as having direct impact upon the forms of human social, political and economic life.

But differences also exist in these readings. Whereas liberation theology has contributed greatly to a fresh understanding of the biblical teaching on liberation and God's cause of righteousness and justice in the world, the pacifist reading calls attention to the method by which this is worked out in the biblical text—and such is held to be binding upon the believer's ethical life. Whereas both liberation theology and pacifist hermeneutic call for human participation in God's work in the world, the former stresses action to overthrow oppressive socio-economic structures whereas the latter redefines the human activity as trust, prophetic word, and creative engagement to turn enemies into brothers and sisters. Both readings of the biblical text highlight essential components of God's word to humanity.

The aim of this chapter is to challenge the pacifist tradition with the hermeneutical contributions of liberation theology and to similarly challenge liberation theology with the hermeneutical contributions of the Anabaptist pacifist tradition. An additional goal is to show two forms of hermeneutic within sixteenth-century Anabaptism, thus providing a third hermeneutical perspective which, while not to be espoused, might stimulate a better understanding of the two main alternatives under comparison in this essay. I shall thus summarize and analyze the similarities and differences among the three historical forces denoted in the title of this article.

I. COMPARATIVE FEATURES OF LIBERATION THEOLOGY AND ANABAPTISM

LaVerne Rutschman has helpfully drawn our attention to both similarities and differences between these two movements.[3] My own analysis utilizes some of his insights and reflects my own reading of the situation as well. First, I shall identify some basic similarities.

1. Both movements are radically oriented to the vision of a new order, rooted in the conviction that God is doing a new thing (cf. Isa. 43:19). If one uses the word eschatological broadly, it is fair to say that both movements are strongly eschatological, although differences in eschatological perception do arise, as will become apparent below upon a close analysis of the two movements.
2. Both movements protest against the evils of existing political orders and both contain a variety of responses, from violent revolution on the one hand, to nonviolence, and even nonresistance in Anabaptism, on the other hand.
3. Both movements gain strength from potent socio-economic-political dynamics within the larger culture of the society. Here must be mentioned the rapid literacy development in both sixteenth-century Europe and in many present-day Latin American countries. The economic disparities between the few rich and the many poor provide powerful impetus for major socio-economic changes. In both cases also the rising power of the working class is an important force for social change. Dülmen argues that many Anabaptists were craftsmen and small village *Handwerkers* whose places in society were rising in importance. From this group came the majority of the Anabaptist leaders, and from this group arose also the enormous missionary activity of the Anabaptist movement. Dülmen goes on to say that the special place that the Anabaptists felt God had given them in history compensated for their political and social oppression.[4] Similarly, the rising importance of the day laborers within the Latin American economy, as well as their religious and political place in society, is evident today.

Moreover, the role of Scripture study in the base communities provides a religious basis and authority for social change. In the same way that the small gathered groups of Anabaptists practiced *real* baptism, which was

seen by the authorities as an act of political rebellion, so the base communities in Latin America—as they celebrate the Mass, study the Scripture and organize for political change—threaten the guardians of the existing economic and political order, although both groups are, in comparative socio-economic analyses, in positions of powerlessness.
4. In both movements there is distrust and critique of the dominant socio-political-theological ideology. A new religious commitment provides a dynamic of protest and vision for a new social order.
5. Both movements might be characterized, to borrow Rutschman's phrase, as "on the way" movements with hope for the future. Both manifest a wide variety of emphases and forms through which hope and vision for new social orders are to be realized.
6. Both movements also appear to have polygenetic origins. Just as the Anabaptist movements appear to have originated at a number of places at roughly the same time, with both similar and differing features, so liberation movements are arising in many different communities, spurred forward by a *Zeitgeist* that baffles the careful historian's analysis.
7. Both movements approach the study of Scripture with what might be called a hermeneutical circle. In Anabaptism the circle moved from the community's commitment-to-obedience to study of the biblical text to an experiential discipleship that then reshaped the commitment of the community to obedience. As Hans Denck put it, no one can know or understand the will of God apart from following or obeying and conversely no one can know or obey apart from understanding the will of God as revealed in Scripture.

In liberation theology the hermeneutical circle consists basically of movement from praxis to the reading of the text and then back to the reshaping of the praxis. Here praxis often includes as analysis of the social situation with pre-commitment to change that situation in the direction of justice. Praxis thus means exposure to real life, and especially to the experiences of oppression within the socio-economic situation. Gustavo Gutiérrez inserts a third point within the circle, namely, theological reflection upon the social situation. This must interact with the reading of the biblical text.[5] Carlos Mesters describes the Bible reading of base communities as interaction among three points in the hermeneutical circle: community as the context, the Bible text itself, and social reality (the real life situation of the people). As these three interact, the word of God is heard by the people.[6]

In both of these approaches to Scripture, Anabaptist and liberationist, a strong relationship exists between action-commitment on the part of the community and the study of the biblical text. But, between these two movements some basic differences are also to be observed:
1. The eschatological viewpoints of the two movements, as these interacted with Scripture study, are essentially different. This will be explored in more detail below.
2. The Anabaptists, for the most part, lived with a strong church-world

dualism. Akin to the tradition of the Qumran community, they saw themselves as the faithful remnant and the forerunners of the messianic hope to be realized within, but only partially within, human historical structures. They made a clear distinction between the expected behavior of the authentically baptized believers and the life of the larger society. In contrast, liberation theology seeks change for the entire social order. No clear distinction between the life and ethic of the church and the life and ethic of the social order emerges in most of the literature. Hence liberation theology continues to operate within the Constantinian structured vision for society whereas the Anabaptist movement called for a post-Constantinian alternative, a separation between the church and the larger social order, which included the state's political rule.

3. Growing out of the above emphases, the ecclesial understandings of both Anabaptism and liberation theology are essentially different. Some of the major concerns within Anabaptist theology and life had to do with mutual aid among its members, brotherly/sisterly discipline according to Matthew 18:15-18, and mutual encouragement in the life of cross-bearing. On the front burner of the ecclesial agenda of liberation theology, however, appears to be the effective organization of the community for the establishment of justice in the social order. Scripture study, publication activity and tactical organizational strategies are oriented to that end.

4. As both the preceding article by LaVerne Rutschman and his earlier article in *Mennonite Quarterly Review* point out, both movements have differing views on biblical authority. The Anabaptists gave greater priority to the place of Scripture, but used it less critically (in keeping with the wider use of the Scripture in the sixteenth century, in a pre-historical, critical age). Liberation theology, however, uses Scripture quite critically but in relation to analysis of the social situation, which for numerous writers takes precedence over Scripture study itself.

Until now the comparative analysis has focused upon the main Anabaptist tradition; it has not taken into account the Münsterite strand of violence with its distinctive eschatological and hermeneutical conceptions. The next stage of analysis will attempt a threefold, rather than a twofold comparison.

II. PROMINENT HERMENEUTICAL ISSUES AMONG THE THREE MOVEMENTS

Especially when an analysis of the Münsterite theology (1530–36) comes into focus (to be distinguished from Thomas Müntzer and the Peasants' Revolt), one of the primary considerations consists of the influence of biblical eschatology and/or apocalyptic on the movement. While more must be said in order to fine tune the subsequent analysis, I identify some of the striking similarities and differences among the three movements in their appeal to various emphases in the Bible:

Swiss Brethren and Menno	Münster Theology (1534-35)	Liberation Theology Today
Patient waiting and enduring, suffering until the end.	End of age is here and calls for a special program (Hoffman & Rothmann).	The new order of the kingdom liberates from oppression. The Exodus is pivotal in the reading of the Bible.
Nonresistance and love for enemy are hallmarks of the new life.	God's endtime, now arrived, calls believers to avenge God's wrath against evil doers.	The new order calls for justice in the economic and political sphere, even the violent overthrow of the oppressor.
The church separates itself from the evils of political and economic power, specifically the use of the sword.	The believers use divine power through the sword to crush the head of evil (strong apocalyptic imagery).	The death/resurrection paradigm calls for destruction of the old that the new might be born.

As one reflects upon this simplified typology, it is clear that various parts of the Bible can be used to adduce support for each of these positions. As Hans Jürgen Goertz has argued, the violence of both Münster and liberation theology is to be understood as counter-violence, which arises out of God's call for justice in judgment upon the violence of the established order.[7] But even though this link stands *prima facie,* a closer analysis indicates widely differing understandings of eschatology between Münsterite theology and liberation theology. The justification for the use of violence by the Münsterite Anabaptists depended upon the eschatological vision that they indeed were called to establish the New Jerusalem upon earth (the historical evidence indicates that they had earlier intended to make Amsterdam the permanent home of the New Jerusalem—and this is not metaphorical theology!). They believed that the endtime had come and the almighty God had chosen them as the elect to carry out the work of God's final judgment upon the wicked. Remarkable indeed is the Münster leaders' appeal to the Old Testament (contrary to mainline Anabaptist hermeneutic) for the establishment of the death penalty, polygamy and the rule of the community under twelve elders with Jan van Leiden regarded as King David *redivivus.* Put in the words of the Qumran Covenanters, it was the time for "the War of the Sons of Light and [Against] the Sons of Darkness." Within the mainstream of the Anabaptist tradition, this has been regarded rightly as an aberration in eschatological perception. It stands in sharp contrast to the continuing emphasis of most Anabaptists to practice nonresistance toward the enemy and to suffer wrong rather than retaliate. Precisely at this point a very sharp difference arises among the three movements under discussion. When choosing between violence or nonviolence, liberation theology is different from either of the above in that it is more socio-economically analytical and politically pragmatic rather than eschatologically oriented.

Of second importance in this comparison of the three movements is the influence of social, economic and political factors upon the use of the Bible. Both the Anabaptist movement and liberation theology depend upon the rising of the lower class into what is regarded as the middle class in the European and American economic structure. Because of this feature, Marxian analysis has proposed a distinctive interpretation of Anabaptism, and Marxian ideology plays a significant role in liberation theology as well. Some have seen Thomas Müntzer and the Peasants' Revolt of 1524 as part of the larger Anabaptist story. Certainly it is related to the *Zeitgeist* of the times, but the distinguishing nonviolent feature of mainline Anabaptism, in contrast to the Peasants' Revolt, must be clearly noted.[8]

Another striking difference to be noted in this level of analysis is that while some of the early Anabaptist leaders (Grebel, Sattler and Marpeck) were scholars, the leaders of the Münster rebellion were mostly of the guild class. Jan Matthijs was a baker from Haarlem and Jan (Bokelson) van Leiden was a tailor. Most of the leaders in the liberation theology movement, however, are priests and scholars, more similar to the *early* leaders of the Anabaptist movement (who were shortly martyred off the scene). Hence the class status of the leaders in the movement shows considerable variety, with liberation theology representing the most educated leadership, the nonresistant/pacifist Anabaptist movement representing a mixture of educated leadership and uneducated (in fact, the Anabaptists came to be very suspicious of the school men because they used rational maneuvers to obscure the clear truth of God's word[9]) and the leaders of the Münsterite experiment least educated.

To what extent are these socio-economic factors in these movements determinative for their use of Scripture? Although Ernesto Cardenal's four volumes portraying the Scripture study of the Solentiname base communities indicate that the impetus for the social vision arises out of direct reading of the biblical text, most of the literature on liberation theology is oriented to university students at the graduate level, with much traffic between Scripture exegesis and Marxian social analysis. This kind of ideological construct, operating upon scriptural exegesis, would have been anathema to most of the Anabaptist leaders. According to Walter Klaassen's description, Anabaptism stood against Idealism (which identified reality with ideas). Quite certainly then, Anabaptism would also have been opposed to reading the Bible through the lenses of any ideological value system other than the Gospel itself.[10] Emphasizing obedience in life, it called for costly discipleship, even suffering and death for the sake of the Gospel.

The import of the endtime eschatological scheme upon the Münsterite community might be seen as a religious ideology, distinguishing it from mainline Anabaptism and associating it more closely to those liberation theologians who employ Marxian ideology as both apologetic and vision for the future.

Although similarities exist at some points in the class status of the leaders of liberation theology and Anabaptism, it is my judgment that the critical distinctions and similarities do not lie at this point. Rather, the critical distinctions—and differences—are to be designated by the cross-bearing discipleship orientation of Anabaptism, the avenging triumphalism of Münsterite theology and the revolutionary social justice of liberation theology. Further, the differences among these three are not superficial, but deep—and determinitive of the substantive nature of each of the three movements.

III. BEYOND COMPARISONS: TOWARD LIBERATION WITH DISCIPLESHIP

In this section I would like to work toward a more normative statement of hermeneutical perception, arising out of these comparisons, that can be instructive for those of us who wish to be faithful to both the liberationist and discipleship strands within the biblical tradition.

1. We must recognize clearly that the Gospel narrative is permeated with liberation events. Jesus came in the power of the Spirit to crush the head of Satan, to conquer evil in both its personal and structural manifestations. Two of the predominant emphases in Mark's Gospel are exorcisms, in which people are freed from the power of the demonic, and judgment upon both the religious leaders and the religious institutions, especially the Temple.[11]

Essential to the Gospel and our response to it must be commitment to the liberating power of Jesus Christ. Oppressive forces, both in personal and structural dimensions of life, are to be joyously repudiated in the name and power of the Gospel.

2. At the heart of the same Gospel story lies the costly call to discipleship, following Jesus in the way of the cross.[12] Unless this emphasis is held in close conjunction with the call to liberation, the Gospel of Jesus Christ is distorted, aborted and finally repudiated.

3. Specifically and crucially, Jesus' teaching regarding love for the enemy must be seen as a critical test put to all of the above movements. Nonresistant/pacifist Anabaptism alone passes this test, in my judgment. The Münsterite violence is a direct repudiation of Jesus' command to love the enemy; those within the liberation theology movement who call for the violent overthrow of the oppressor are called hereby also to account. Granted it may be justified as counter-violence, yet it is not the way of the slain Lamb (Rev. 5:8) who through a martyr's death reconciles hostile peoples into one body of peace (Eph. 2:13-14).[13]

4. Our approach to Scripture via the hermeneutical circle should continue and be informed by both the contribution of liberation theology and Anabaptism. Utilizing elements noted earlier in both approaches to Scripture, I would suggest the following four-point engagement: 1) the community's commitment to discipleship and God's establishment of justice; 2) reading and study of the

text corporately as a community of faith; 3) theological reflection upon the text in light of the community's reality; and 4) praxis-reflection, consisting of discernment on the part of the community on how to live out the will of God within the social situation of the community, both internally and externally.

Analysis of the social situation itself, just as knowledge of the historical-critical method and options to it, should not be a phase in the hermeneutical process itself. Rather the faith of the community, the Bible study process, the theological reflection and then the praxis-response should all be in active tension with informed awareness of various methodologies for both social analysis and Scripture study. Any one form of social analysis or Bible study method must not dominate the hermeneutical process, but be constantly scrutinized by the Bible study process itself.

As I have argued in my larger hermeneutical study, we as interpreters must be as self-conscious as possible about the ways in which political, economic, social and religious traditions influence our readings of the biblical text, while at the same time we must stand ever firm on our commitment to the biblical text as the final arbiter and guide for our lives. Granted the truth in what the European materialist biblical scholars tell us—that only by coming to the Bible through the hands of economic reality, the feet of political praxis, and the eyes of ideological vision can we understand the Scripture[14]—yet it is truer still that we can only understand economic reality, political praxis and ideological vision as we submit ourselves to the critical scalpel of the divinely authoritative word for our lives. That word includes the costly way of discipleship. And that call to obedience begins with me, in my specific social situation and must affect the decisions I make in relation to my brother, my sister and to the larger world in which I live.

5. God's people must recognize their ongoing need for internal renewal and self-criticism, which arises from submission to the word and the Spirit. This need certainly exists for the church as a whole but also for those of us committed to liberation and discipleship, since self-serving unjust interests can quickly take over revolutionary movements even in the name of peace and equity.

This call to self-critical reflection was one of the major conclusions of an extensive study of Scripture in order to ascertain its significance for peace-praxis in today's world. The results of this fifteen-year study, written by four different scholars, correlate peace-praxis with biblical eschatological hope and conclude with a call to the church: "Is it not in the self-critical reflection of the church upon its own commission and its reformation of both its leaders and members that the most important (at least foundational) aspect of its contribution to peace might be given?"[15]

Only as the church is continually reborn and reformed, discipled and vindicated by God, will it become a prophetic voice for liberation, justice and peace in the world today.

NOTES

1. Such an analysis of social class structure had been done by Claus-Peter Clasen, *Anabaptism: A Social History, 1525-1618* (Ithaca, N.Y.: Cornell University Press, 1972). For an interpretation which links the Münsterite violence directly with Anabaptism, see James M. Stayer, *Anabaptists and the Sword* (Lawrence, Kan.: Coronado Press, 1972, 1976 [note the "Reflections and Retractions" in the 1976 edition]).
2. For fuller presentation of these uses of Scripture, see Willard M. Swartley, *Slavery, Sabbath, War and Women: Case Issues in Biblical Interpretation* (Scottdale, Pa: Herald Press, 1983), ch. 3.
3. LaVerne Rutschman, "Anabaptism and Liberation Theology," *Mennonite Quarterly Review* 55, 3 (July 1982): 255-70.
4. Richard van Dülmen, "Das Täufertum und das Königreich Sion in Münster 1534/5 ," in *Reformation als Revolution: Soziale Bewegung und religiöser Radikalismus in der deutschen Reformation* (München: Deutscher Taschenbuch Verlag, 1977), pp. 179-84.
5. Gustavo Gutiérrez, *A Theology of Liberation,* trans. and ed. Sister Caridad Inda and John Eagleson (Maryknoll, N.Y.: Orbis Books, 1973). See also Norman Gottwald, ed., *The Bible and Liberation: Political and Social Hermeneutics,* Part 2 (Maryknoll, NY: Orbis Books, 1983).
6. Carlos Mesters, "The Use of the Bible in Christian Communities of the Common People," in Gottwald, pp. 119-33.
7. Hans Jürgen Goertz, *Profiles of Radical Reformers* (Scottdale, Pa.: Herald Press, 1982), pp. 200-202.
8. See Conrad Grebel's letter to Thomas Müntzer for this distinction: Leland Harder, ed., *The Sources of Swiss Anabaptism: The Conrad Grebel Letters and Related Documents* (Scottdale, Pa.: Herald Press, 1985), pp. 292-94.
9. Walter Klaassen, *Anabaptism: Neither Catholic Nor Protestant* (Waterloo, Ont.: Conrad Press, 1973), pp. 37-47.
10. Klaassen, p. 38.
11. Willard M. Swartley, *Mark: The Way for All Nations* (Scottdale, Pa.: Herald Press, 1979, 1981), ch. 9.
12. Swartley, *Mark,* ch. 7-8.
13. Oscar Romero's death stands in this tradition. See the exposition of Pauline theology on this point by Ulrich Luz, "Eschatologie und Friedenshandeln bei Paulus" in *Eschatologie und Friedenshandeln,* ed. Luz, et al. (Stuttgart: Verlag Katholisches Bibelwerk, 1981), pp. 153-94.
14. Michel Clevenot, *Materialist Approaches to the Bible* (Maryknoll, N.Y.: Orbis Books, 1984).
15. The four authors of this final phrase of the study are Jürgen Kegler ("Prophetisches Reden von Zukünftigem"), Peter Lampe ("Die Apokalyptiker—ihre Situation und ihr Handeln"), Paul Hoffmann ("Eschatologie und Friedenshandeln in der Jesusüberlieferung) and Ulrich Luz ("Eschatologie und Friedenshandeln bei Paulus"). Luz writes the concluding chapter under the heading "The Significance of the Biblical Witness for the Church's Peace-Praxis" (my translation). The quotation (my translation) comes from page 193 (see note 13 for bibliographic detail).

6

Withdrawal and Diaspora: The Two Faces of Liberation

JOHN H. YODER

It is widely agreed that the story of the Exodus has in the Old Testament a fundamental position that is of far greater theological importance than its merely standing at the beginning of the story of the Hebrew people. Even the superficial reader of the Old Testament can observe how this formative story continues to cast its light on the identity and the path of Israel. The rise of critical Old Testament scholarship in recent decades has simply reinforced this already present awareness of the centrality of the Exodus story.

There is an equal self-evidence in our time to preoccupation with the theme of the liberation of the oppressed. Our age is the heir to four different formulations of the call to liberation. There is the Protestant experience from the Huguenots through Cromwell to the American Revolution. There is the democratic vision of enlightenment rationalism, with its fruition in the French Revolution. Thirdly, Latin America is heir, as the rest of the so-called Third World is not, to what we might call the Bolivarian vision. This vision, undertaken in the name of an ideal that drew freely from the two older traditions named above, could not by the nature of the case arise out of the same kind of democratic base; therefore it took the form of creating independent "national" units that withdrew from European control under the initiative of a militant elite.

Beyond the three models just identified, and claiming a different level of analysis, there is the Marxist vision of liberation, arising in Western Europe out of the same cultural resources as the other three streams, but moving beyond them in two fundamental respects: in undertaking a broader analysis of the economic forms of oppression, and in finding its greatest political successes not in its birthplace, industrialized Western Europe, but in two great empires of the East.

It is hardly necessary in this context to review how those four cultural traditions, all of them present for over a century, have come to have increasingly wide recognition as the awareness of oppressive situations has grown, as the oppressiveness of economic colonialism has become not only more visible but also quantatively greater despite all the promised progress and all the attempted revolutions of the past centuries.

It is thus completely fitting, in the effort of the Christian community to deepen the actualization of her presence in a world where the demand for change is omnipresent, that the evident analogy between the basic image of social criticism in our time and the root image of Hebrew faith should have led to a widespread appeal by both preachers and theorists to the image of the Exodus (not only the language but also the myth) as a key to interpret our age and to spark the Christian community into vital involvement and risk. There has thus arisen a vast literature, which although popularly labeled as "theology of liberation" might more precisely (and in a favorable sense) be called a "proclamation of liberation," in which the centrality of the Exodus story for biblical faith is juxtaposed with formulations of the revolutionary vision drawn from Marx and Bolívar and to a lesser extent from Cromwell and Rousseau.

It cannot be the intention of this analysis to call into question the creative leap that the preacher must make from the Bible to the present, which must always mean some kind of selectivity within the materials of the biblical witness and some kind of selectivity within the concerns of the present. The task of this study, rather, takes for granted not only that there must be such a leap, but also that the selectivity, which links liberation today with Exodus then, is proper. It is however the task of theology, now not in the sense of proclamation and creative leap but in the sense of critical reflection, to inquire within what limits and to what extent this particular creative juxtaposition may claim theological validity reaching beyond the limits of partisan ideology.

Neither can it be the function of this present study to relate the Old Testament to the New or study the variety of ways in which this Hebrew tradition has to be related to the New Testament. If Christians confess in Jesus one greater than Moses, their confession must both confirm and transcend the story whose foundation is the Pentateuch events. This real question is likewise properly identified as beyond our present assignment.

It would be possible, and of course it would be very fitting and fruitful, to bring to such a theological critique the perspective of critical analysis of the authorship of the various Pentateuch accounts or of the diversity of interpretations of the Exodus model through the prophets and the later Israelite writers of chronicles. But as a minimum specimen, this outline will need to accept the limits of the present canonical testimony as a guide to the definition of the tests of consistency and balance that we are responsible to undertake.

It is evident that such a critical undertaking cannot be based upon a thorough survey of all the vast literature in which the imagery in question is exploited.[1] Thus this meditation on the validity of certain images must not be misunderstood as a specific criticism of any one particular text or texts on "liberation." Nor could it be claimed that all the writing that is being done falls into the particular temptations or errors here recognized as possible.

EXODUS IS NOT A PROGRAM BUT A MIRACLE

The Exodus experience is a part of the ancient Hebrew vision of the wars of Yahweh. These events were not rationally planned, pragmatically executed military operations in which success was dependent on the shrewdness of the planners or the number of their weapons; they were rather cultic events and miracles. Sometimes (and the Red Sea is one such case) the Israelites did not even participate in the destruction of the enemy. Even when they did, the real combat was not a liberation front or a terrorist commando but Yahweh himself.

We misunderstand the meaning of the wars of Yahweh if we moralistically try to interpret them as a part of the debate about the legitimacy of war and violence.[2] The legalistic argument would run that killing must not be wrong because God commanded it in the case of the Amalekites, but we recognize that nowhere else do we argue in that way from ancient Israel to contemporary ethics. The legitimate lesson of the wars of Yahweh for contemporary ethics, in line with the interpretation already worked out by the prophets, is that because "Yahweh will fight for us," entering upon a conflict was not a matter of human strategizing and winning. It was not the effect of preponderant human power. The Red Sea event is for the whole Old Testament the symbol of the confession that the Israelites do not raise a hand to save themselves. They trust and venture out.

EXODUS PRESUPPOSES THE PREVIOUS "LIBERATION" OF THE COMMUNITY OF THE OPPRESSED

The Exodus event was not the creation of a community. There had to be a community first. For generations the Hebrews had been reciting the stories of Abraham, Isaac and Jacob as they had been led by the "God of the fathers" before reaching Egypt. This history of recitation and celebration provided Moses not only with an audience for his call to mobilization but also with the means whereby he could be accredited as the one whom they should hear, because the "God of the fathers" had sent him. Thus there is a prerequisite for the going out. The people could not have been gathered to go if they had not been a people before.

This would suggest that those particular interpretations of liberation are inadequate that hold out the promise that a great event of revolution or some destruction of a particular oppressor will *by itself* create the community in which freedom is real. Such a promise is cruel in its avoidance of historical seriousness. It makes promises that events will not keep.

THE EXODUS IS THE WORK OF A CULTURALLY PREPARED LEADER

Although all of the streams of revolutionary tradition identified above (except the Bolivarian) project liberation and revolution in terms of a social process whose legitimacy and power arise from "the people" or from the dialectic of historical structures, the Exodus event is very much the product of the personal uniqueness of Moses. Moses was not simply a prophet claiming God-given authority. He was at the same time a very rare cultural event. He was identified by blood and emotion with the suffering of his own people, yet he had also had the education of an Egyptian prince and the experience of a Bedouin shepherd. His personality included a deep understanding of the enemy culture and a broad acquaintance with the desert into which he was to go.

Whether this image of leadership is applied by analogy today to the individual leader or to the collective elite, the cause of genuine liberation is ill-served when suffering communities are offered the hope that they can be led out of captivity by persons whose accreditation is only their claims of personal power or only their identification with the people. Of course Moses could not have liberated his people if he had not been a genuine Hebrew. But it is more important (because it is more rare) that he was also a genuine Egyptian and a genuine Arabian. Of course the liberation of Latin America must be realized by leaders who are genuinely Latin American. But it is more nearly indispensable (because it is more rare) that such leadership be intimately and wisely informed about the culture that oppresses and about the desert in the future.

It is not without importance that Mohandas K. Gandhi was a British lawyer, who first developed his skills and his theory not in his homeland but in Africa where Indians were a minority. Martin Luther King Jr. studied Gandhi and Paul Tillich in a liberal Methodist theological faculty. Something analogous can be said of the apostle Paul or of Tupac Amaru. There will be no liberation if the leadership is not autochthonous. But the liberation will not be legitimate and will not live if the leadership is not cosmopolitan.

It is not sufficient, in explaining the uniqueness of Moses (or of the other leaders just mentioned), to say that he is informed about the oppressing culture or the future desert. His information is more than that: it is a capacity to communicate. Martin Luther King was able to speak to white America in the terms of the "American Dream," forcing a recognition of the legitimacy of the demands of his people. Gandhi similarly could talk back to imperial England in terms of the language and the values of British legal ideals. King did it in Washington, Gandhi in London. Moses before Pharaoh was not a spy in the enemy camp. He was proclaimer in the public arena. He made it visible beyond the confines of his own community that the release the people demanded was theirs by right, and he did it in the language of the wider world.

The identity of the God of the fathers was not simply recounted as an ancient tradition, but proclaimed as a potentiality for new events. The prophetic ministry of the one sent by the God of the fathers is not simply *conscientization*, bringing to awareness the contradiction and the injustice of the present; the proclaimed word rather creates new possibilities beyond what our critical analysis of the situation could invent.

EXODUS IS BUT THE BEGINNING OF PROBLEMS

The Red Sea was not the Jordan. On the other side of the water, beyond the destruction of Pharaoh, there lay not the land of liberty but another temptation to worship the gods of Egypt, or to picture the Yahweh who had freed them in forms borrowed from Egypt (the bullock) and with gold stolen from Egypt. The end of the oppression was not freedom. The death of the oppressor was not liberty but only the occasion for a new testing and a new enslavement. This new enslavement was not the direct product of the oppressor, but rather shows the acceptance, by the oppressed, of the oppressor's values, making them unwilling to wait for the grace of the new order being carved out for them on the mountain.

EXODUS IS WITHDRAWAL

The simplest application of the imagery of Exodus as liberation is often its juxtaposition with examples of the seizure of power in or from the state after the model of Bolívar or Lenin. The parallel is, however, by no means so evident. Perhaps it would have been very possible for Moses and his colleagues to take over Egypt. That had been done before in Egypt by immigrant groups. As the Exodus account describes the desperation of Pharaoh and the moral authority of Moses, a takeover of the country by the brickmakers would have been conceivable. But instead the alternative was literally an exodus, a going out, an escape from the situation of oppression rather than a seizure of power in that same place. The death of Pharaoh was not a revolutionary goal, or even a revolutionary means *à la* Bonhoeffer, but rather the self-inflicted defeat brought upon him by his refusal to let the Israelites leave peaceably. Exodus did not mean destroying the oppressive order. It meant forsaking it and creating an alternative.

This observation that the alternative to the oppressive order is another order and not the assassination of the oppressor would preserve many liberation movements, especially in a context like that of Latin America, from the cruel disappointment of revolutions that fail to liberate, not simply because of ill will or stupidity on the part of a revolutionary elite, but because of deep flaws in the structure of the effort itself.

EXODUS IS FULFILLED IN THE COVENANT

When we observe the account of the lights and the noises on Sinai, the people's fear and the coming of sacred words, we may be tempted to accentuate in our interpretation the similarities with the cosmological myth of other cultures. But what happened at Sinai was not mere cosmic magic. It was the constitution of a community under law. This consolidation of the community is indispensable to the meaning of liberation. Not only the divinely chiseled tablets of Torah, but also the commonsensical borrowing from Moses' father-in-law of a model of grassroots government was needed for the "mixed multitude" to become a people. Exodus was the leap of faith, but Sinai was its landing. Historically Exodus was the prerequisite of Sinai; morally it is the other way around. Liberation is *from* bondage and *for* covenant, and *what for* matters more than *what from*.

If Exodus was the prerequisite of Sinai, in terms of movement, Sinai was the prerequisite of Exodus in terms of motive. It was the reason given to the Egyptians (Ex. 8:2, 20, 26f, etc.). Even before the arrival at Sinai, the column of fiery cloud was a symbol of Sinai leading them. Liberation after the model of Exodus issues in the reconstitution of community around the liberator.

This is then another point at which to take the contemporary rhetoric seriously. Can the various fronts and movements, which today call themselves "liberation," point us with confidence, on the basis of experiences elsewhere or of the inherent quality of their vision, to a constitutive event *following* the "exodus" that will give substance to their separate existence? Or is what is today called liberation sometimes sparked and justified mostly by the wrongness of the oppression it denounces, while sharing with the oppressor many ethical assumptions about how to deal with dissent, about the use of violence, about the political vocation of a liberating elite?

So liberation has its postrequisites as well as its prerequisites. It is not a once-and-for-all revolution but only a threshhold linking two phases of pilgrim peoplehood.

THERE IS ONLY ONE EXODUS

The event of Exodus is central, but it is also unique. It is not repeated in the Old Testament story. The community that derives its identity from that Exodus event does not continue it in a chain of further Exodus events but rather in a new identity in a new relation to the God who called it into covenant. From now onward, the meaning of that covenant goes far beyond the event of liberation. On the basis of the total witness of Scripture we would have to say that the event of covenant gives a new form to liberation in such a way that no more Exodus is needed. The call of the prophets is never to go out of Egypt again but rather to realize in contemporary community forms the purpose of the God who freed them. For a while the social form of the realization of liberty was the relative anarchy of the period of the judges. The most ambivalent form of that covenant expression was the attempted state structures of the two Israelite kingdoms, which neither the biblical historians nor the prophets considered very successful. The conclusion of the matter in the experience of Israel, and the basis from which the fulfillment that came in Jesus moves on, was not the national identity, which the Maccabees resurrected once and which the various zealot movements before and after the time of Jesus attempted again and again unsuccessfully. It was rather the community in the dispersion. Especially the message of Jeremiah (chapter 29) demonstrates that for the community that lives in the memory of Exodus, the acceptance of Diaspora existence is not a lesser evil, not resignation where nothing else is possible, but the path of obedience, a safeguard of identity, protection against the "lying dreams" of those who would trouble the exiles with unreal promises of restored national pride. The command "to seek the peace of that city" is not a denial but a definition of the meaning for now of the Exodus and the covenant. The renunciation of national identity in the form of the state is definitive: when Ezra and Nehemiah return to Jerusalem it will be without national independence.

DIASPORA IS THE SCENE OF MISSION

The community in the exile does not simply seek to survive in that hostile world. It "seeks the peace of that city." Joseph and Daniel and Mordecai come to power, not because they seek or struggle for power, but because their faithfulness to Yahweh in the midst of suffering prepares them to be elevated (by the same God and the same power that worked at the Red Sea) and enabled to improve the pagan order so as to make it a protection for its people and viable as an administration. This is done by forcing the pagan power to renounce its self-mythologizing national religious claims and to recognize the higher sovereignty proclaimed by the Hebrew monotheist. So recurrent is the Joseph/Daniel/Mordecai pattern in the Old Testament that we must recognize it as a kind of model. The contribution of a suffering but resolutely monotheistic elite to the renewal of the existing system is as representative of the people of the Exodus as is the traumatic withdrawal of Exodus, and more so than the theocratic takeover.

In terms of the number of years it lasted, the number of places it was followed, the place of the exemplary figures in canonical literature, and their concordance with other prophetic and sapiential teaching, we must conclude that it is the models of Joseph and Daniel, Mordecai and Jonah, rather than the state sovereignty of David and his followers, that had become in the Jewish Scriptures by the time of Jesus the standard for the life of the community living in the covenant produced by liberation.

Our present culture's impatience with intrasystemic contributions to social change should not lead us to think that when the Jews "sought the peace of that city" they were simply supporting and moderately improving the existing oppressive order in the way that today would be called "developmentalist." By no means. The stories of Joseph and Daniel and Mordecai are all stories of radical changes of social structure. By no stretching of the imagination could the Jews, with their radical rejection of the cultic unity of the pagan empire, be considered as morally supporting the existing system even after they had saved it. The ongoing presence of liberation is the countercultural community with its radically different God and Torah.

The fact that the exiles accepted their situation in Diaspora does not mean that they identified emotionally or religiously with their oppressors. The nonconformity remained. To "seek the peace of the city" did not mean being blinded by its glory. Even less did it mean being taken in by Babylon's rhetoric. With the message of Jeremiah that national sovereignty was to be abandoned was constantly linked the lamentation, the dramatic reminder that Babylon is a strange and hostile world. With the story of Daniel being vindicated by God in the eyes of the king was linked the vision of a new kind of divine liberation, now in the language of apocalypse, which by its very imagery is proclaimed as beyond the boundaries of present historical existence and beyond the planning of human agency.

This effort to perceive the place of Exodus at the heart of the identity of Israel, in a more rounded way than is often done could provide the foundation for a far more flexible and hopeful approach to concrete projects of liberation than does the habitual accent upon a single stroke (*golpe*) or a single leap *(salto)* as the universally applicable definition of the liberating event. That demand, or that promise, although apparently optimistic and humanistic, in fact destroys genuine hope and challenge by its distance from present reality. The recognition of many more stages and levels before and after Exodus, partaking with the same realism and seriousness in the same historical process, can illuminate the reality in which most of the oppressed find themselves more soberly and therefore more constructively.

The agents of change and moral awakening, if they are enabled to therefore understand their ministry in the fuller imagery of the long story of elect peoplehood, might well be freed from the *guerrillero* impatience, from the terrorist self-righteousness and from the adolescent anger, which so easily play into the hands of the oppressors when the preoccupation with the heroic seizure of power becomes the only language for hope. Thus the language of hope will be more authentic, neither an opiate nor a stimulant, and ultimately more hopeful than a proclamation that exhausts itself with only one image.

This meditation leaves us with material for further debate. There is a serious need to study whether it is never or always fitting to transfer biblical imagery, whether that of Exodus or that of Diaspora, beyond the history of the biblical community without falling into a nonhistorical idealism. Such an investigation has begun within the liberation literature under such headings as "masses and minorities" or "neo-Constantinianism." Is every oppressed people the people of God? Or must there be some connection to Abraham and Jeremiah and Jesus? Can Christian ethics be generalized as a pattern for all decent human beings, or does it retain some particular historic identification with the history of the Jews and Jesus? And if there should be some permanent linkage with the meaning or the name of Jesus, what does that mean after centuries of the Constantinian alliance of the church with power have clouded the face of

Jesus? Is there such a thing as an incognito Christ apart from the presence and witness of Christians; and if so, how is his working to be identified? These questions need to be named if only to avoid the impression that we ignore them: to discuss them here would involve a different set of questions and procedures than does our present concern.

In summary, the seriousness with which we should take the centrality of Exodus in the Hebrew Canon forbids our distilling from it a timeless idea of liberation that we would then use to ratify all kinds of liberation projects in all places and forms. God does not merely "act in history." God acts in history *in particular ways*. It would be a denial of the history to separate an abstract project label like *liberation* from the specific meaning of the liberation God has brought.

The *form* of liberation in the biblical witness is not the guerrilla campaign against an oppressor culminating in his assassination and military defeat, but the creation of a confessing community that is viable without or against the force of the state and that does not glorify that power structure even by the effort to topple it.

The *content* of liberation in the biblical witness is not the "nation-state" brotherhood engineered after the takeover but the convenantal peoplehood already existing because God has given it, and sure of its future because of the Name ("identity") of God, not because of trust in the success of a coming campaign.

The *means* of liberation in the biblical witness is not prudentially justified, tactically guided violence, but "mighty Acts," which may come through the destruction at the Red Sea—but may also come when the king is moved to be gracious to Esther, or to Daniel, or to Nehemiah.

The *atmosphere* of liberation is not compulsive management of events, not calculation of effects in proportion to effort, but wonderment and praise, doxology.

NOTES

1. A version of the present text was originally commissioned in 1974 for a South American journal. It is intended as a communication from and to the South American world, which I was privileged to visit several times between 1966 and 1973. Nothing in the text is intended as defense of my own geographical or denominational orientation, though I seek neither to deny or to disavow my location.

2. See John Howard Yoder, *Politics of Jesus* (Grand Rapids, Mich.: Eerdmans, 1974), pp. 78ff., and *Original Revolution* (Scottdale, Pa.: Herald Press, 1971), pp. 85ff.

7

Mennonites and the Poor: Toward an Anabaptist Theology of Liberation

RONALD J. SIDER

A serious dialogue between Anabaptism and liberation theology must focus major attention on at least two crucial areas: the question of violence, and the question of God's attitude toward the poor. This essay treats only the second.

On the question of God's and therefore the church's attitude toward the poor, Anabaptism and liberation theology pose an important question for each other. Liberation theology rightly wants to know if the wealthy Mennonite church in North America and Western Europe has any intention of living what the Bible teaches about the poor. And Mennonites want to ask whether liberation theologians are willing to let the Bible, rather than Karl Marx, provide the decisive definition of the proper Christian attitude toward the oppressed.

This dialogue between Mennonites and liberation theologians will also be significant for pressing internal debate within the Mennonite church in North America. Some more conservative folk fear that the Mennonite social activists are developing an unbiblical agenda for the church. They fear secular thought, perhaps even Marxist analysis, is becoming dominant in activist Mennonite circles. These conservative questioners want to know whether the Scriptures are really still the norm for those who talk loudly about justice for the poor.

The activists, on the other hand, fear that the conservative critique of Mennonites who have adopted themes from liberation theology may just be an excuse for ignoring the Bible's radical summons to seek justice for the poor. Is the objection that liberation theology has Marxist elements merely an easy way to justify the status quo and ignore the challenge from the Third World church?

There is a way to work at these mutual suspicions. It is to attempt to listen anew to what the Scriptures say about God's attitude and therefore his people's attitude toward the poor and oppressed. By doing that I hope to help define one crucial aspect of an Anabaptist theology of liberation. I believe that the Bible teaches that God is on the side of the poor. Some liberation theologians have misinterpreted what this central biblical teaching means. Many comfortable Mennonites, on the other hand, have simply ignored it.

What is the biblical attitude? We must begin by asking who the poor are. The Scriptures sometimes tell us that some folk are poor because they are lazy and slothful (for example, Prov. 6:6-11; 19:15; 20:13; 21:25; 24:30-34). And the Bible knows of voluntary poverty for the sake of the kingdom. The most common biblical connotation of "the poor," however, is of those who are economically impoverished because of calamity or exploitation. In this chapter I use this last meaning of "the poor."

In what sense is God on the side of the economically poor? I want to start by saying what I do *not* mean when I say God is on the side of the poor and oppressed.[1]

I do not mean that material poverty is a biblical ideal. This glorious creation is a wonderful gift from our Creator. He wants us to revel in its glory and splendor.

Second, I do not mean that the poor and oppressed are, because they are poor and oppressed, to be idealized or automatically included in the church. The poor sinfully disobey God in the same way that we wretched middle-class sinners do, and they therefore need to enter into a living personal relationship with Jesus Christ. Only then do they become a part of the church. One of the serious weaknesses in much of liberation theology is an inadequate ecclesiology, especially the tendency to blur the distinction between the church and the world. And one can understand why. It is understandable that black and Latin American theologians would be impressed by the double fact that whereas most of the organized church regularly ignores the injustice that causes poverty and oppression, those who do care enough to risk their lives for improved conditions are often people who explicitly reject Christianity. Hence one can understand why someone like Hugo Assmann would conclude that

> the true Church is "the conscious emergence and the more explicit enacting of the one meaning of the one history," in other words, a revolutionary consciousness and commitment. The explicit reference to Jesus Christ becomes in this view gratuitous in the original sense of the word—something which is not demanded by or needed for the struggle [of socio-economic liberation]. . . . The reference to Jesus Christ does not add an "extra" to the historical struggle but is totally and without rest identified with it.[2]

In spite of deep appreciation for the factors that lead to an identification of the church with the poor and oppressed or the revolutionary minority that seeks liberation for them, one must insist that such a view is fundamentally unbiblical.

Third, when I say that God is on the side of the poor and oppressed, I do not mean that God cares more about the salvation of the poor than the salvation of the rich or that the poor have a special claim to the Gospel. It is sheer nonsense to say with Enzo Gatti:

> The human areas that are poorest in every way are the most qualified for receiving the Saving Word. They are the ones that have the best right to that Word; they are the privileged recipients of the Gospel.[3]

God cares equally about the salvation of the rich and the poor. To be sure, at the psychological level, Gatti is partly correct. Church growth theorists have discovered what Jesus alluded to long ago in his comment on the camel going through the eye of the needle. It *is* extremely difficult for rich persons to enter the kingdom. The poor *are* generally more ready to accept the Gospel than the rich.[4] But that does not mean that God desires the salvation of the poor more than the salvation of rich.

Fourth, to say that God is on the side of the poor is not to say that knowing God is nothing more than seeking justice for the poor and oppressed. Some—although certainly not most—liberation theologians do jump to this radical conclusion. José Miranda says bluntly, "To know Yahweh is to achieve justice for the poor."[5] "The God who does not allow himself to be objectified, because only in the immediate command of conscience is he God, clearly specifies that he is knowable *exclusively* in the cry of the poor and the weak who seek justice."[6] Tragically it is precisely Miranda's kind of one-sided, reductionist approach that offers comfortable North Americans a plausible excuse for ignoring the radical biblical word that seeking justice for the poor is inseparable from—even though it is not identical with—knowing Yahweh.

Finally, when I say that God is on the side of the poor, I do not mean that hermeneutically we must start with some ideologically interpreted context of oppression (for instance, a Marxist definition of the poor and their oppressed situation) and then reinterpret Scripture from that ideological perspective. Black theologian James H. Cone's developing thought is interesting at this point. In 1969 in *Black Theology and Black Power* he wrote,

> The fact that I am Black is my ultimate reality. My identity with *blackness*, and what it means for millions living in a white world, controls the investigation. It is impossible for me to surrender this basic reality for a "higher more universal reality."[7]

By the time Cone wrote *God of the Oppressed,* however, he realized that such a view would relativize all theological claims, including his own critique of white racist theology.

> How do we distinguish our words about God from God's Word . . . ? Unless this question is answered satisfactorily, black theologians' distinction between white theology and Black Theology is vulnerable to the white contention that the latter is merely the ideological justification of radical black polities.[8]

To be sure, Cone believes as strongly as other liberation theologians that the hermeneutical key to Scripture is God's saving action to liberate the oppressed. But how does he know that?

> In God's revelation in Scripture we come to the recognition that the divine liberation of the oppressed is not determined by our perceptions but by the God of the Exodus, the prophets, and Jesus Christ who calls the oppressed into a liberated existence. Divine revelation *alone* is the test of the validity of this starting point. And if it can be shown that God as witnessed in the Scriptures is not the liberator of the oppressed, then Black Theology would have either to drop the "Christian" designation or to choose another starting point.[9]

One can only wish that all liberation theologians agreed with Cone!

Thus when I say that God is on the side of the poor, I do not mean that poverty is the ideal; that the poor and oppressed, *qua* poor and oppressed, are the church or have a special right to hear the Gospel; that seeking justice for the oppressed is identical with knowing Yahweh; or that hermeneutically one should begin with some ideologically interpreted context of oppression and then reinterpret Scripture from that perspective.

In what sense then *is* God on the side of the poor and oppressed? I want to develop three points:[10] 1) At the central points of revelation history, God also acted to liberate the poor and oppressed; 2) God acts in history to exalt the poor and oppressed and to cast down the rich and oppressive; and 3) God's people, if they are truly God's people, are also on the side of the poor and oppressed.

GOD ACTS TO LIBERATE THE POOR AND OPPRESSED

First, I want to look briefly at three central points of revelation history—the Exodus, the destruction of Israel and Judah, and the incarnation. At the central moments when God displayed his mighty acts in history to reveal his nature and will, God also intervened to liberate the poor and oppressed.

God displayed his power at the Exodus in order to free oppressed slaves! When God called Moses at the burning bush, he informed Moses that his intention was to end suffering and injustice: "I have seen the affliction of my people who are in Egypt, and have heard their cry because of their taskmasters; I know their sufferings, and I have come down to deliver them out of the hand of the Egyptians" (Exod. 3:7-8). Each year at the harvest festival, the Israelites repeated a liturgical confession celebrating the way God had acted to free a poor, oppressed people.

> A wandering Aramean was my father; and he went down into Egypt and sojourned there. . . . And the Egyptians treated us harshly and afflicted us, and laid upon us hard bondage. Then we cried to the Lord, the God of our fathers, and the Lord heard our voice, and saw our affliction, our toil, and our oppression; and the Lord brought us out of Egypt with a mighty hand (Deut. 26:5ff).

Unfortunately some liberation theologians see in the Exodus only God's liberation of an oppressed people and miss the fact that God also acted to fulfill his promises to Abraham, to reveal his will and to call out a special people. Certainly God acted at the Exodus to call a special people so that through them he could reveal his will and bring salvation to all people. But his will included the fact, as he revealed ever more clearly to his covenant people, that his people should follow him and side with the poor and oppressed. The fact that Yahweh did not liberate all poor Egyptians at the Exodus does not mean that he was not concerned for the poor everywhere anymore than the fact that he did not give the Ten Commandments to everyone in the Near East means that he did not intend them to have universal significance. Because God chose to reveal himself in history, he disclosed to particular people at particular points in time what he willed for all people everywhere.

At the Exodus God acted to demonstrate that he is opposed to oppression. We distort the biblical interpretation of the momentous event of the Exodus unless we see that at this pivotal point the Lord of the universe was at work correcting oppression and liberating the poor.

The prophets' explanation for the destruction of Israel and then Judah underlines the same point. The explosive message of the prophets is that God destroyed Israel not just because of idolatry (although certainly because of that), but also because of economic exploitation and mistreatment of the poor!

The middle of the eighth century B.C. was a time of political success and economic prosperity unknown since the days of Solomon. But it was precisely at this moment that God sent his prophet Amos to announce the unwelcome news that the northern kingdom would be destroyed. Why? Penetrating beneath the facade of current prosperity and fantastic economic growth, Amos saw terrible oppression of the poor. He saw the rich "trample the head of the poor into the dust of the earth" (2:7). He saw that the affluent lifestyle of the rich was built on oppression of the poor (6:1-7). Even in the courts the poor had no hope because the rich bribed the judges (5:10-15).

God's word through Amos was that the northern kingdom would be destroyed and the people taken into exile (7:11, 17). Only a very few years after Amos spoke, it happened just as God had said. Because of their mistreatment of the poor, God destroyed the northern kingdom. If there were room, it would be easy to document the same point with reference to the destruction of the southern kingdom (e.g., Jer. 5:26-29; 34:3-17). The cataclysmic catastrophe of national destruction and captivity reveals the God of the Exodus still at work correcting the oppression of the poor.

When God acted to reveal himself most completely in the incarnation, he continued to demonstrate his special concern for the poor and oppressed. St. Luke used the programmatic account of Jesus in the synagogue at Nazareth to define Jesus' mission. The words which Jesus read from the prophet Isaiah are familiar to us all:

> The Spirit of the Lord is upon me,
> because he has anointed me to preach good news to the poor.
> He has sent me to proclaim release to the captives
> and recovery of sight to the blind,
> to set at liberty those who are oppressed,
> to proclaim the acceptable year of the Lord (Luke 4:18-19).

After reading these words he informed the audience that this Scripture was now fulfilled in himself. The mission of the Incarnate One was to preach the good news to the poor and free the oppressed.

Many people spiritualize these words either by simplistically assuming that he was talking about healing blinded hearts in captivity to sin or by appealing to the later Old Testament and intertestamental idea of "the poor of Yahweh" (the *'anawim*). It is true that the later psalms and the intertestamental literature use the terms for the poor (especially 'anawim) to refer to pious, humble, devout Israelites who place all their trust in Yahweh.[11] But that does not mean that his usage had no connection with socio-economic poverty. Indeed, it was precisely the fact that the economically poor and oppressed were the faithful remnant that trusted in Yahweh that led to the new usage where the words for the poor designated the pious faithful.

The Hebrew words for the poor were *'ani, 'anaw, 'ebyon, dal* and *ras. 'Ani* (and *'anaw,* which originally had approximately the same basic meaning) denotes one who is "wrongfully impoverished or dispossessed."[12] *'Ebyon* refers to a beggar imploring charity. *Dal* connotes a thin, weakly person, for example, an impoverished, deprived peasant.[13] Unlike the others, *ras* is an essentially neutral term. In their persistent polemic against the oppression of the poor the prophets used the terms *'ebyon, 'ani* and *dal.*

Later these same words (especially *'anawim*) were used to designate the faithful remnant, the "pious poor" who trust solely in Yahweh.[14] But that does not mean that the older socio-economic connotations were lost. Richard Batey puts it this way:

> Beginning with the experience that the poor were often oppressed by the wicked rich, the poor were considered to be the special objects of Yahweh's protection and deliverance (Pss. 9:18, 19:1-8 . . .). Therefore the poor looked to Yahweh as the source of deliverance from their

enemies and oppressors. This attitude of trust and dependence exemplified that piety that should have characterized every Israelite. In this way the concept of the "pious poor" developed.[15]

Zondervan's *New International Dictionary of the New Testament* makes the same point:

> Only in the setting of this historical situation can we understand the meaning in the Psalm of "poor" and "needy." The poor man is the one who suffers injustice; he is poor because others have despised God's law. He therefore turns, helpless and humble, to God in prayer. . . . Through the self-identification, generation after generation, of those who prayed with the poor in psalms of individual lamentation and thanksgiving . . . there gradually developed the specific connotation of "poor" as meaning all those who turn to God in great need and seek his help. God is praised as the protector of the poor (e.g. Pss. 72:2, 4, 12f; 132:15), who procures justice for them against their oppressors.[16]

This same usage is common in intertestamental literature. When Greece and then Rome conquered Palestine, Hellenistic culture and values were foisted upon the Jews. Those who remained faithful to Yahweh often suffered financially. Thus the term *poor* was, as J. A. Ziesler says, "virtually equivalent to pious, God-fearing, and godly and reflects a situation where the rich were mainly those who had sold out to the incoming culture and had allowed their religious devotion to become corrupted by the new ways. If the poor were the pious, the faithful and largely oppressed, the rich were the powerful, ungodly, worldly, even apostate."[17] Thus the faithful remnant at Qumran called themselves "the poor" (*'ebyon*).[18] They and other first-century Jews yearned eagerly for the new age when the Messiah would come to fulfill the messianic promises (e.g., Isa. 11:4) and bring justice to the poor.[19]

Thus when Jesus read from Isaiah 61 in the synagogue at Nazareth and proclaimed good news to the poor, he was announcing to the faithful remnant who trusted in Yahweh and therefore were also poor socio-economically that the messianic age of justice for the poor had arrived.

Luke 7:18–23 confirms the argument that Luke 4:18f dare not be given a primarily spiritualized meaning. John sends his disciples to see if Jesus is the long-expected Messiah. Jesus' response is to heal the sick and blind and then tell John's disciples to report what they had seen:

> "Go and tell John what you have seen and heard: the blind receive their sight, the lame walk, lepers are cleansed, and the deaf hear, the dead are raised up, the poor have good news preached to them" (Luke 7:22).

This passage mentions many of the things outlined in Luke 4:18. Since Jesus had just healed those physically sick and blind, it is entirely clear that Jesus is referring to physical blindness and poverty. The same is undoubtedly the case in the parallel text of Luke 4:18f.[20] The new age that Jesus saw himself inaugurating had specific economic and social content of great interest for the poor and oppressed.

Other aspects of Jesus' teaching support this interpretation. The Lucan beatitudes promise blessing to the poor and hungry. The messianic kingdom in which the pious, but therefore also socio-economically poor, will receive justice is now coming in the person of Jesus. Nor does Matthew represent a spiritualized version of the beatitudes.[21] The poor "in spirit" are the pious poor who are also socio-economically deprived. And they hunger and thirst for righteousness—that is justice! As Herman Ridderbos rightly insists, the word *righteousness* here "must not be understood in the Pauline forensic sense of imputed forensic righteousness, but as the kingly justice which will be brought to light one day for the salvation of the oppressed and the outcasts, and which will be executed especially by the Messiah. . . . It is *this* justice to which the 'poor in spirit' and the 'the meek' look forward in the Sermon on the Mount."[22]

Now I do not in any way want to imply that Jesus' message was focused exclusively on socio-economic concerns. His message included a central concern for forgiving sinners, and he came to die on the cross for our sins. But it simply will not do to spiritualize Jesus' message and overlook the fact that right at the heart of the mission of the Incarnate One was a concern for justice for the poor and oppressed. His strong warning that those who do not feed the hungry, clothe the naked, and visit the prisoners will experience eternal damnation (Matt. 25:31ff) does not represent a peripheral concern. It represents a central focus of his messianic mission.

At the supreme moment of history when God himself took on human flesh, we see the God of Israel still at work liberating the poor and oppressed and summoning his people to do the same.

GOD EXALTS THE POOR AND OPPRESSED AND CASTS DOWN THE RICH AND OPPRESSIVE

The second aspect of the biblical teaching that God is on the side of the poor and oppressed is that God works in history to cast down the rich and exalt the poor. Mary's Magnificat puts it simply and bluntly:

> My soul magnifies the Lord. . . .
> He has put down the mighty from their thrones
> and exalted those of low degree;
> he has filled the hungry with good things,
> and the rich he has sent empty away (Luke 1:46–53).

James 5:1, "Come now, you rich, weep and howl for the miseries that are coming upon you," is a constant theme of biblical revelation.

Why does Scripture declare that God regularly reverses the good fortunes of the rich? Is God engaged in class warfare? Actually our texts never say that God loves the poor more than the rich. But they do constantly assert that God lifts up the poor and disadvantaged. And they persistently insist that God casts down the wealthy and powerful. Why? Precisely because, according to Scripture, the rich often become wealthy by oppressing the poor and because they fail to feed the hungry.

Why did James warn the rich to weep and howl because of impending misery? Because they had cheated their workers: "You have laid up treasures for the last days. Behold, the wages of the laborers who mowed your fields, which you kept back by fraud, cry out; and the cries of the harvesters have reached the ears of the Lord of hosts. You have lived on the earth in luxury and in pleasure; you have fattened your hearts in a day of slaughter" (5:35). God does not have class enemies. But he hates and punishes injustice and neglect of the poor. And the rich, if we accept the repeated warnings of Scripture, are frequently guilty of both.

Long before the days of James, Jeremiah knew that the rich were often rich because of oppression.

> Wicked men are found among my people;
>   they lurk like fowlers lying in wait.
> They set a trap;
>   they catch men.
> Like a basket full of birds,
>   their houses are full of treachery;
> *therefore they have become great and rich,*
>   *they have grown fat and sleek.*
> They know no bounds in deeds of wickedness;
>   they judge not with justice
> the cause of the fatherless, to make it prosper,
>   and they do not defend the rights of the needy.
> Shall I not punish them for these things?
>   says the Lord (Jer. 5:26-29, *RSV*).

Hosea and Micah made similar charges:

> A trader in whose hand are false balances,
>   he loves to oppress.
> Ephraim has said, "Ah, but I am rich,
>   I have gained wealth for myself";
> but all his riches can never offset
>   the guilt he has incurred (Hos. 12:7-8, *RSV*).

> The voice of the Lord cries to the city . . . .
> Can I forget the treasures of wickedness in the house of the
>   wicked,
> and the scant measure that is accursed?
> Shall I acquit the men with wicked scales and with a bag of
>   deceitful weights?
> Your rich men are full of violence (Mic. 6:9-12, *RSV*).

Job 24:1-12, Psalm 73:2-12, Ezekiel 22:23-29 and Amos 8:4-8—to cite just a few more texts—all repeat the same point.

One more example from Isaiah is important. Through his prophet Isaiah, God declared that the rulers of Judah were rich because they had cheated the poor. Surfeited with affluence, the wealthy women had indulged in self-centered wantonness, oblivious to the suffering of the oppressed. The result, God said, would be devastating destruction.

> The Lord enters into judgment
>   with the elders and princes of his people:
> "It is you who have devoured the vineyard,
>   *The spoil of the poor is in your houses.*
> What do you mean by crushing my people,
>   by grinding the face of the poor?" says the Lord of hosts
>   (Isa. 3:14ff., *RSV*).

Because the rich oppress the poor and weak, the Lord of history is at work pulling down their houses and kingdoms.

Sometimes Scripture does not charge the rich with direct oppression of the poor. It simply accuses them of failure to share with the needy. But the result is the same.

The biblical explanation of Sodom's destruction provides one illustration of this terrible truth. If asked why Sodom was destroyed, virtually all Christians would point to the city's gross sexual perversity. But that is a one-sided recollection of what Scripture actually teaches. Ezekiel shows that one important reason God destroyed Sodom was because she stubbornly refused to share with the poor!

> Behold, this was the guilt of your sister Sodom: she and her daughters had pride, *surfeit of food, and prosperous ease, but did not aid the poor and needy.* They were haughty, and did abominable things before me; therefore I removed them when I saw it (Ezek. 16:49-50, *RSV*).

The text does not say that they oppressed the poor (although they probably did). It simply accuses them of failing to assist the needy.

GOD'S PEOPLE ARE ON THE SIDE OF THE POOR AND OPPRESSED

The third aspect of the biblical teaching that God is on the side of the poor and oppressed is that the people of God, if they are really the people of God, are also on the side of the poor and oppressed. Those who neglect the poor and the oppressed are not really God's people at all—no matter how frequent their religious rituals or how orthodox their creeds and confessions. The prophets sometimes made this point by insisting that knowledge of God and seeking justice for the oppressed are inseparable. At other times they condemned the religious rituals of the oppressors who tried to worship God and still continue to oppress the poor.

Jeremiah announced God's harsh message that King Jehoiachim did not know Yahweh and would be destroyed because of his injustice:

> Woe to him who builds his house by unrighteousness,
>   and his upper rooms by injustice;
> who makes his neighbor serve him for nothing,
>   and does not give him his wages; . . .
> Did not your father eat and drink
>   and do justice and righteousness?
>   Then it was well with him.
> He judged the cause of the poor and needy;
>   then it was well.
> Is not this to know me?
>   says the Lord (Jer. 22:13-16, *RSV*).

Knowing God necessarily involves seeking justice for the poor and needy (cf. also Hos. 2:19-20).

The same correlation between seeking justice for the poor and knowledge of God is equally clear in the messianic passage of Isaiah 11:1-9. Of the shoot of the stump of Jesse the prophet says: "With righteousness he shall judge the poor and decide with equity for the meek of the earth" (v. 4, *RSV*). In this ultimate messianic shalom, "the earth shall be full of the knowledge of the Lord as the waters cover the sea" (v. 9, *RSV*).

The prophets also announced God's outrage against worship in the context of mistreatment of the poor and disadvantaged. Isaiah denounced Israel (he called her Sodom and Gomorrah!) because she tried to worship Yahweh and oppress the weak at the same time (1:10-17).

> "Why have we fasted, and thou seest it not?
>   Why have we humbled ourselves and thou takest no knowledge of it?"
> Behold, in the day of your fast you seek your own pleasure,
>   and oppress all your workers. . . .

> Is not this the fast that I choose:
>> to loose the bonds of wickedness,
>> to undo the thongs of the yoke,
> to let the oppressed go free,
>> and to break every yoke?
> Is it not to share your bread with the hungry,
>> and bring the homeless poor into your house?
>>> (Isa. 58:3-7; likewise Isa. 1:10-17, *RSV*).

God's words through the prophet Amos are also harsh:

> I hate, I despise your feasts,
> and I take no delight in your solemn assemblies.
> Even though you offer me your burnt offerings
> and cereal offerings, I will not accept them . . .
> But let justice roll down like waters,
> and righteousness like an overflowing stream (Amos 5:21-24, *RSV*).

Earlier in the chapter Amos had condemned the rich and powerful for oppressing the poor. They even bribed judges to prevent redress in the courts. God wants justice, not mere religious rituals, from such people. Their worship is a mockery and abomination to the God of the poor.

Nor has God changed. Jesus repeated the same theme. He warned the people about scribes who secretly oppress widows while making a public display of their piety. Their pious-looking garments and frequent visits to the synagogue are a sham. Woe to religious hypocrites "who devour widows' houses and for a pretense make long prayers" (Mark 12:38-40). Like Amos and Isaiah, Jesus announced God's outrage against those who try to mix pious practices and mistreatment of the poor.

The prophetic word against religious hypocrites raises an extremely difficult question. Are the people of God truly God's people if they oppress the poor? Is the church really the church if it does not work to free the oppressed?

We have seen how God declared through the prophet Isaiah that the people of Israel were really Sodom and Gomorrah rather than the people of God (1:10). God simply could not tolerate their idolatry and their exploitation of the poor and disadvantaged any longer. Jesus was even more blunt. To those who do not feed the hungry, clothe the naked, and visit the prisoners, he will speak a terrifying word at the final judgment: "Depart from me, you cursed, into the eternal fire prepared for the devil and his angels" (Matt. 25:41). The meaning is clear and unambiguous. Jesus intends his disciples to imitate his own special concern for the poor and needy. Those who disobey will experience eternal damnation.

But perhaps we have misinterpreted Matthew 25. Some people think that "the least of these" (v. 45) and "the least of these my brethren" (v. 40) refer only to Christians. This exegesis is not certain. But even if the primary reference of these words is to poor believers, other aspects of Jesus' teaching not only permit but require us to extend the meaning of Matthew 25 to both believers and unbelievers who are poor and oppressed. The story of the good Samaritan (Luke 10:29ff.) teaches that anybody in need is our neighbor. Matthew 5:43ff. (*RSV*) is even more explicit:

> You have heard that it was said, "You shall love your neighbor and hate your enemy." But I say to you, love your enemies and pray for those who persecute you, so that you may be sons of your Father who is in heaven; for he makes his sun rise on the evil and on the good, and sends rain on the just and on the unjust.

The ideal in the Qumran community (known to us through the Dead Sea Scrolls) was indeed to "love all the sons of light" and "hate all the sons of darkness" (I QS 1:9-10). Even in the Old Testament Israelites were commanded to love the neighbor who was the son of their own people and ordered not to seek the prosperity of Ammonites and Moabites (Lev. 19:17-18; Deut. 23:3-6). But Jesus explicitly forbids his followers to limit their loving concern to the neighbor who is a member of their own ethnic or religious group. He explicitly commands his followers to imitate God who does good for all people everywhere.

As George Ladd has said, "Jesus redefines the meaning of love for neighbor; it means love for any man in need."[23] In light of the parable of the Good Samaritan and the clear teaching of Matthew 5:43ff., one is compelled to say that part of the full teaching of Matthew 25 is that those who fail to aid the poor and oppressed (whether they are believers or not) are simply not the people of God.

Lest we forget the warning, God repeats it in 1 John. "But if any one has the world's goods and sees his brother in need, yet closes his heart against him, how does God's love abide in him? Little children, let us not love in word or speech but in deed and truth" (3:17-18, *RSV*; cf. also, James 2:14-17). Again, the words are plain. What do they mean for Western Christians who demand increasing affluence each year while people in the Third World suffer malnutrition, deformed bodies and brains, even starvation? The text clearly says that if we fail to aid the needy, we do not have God's love—no matter what we may say. The text demands deeds, not pious phrases and saintly speeches. Regardless of what we do or say at 11:00 A.M. Sunday, those who neglect the poor and oppressed are not the people of God.

But still the question persists. Are professing believers no longer Christians because of continuing sin? Obviously not. The Christian knows that sinful selfishness continues to plague even the most saintly. We are members of the people of God not because of our own righteousness but solely because of Christ's death for us.

That response is extremely important and very true. But it is also inadequate. All the texts from both testaments, which we have just surveyed, surely mean more than that the people of God are disobedient (but still justified all the same) when they neglect the poor. These verses pointedly assert that some people so disobey God that they are not his people at all in spite of their pious profession. Neglect of the poor is one of the oft-repeated biblical signs of such disobedience. Certainly none of us would claim that we fulfill Matthew 25 perfectly. And we cling to the hope of forgiveness. But there comes a point—and, thank God, God alone knows where!—when neglect of the poor is no longer forgiven. It is punished. Eternally.

The biblical teaching that Yahweh has a special concern for the poor and oppressed is unambiguous. But does that mean, as some assert today, that God is biased in favor of the poor? Not really. Scripture explicitly forbids being partial. "You shall do no injustice in judgment; you shall not be partial to the poor or defer to the great, but in righteousness shall you judge your neighbor" (Lev. 19:15; also Deut. 1:17). Exodus 23:3 contains precisely the same injunction: "Nor shall you be partial to a poor man in his suit." God instructs his people to be impartial because God is not biased.

The most crucial point for us, however, is not God's impartiality, but rather the result of God's freedom from bias. The text declares Yahweh's impartiality and then immediately portrays God's tender care for the weak and disadvantaged. "For the LORD your God is God of gods and LORD of lords, the great, the mighty, and the terrible God, *who is not partial* and takes no bribe. He executes justice for the fatherless and the widow, and loves the sojourner, giving him food and clothing" (Deut. 10:17-18).

God is not partial. God has the same loving concern for each person God has created. Precisely for that reason God cares as much for the weak and disadvantaged as for the strong and fortunate. By contrast with the way you and I, as well as the comfortable and powerful of every age and society, always act toward the poor, God seems to have an overwhelming bias in favor of the poor. But it is biased only in contrast with our sinful unconcern. It is only when we take our perverse preference for the successful and wealthy as natural and normative that God's concern appears biased.

If the preceding analysis is right, some important conclusions follow for the two dialogues mentioned at the beginning of this essay.

It is crucial to let the Scriptures, rather than secular ideology of left or right, define our attitude toward the poor. Knowing God involves much more than seeking justice for the oppressed—although it does not involve less. People enter into a right relationship with God and enter the church not by caring for the poor but by confessing their sins and accepting Jesus Christ as Lord and Savior. Any tendency, whether on the part of liberation theologians or North American activists, to ignore or deny these important points should be vigorously resisted. The Bible is our norm.

On the other hand, and precisely for that reason, the Mennonites of North America and Western Europe dare not allow surrounding materialistic values to become the decisive factor in their lifestyles, thinking and teaching. The temptation to do that is enormous. If some activists run the danger of granting too large a role to secular social analysis, then many conservative Mennonites are dreadfully close to selling out totally to rampant materialism. Until conservative critics of Mennonite or liberation theology activists begin to demonstrate their freedom from materialistic values by the kind of costly identification with the poor demanded by the prophets and modeled by Jesus, they would be wise to remain silent. Unless the Mennonite leadership in North America and Western Europe revamps our church organizations—our publications, colleges, mission agencies and seminaries—so they reflect the same concern for the poor and oppressed described in the Bible, Third World theologians will have every right to charge that our proud claim to follow the Scriptures is dishonest.

A viable Anabaptist theology of liberation cannot be developed in ivory towers. It can only be constructed congregation by congregation as the united membership together hammers out a faithful implementation of Jesus' call to identify with the poor and oppressed. If we do that, we will faithfully hand the Anabaptist vision on to the next generation and be an instrument of shalom in contexts of agony. We will also glorify the One revealed in the Scriptures as the defender of the poor and oppressed.

NOTES

1. The major part of the following text is reprinted from Ronald J. Sider, "An Evangelical Theology of Liberation," in *Perspectives on Evangelical Theology: Papers from the Thirteenth Annual Meeting of the Evangelical Theological Society,* ed. Kenneth S. Kantzer and Stanley N. Gundry (Grand Rapids, Mich.: Baker Book House, 1979), pp. 117-34.

2. Quoted in José Míguez Bonino, *Doing Theology in a Revolutionary Situation* (Philadelphia: Fortress Press, 1975), pp. 161-62.

3. Enzo Gatti, *Rich Church—Poor Church* (Maryknoll, N.Y.: Orbis Books, 1974), p. 43.

4. See Samuel Escobar's summary of Donald McGavran in S. Escobar and J. Driver, *Christian Mission and Social Justice* (Scottdale, Pa.: Herald Press, 1978), pp. 45-47.

5. José P. Miranda, *Marx and the Bible* (Maryknoll, N.Y.: Orbis Books, 1974), p. 44.

6. Miranda, p. 48

7. James H. Cone, *Black Theology and Black Power* (New York: Seabury, 1969), pp. 32-33. But see a conflicting, more biblical emphasis on pp. 34, 51.

8. James H. Cone, *God of the Oppressed* (New York: Seabury, 1975), p. 84.

9. Cone, *God of the Oppressed,* p. 82; Cone's italics.

10. The following section relies heavily on chapter three of Ronald J. Sider, *Rich Christians in an Age of Hunger,* rev. ed. (Downers Grove: InterVarsity Press, 1977, 1984).

11. See Richard A. Batey, *Jesus and the Poor: the Poverty Program of the First Christians* (New York: Harper, 1972), pp. 83-97; Albert Gélin, *The Poor of Yahweh* (Collegeville, Minn.: Liturgical Press, 1964). See too, C. Schultz, " 'Ani and 'Anaw in Psalms" (unpublished Ph.D. dissertation, Brandeis University, 1973); P. D. Miscall, "The Concept of the Poor in the Old Testament" (unpublished Ph.D. dissertation, Harvard University, 1972).

12. *Theological Dictionary of the New Testament,* ed. Gerard Kittel, 9 vols. (Grand Rapids, Mich.: Eerdmans, 1964), v. 6, p. 888.

13. Gélin, pp. 19-20.

14. Gélin, p. 50.

15. Batey, p. 92.

16. *The New International Dictionary of New Testament Theology,* ed. Colin Brown, 3 vols. (Grand Rapids, Mich.: Zondervan, 1976), v.2, pp. 822-23.

17. J. A. Ziesler, *Christian Asceticism* (Grand Rapids, Mich.: Eerdmans, 1973), p. 52.

18. *Theological Dictionary of the New Testament 6.* 986-89.

19. Batey, p. 93; *Theological Dictionary of the New Testament* 6. 905.

20. If Jesus announced the Jubilee, then we have further confirmation of this argument. See Robert Sloan, *The Acceptable Year of the Lord* (Austin: Schola, 1977), and Donald Wilford Blosser, "Jesus and the Jubilee . . ." (unpublished dissertation, University of St. Andrews, 1979).

21. See *Theological Dictionary of the New Testament* 6. 904, n.175.

22. Herman N. Ridderbos, *The Coming of the Kingdom* (Philadelphia: Presbyterian and Reformed, 1961), p. 190.

23. George E. Ladd, *A Theology of the New Testament* (Grand Rapids,: Mich.: Eerdmans, 1974) p. 133.

8

The Anabaptist Vision and Social Justice

JOHN DRIVER

This study represents an attempt to understand the church's attitude toward, and role in, the contemporary struggle for social justice in Latin America from the perspective of radical Anabaptism and its vision of the church and the social order. It is not so much a historical study focusing on sixteenth-century Anabaptism as it is an attempt to understand the current struggle from that perspective.

ANABAPTISM AND THE STRUGGLE FOR SOCIAL JUSTICE

A concern for social justice was probably more central to the genius of radical Anabaptism of the sixteenth century than most of the modern heirs of the movement would imagine. While sixteenth-century Anabaptism was certainly a religious movement, it was also a social movement.

It is generally recognized that Anabaptism was one of a whole series of socio-religious movements throughout Europe during the Middle Ages that focused their social protest in terms of a call to "apostolic simplicity" in life and worship. This mood was shared by such diverse movements as medieval monasticism, the Waldensians, the renewal movement among the Franciscans and Joaquin de Fiore in Italy, the English Lollards, Peter Chelcicky and the Bohemian Brethren, and Anabaptism. In these movements the concern for a return to "apostolic simplicity" responded in one way or another to fundamental social and economic dissatisfaction. While the Bible seemed to put a premium on poverty, the church came to own one-third of the real estate in Europe and the income from it. The New Testament spoke of brotherhood, but this was contradicted by the church, which legitimized class differences. These socio-economic contradictions produced tensions that led to revolutionary ferment.

Human misery was no doubt a prime cause of the social dissatisfaction that led many to question the papacy, the hierarchy and the church's social practices as well as its doctrines. One of the concrete expressions of this general mood of dissatisfaction was the series of peasant uprisings that took place in Europe in the late fifteenth and early sixteenth centuries, culminating in the Peasant Revolt of 1524-25. Recent studies have shown that the religious and social views held by the peasants and the Anabaptists overlapped considerably.[1] For our purposes a brief review of common social concerns will suffice.

1) Both groups insisted that the Gospel is relevant to social and economic realities.

2) Both protested against the payment of tithes (since this merely increased the wealth of the church) as well as against the charging of interest (since this oppressed the poor and was also forbidden in Scripture). The peasants were willing to continue their payments if they were used to support local pastors and as relief for the poor.

3) Both rejected structures that perpetuated class distinctions. This led to the rejection of the use of titles among the Anabaptists and to the creation of brotherhood structures for the congregation. Among the peasants it meant that common woodlots, pastures and waters should no longer be sequestered by the feudal lords for their exclusive use, but be available to all who needed them.

4) Both called for human freedom. For the peasants this meant freedom from serfdom. For the Anabaptists it meant freedom to act and to believe according to one's own conscience without coercion.

5) Both sought independence from ecclesiastical control. The peasants asked freedom to choose (and dismiss) their own pastors and to hear the pure preaching of the word of God. Anabaptists not only demanded the same things, but set about to realize them in their clandestine conventicles.

6) Both were movements of resistance to the established authorities (church and state). Peasants resisted the increasing economic demands of their feudal masters. Anabaptists resisted the claim of church hierarchies (both Catholic and Protestant) on their unquestioning obedience as well as rejecting the sacral claims of secular authorities. Their commitment to Christ and to his "law" led them, in certain cases, to both ecclesiastical and civil disobedience.

7) Both groups wanted nonviolent change to fuller social justice and equality. But the peasants were prepared to use force if necessary. As for the Anabaptists, there was some ambivalence among them prior to Schleitheim,[2] noted especially in Hubmaier, Hut and Anabaptists in the Tyrol. However, under the pressures of official persecution and through study of the Scriptures, the doctrine of the two kingdoms established itself among Anabaptists. It became clear to them that there are two realms and that different sets of rules are operative in these two spheres: violence in one and nonresistance in the other.[3]

It is possible that many of those who originally participated in peasant movements found their way into Anabaptist conventicles after their uprisings were crushed by authorities. The remarkable growth of Anabaptism in areas in which peasant revolts had been forcibly repressed points to this possibility. The brotherhood communities of sharing and justice, which characterized Anabaptists of all types, the more formally structured communities of the Hutterites as well as the less structured congregations of the Swiss and Dutch, gave concrete expression to the fundamental social concerns of the movement and assured its survival in the face of official persecution.

CONCERN FOR SOCIAL JUSTICE IN LATIN AMERICA

The struggle for social justice in Latin America is as old as Spanish imperial domination itself. This fact is illustrated by a sermon preached in a straw-thatched church in Santo Domingo in the year 1511 by a Dominican Friar, Antonio de Montesinos. Preaching from the text, "A voice cries in the wilderness . . . ," Montesinos delivered the first deliberate and important public protest against social injustices in the New World. The following lines are excerpted from the sermon:

> In order to make your sins against the Indians known to you. . . I am a voice of Christ crying in the wilderness of this island. . . . This is going to be the strangest voice that ever you heard, the harshest and hardest and most awful and most dangerous that ever you expected to hear. . . . This voice says that you are in mortal sin, that you live and die in it, for the cruelty and tyranny you use in dealing with these innocent people. Tell me, by what right or justice do you keep these Indians in such a cruel and horrible servitude? . . . Why do you keep them so oppressed and weary, not giving them enough to eat nor taking care of them in their illness? For with the excessive work you demand of them they fall ill and die, or rather you kill them with your desire to extract and acquire gold every day. . . . Be certain that, in such a state as this, you can no more be saved than the Moors and Turks. [4]

Within three months orders issued in Spain called for the cessation of such scandalous protests. But voices raised in behalf of the Indians would not be silenced. The loudest of these was, without doubt, that of Bartolomé de las Casas. Las Casas was originally a colonist who worked his mines and cultivated his estate with Indian slaves. Converted at the age of forty into a defender of the Indians, he dedicated the rest of his life (more than fifty years) to the struggle for justice. Las Casas insisted to his dying day that the Spanish conquest of the Americas was being waged by unjust means. He held that the only way to commend the Gospel to the heathen is through peaceful means.

It is not surprising that today, almost five centuries later, Las Casas' writings still strike a sympathetic chord in Latin America. The very same injustices denounced by Montesinos are those which, in our times, have given rise to the development of a "theology of liberation." In the present "situation of sin" the exploitation may be less direct and the oppressors may be farther removed from the suffering, but it is no less real.

Liberation theology is characterized by a fundamental concern for social justice. It is basically "reflection based on the Gospel and the experiences of men and women committed to the process of liberation in the oppressed and exploited land of Latin America . . . of shared efforts to abolish the current unjust situation and to build a different society, freer and more human."[5] It questions radically the prevailing social system in Latin America: one of economic, social, political and cultural dependence from which people must be liberated as a necessary condition for their well-being. This is a system of theological reflection rooted in the oppression and exploitation of the Third World over against those theologies that are the products of the affluent world.

Liberation theology understands salvation largely in terms of socio-economic liberation, and the historic experience of the Exodus in the life of the people of God becomes the paradigm for the political liberation of people in all times. The church is understood dynamically, rather than spatially. It is basically a calling—a vocation. All of humanity is understood as the people of God, and therefore all of human history must be understood as a general history of salvation. The church is called to fulfill a service function within this history.

One is impressed by the way in which the theology of liberation takes very seriously the struggle for social justice. In fact, human injustices constitute its point of departure. Its insistence on applying seriously the biblical message to the concrete socio-political situation in which Christians find themselves is perhaps its greatest strength.

CONTEMPORARY STRATEGIES ADOPTED BY CHRISTIANS CONCERNED FOR SOCIAL JUSTICE IN LATIN AMERICA

1) The first of these might be called the option of justifiable recourse to violence in the struggle for justice. As we have just noted, the movement characterized by the theology of liberation understands that the prevalence of socio-economic injustices in Latin America is the basic problem around which the church should orient itself. "To struggle to establish justice among men is to begin to be just before the Lord; love of God and love of neighbor are inseparable."[6] However, violence is not necessarily implicit in this struggle for justice. The nonviolent strategies followed by the movement of Catholic base communities in Brazil bear witness to this fact. But "when a government adopts repressive policies . . . uses violence and even torture on the men who are fighting for the liberation of their peoples, we propose that the church condemn such repressive methods, that it recognize the right these men possess to fight for justice, and that it manifest solidarity with their ideals, even though it may not always approve of their methods."[7] Some Christians, thrust into extreme situations, see no other way but the traditional one of fighting, opposing institutionalized violence with counter-violence.

In reality, this position represents a type of theocratic option. In situations where change cannot be brought about without force, revolutionary violence is justified as a last resort. While traditional moralists have spelled out the necessary conditions for waging a just war, Third World theorists have worked on identifying the criteria for determining when revolutionary violence is justifiable: 1) if oppressors have already utilized violence; 2) if all of the possibilities for legal action and protest have already been exhausted without success; 3) if the existing situation causes more human suffering than will probably result from revolutionary counter-violence; and 4) if there is reasonable assurance of success.

Christian revolutionaries who opt for this strategy are generally persons of high moral sensitivity who are moved out of compassion for, and a feeling of solidarity with, masses who suffer under the effects of institutionalized violence of unjust systems.

2) Another strategy has been the "guerrilla option." Although it has considerable in common with the first strategy (its basic sociological analysis, its commitment to liberation, its understanding of the Gospel and its implications, and so forth), there is at least one fundamental difference. In the doctrine of the just revolution, as in the concept of the just war, violence is not justified unless there is reasonable assurance of success in the venture. Decisions are made on the basis of pragmatic calculations. However, some guerrilla movements have considered the option of violence in terms not unlike those proper of the crusade (holy war). The "cause" is invested with a holy aura that is above ethical or pragmatic scrutiny. It is assigned a quasi-religious, absolute value to which the Christian may give himself fully.[8] In fact there is the possibility of martyrdom. The practical distinction between the just war (or just revolution) and the crusade (or guerrilla) is the latter's disposition to martyrdom. The first requires that justice be accomplished, even at the cost of violence. The second conceives of death as a morally valid sacrifice, not because the ends have been realized, but in the glorious nature of death itself.

The following excerpts from a letter written by a South American Christian *guerrillero* illustrate the guerrilla option:

> On joining the guerrillas . . . I believe that my true priestly consecration is beginning now—a consecration which demands total sacrifice so that all men might live, and live abundantly. (Camilo) Torres' word and example are the banner of redemption . . . and a light on the path of all those who seek total commitment with the revolution. Camilo has not died; he lives in the hearts of the poor and oppressed, within each man who fights for justice and human brotherhood. . . . He was a prophet of our time, a total revolutionary, a new man of that future society which is in gestation. . . . It is to his attitude and thought that I owe the joy of the commitment which I announce, the decision to give myself, to death if necessary, for the liberation of the Colombian people. . . . The masses experience hunger, injustice, and exploitation. They need live examples

to direct their rebelliousness and channel their eagerness for liberation. Camilo has done it. With his glorious sacrifice, he showed once for all the way of redemption for all revolutionaries and oppressed masses. ... From these mountains washed with the blood of our martyrs, I invite all Colombian men and women to organize and prepare for the final struggle, following the banner and example of the great teacher of our people, Camilo Torres Restrepo. With the strength that his glorious death imparts to us, together with my comrades I repeat: Not one step backwards—Liberation or death.[9]

3) A third option is the nonviolent struggle for justice. The International Fellowship of Reconciliation movement is representative of this position. Nonviolence is seen as a strategy for the liberation of persons and the attainment of justice in social relationships. This option is no less critical of the realities in Latin America than those already listed: oppression, both internal and external; unjust economic systems, which favor a few and leave the majority condemned to a marginal existence; education that prepares people to serve the existing unjust systems; and so on.

In the struggle for justice this option attempts to practice the concepts lived and taught by Christ in his Gospel of liberation. It believes that by his incarnation—attacking evil at its root in the conscience of humankind—by the power of truth, by the love and justice of God, and accepting all the consequences of these in his commitment until death, all the while fully respecting the human person, Christ brought the revelation of true liberation to all people. This process of liberation and reconciliation begins in the community of faith. "Christ . . . inspired the conversion of men so that they may be the leaven of the renewal of the world. Concretely, liberative action must be the ability to save ourselves, to transform ourselves in serving our neighbor. By themselves . . . structures do not liberate. . . . Christ proved his messianism by concrete and liberating actions. In the same way, the church must continue the liberating action of Christ among the brethren, the men who in Latin America suffer at present from oppression and dependance."[10]

Nonviolence that does not take a stand regarding the process of liberation of the people will be suspect. The church is called to take this stand in the hope that oppressed peoples will actively participate in their liberation, assume personal and collective responsibility, and thereby make possible the liberation of their oppressors and the transformation of structures as well.

Since nonviolence is understood as a strategy for social change, Christians who take this option will be social activists, engaging in conscientization at all levels, in public manifestations, strikes, civil disobedience, and so forth, convinced that nonviolence will finally prevail over violence. Underlying this strategy is belief in the ultimate efficacy of nonviolence.

4) Another option that has occasionally been assumed by Protestants is a sort of socio-political collaboration with the power structures in what is believed to be the long-term interests of the church. Some Protestant missionaries

in Chile, for example, welcomed the overthrow of Allende's government by the military junta because this assured them of "freedom" to evangelize and plant churches. In Bolivia a bloody revolution lasting three or four days and engineered by rightist military elements, which toppled the government and expelled leftists from places of leadership, was heralded by some as a miraculous event. "Hope brightened for the future. We knew anew that God is sovereign in all circumstances and that He was giving us further opportunity to win this nation to Christ. How thrilling to experience first hand that our 'God only doeth wondrous things'—everything He does is miraculous."[11]

In January 1973 an international group of Christians in Bolivia released a public statement calling for the cessation of a rising "spiral of violence" in that country. In his reply the Minister of Interior, a colonel in the Bolivian army, suggested that the foreigners in the group might do well to leave the country and then cited, with approval, the ministry of a charismatic Catholic healer and evangelist who preaches "peace, love, and the gospel." The preaching and healing of Jesus, which were mighty signs of an inbreaking kingdom characterized by its powerful moving force for both spiritual and social change, somehow failed to come through in all of its radicality and power in this particular instance.

This option assumes the position that if churches are simply left alone to evangelize and grow, the immediate problems of social justice in society can be overlooked in the hope that in the long run the church will be able to penetrate the social structures with its healing influence. Concern for social justice tends to be relegated to a position separate from, and posterior to, church planting concerns.

5) An option that has generally been acceptable to conservative Catholics and Protestants alike in Latin America is one which concerns itself with the conservation and strengthening of Christian social values. One small but militant group representative of this reactionary wing is a quasi-military Catholic movement dedicated to the conservation of "Tradición, Familia y Propiedad."

But many traditional Catholics and a considerable number of Protestants in Latin America would fall into this conservative category. The socio-economic orientation of this group tends toward capitalism rather than socialism; development rather than radical change of system; toward evolution rather than revolution. This orientation generally rejects socialization out of principle. It tends to see society (Latin American vestiges of Christendom, in the case of Catholics, and liberal democracy, in the case of Protestants) as fundamentally Christian and basically sound. Therefore it proposes progressive and gradual changes without endangering the system. Social concerns tend to be individualistic. The rehabilitation of persons in need contributes to the welfare of society. The exercise of repressive power, and even violence, is generally accepted as necessary since it assures the maintenance of order in which this progressive Christianization of social structures can take place. This, of course, represents a fundamentally Constantinian stance.

TOWARD A STRATEGY OF STRUGGLE FOR SOCIAL JUSTICE CONSISTENT WITH A RADICAL ANABAPTIST VISION

It could be argued that the attempt to construct a strategy of struggle for social justice on the basis of the radical Anabaptist vision will prove to be a precarious undertaking. Several clearly distinguishable currents can be detected within what has come to be called the Radical Reformation of the sixteenth century in Europe, with somewhat differing views of the church and its relationship to society. It is apparent that one's own viewpoint tends to determine which of the Anabaptists one reads, as well as the way in which one interprets them. While I make no claim to full objectivity in the following paragraphs, I do feel that my view is based on a generally accepted consensus of what the Anabaptists were about. The fact that an early ambivalence concerning the matter of violence gave way, in the crucible of this sixteenth-century struggle for social justice, to the renunciation of violent means, only strengthens the conviction that nonresistant suffering is fundamental to understanding the Anabaptist vision of the social justice issues.

1) The Anabaptist vision implies, first of all, being a messianic community. An understanding of the church as a messianic community that is in fact the bearer of the real meaning of history, a paradigm of God's intention for all of humankind, as well as the entire created order, is fundamental. The realization that it is by God's act of grace alone that this is so will serve to keep the community humble. The fact that this reconciled and reconciling community is God's pattern for bringing to complete fulfillment God's creation is the fundamental meaning and motivation for mission.

Perhaps the most important task that confronts the church is simply resisting the seductive charms of the world, of being the church in spite of all of the pressures to force it into another mold. The fact that it is already the community in which God's justice is being concretely realized gives it the moral right to denounce the deeds of tyrants, calling them to repentance in relation to specific injustices. Only a community that has been liberated by Christ can denounce with authority the idolatrous bondage to sacral systems. Only a community of reconciliation can denounce with authority the strife of nationalism, racism and classism. Only a community of openness and honesty can denounce with any degree of credibility the deceitful and vicious uses of propaganda from both right and left. Only a community in which recourse to coercion has been renounced in an authentic brotherhood can with authority denounce the violence with which humans persist in their evil desire to dominate others.

2) It implies being a community of testimony. The messianic community understands itself as the bearer of a liberating message. It is a matter of communicating a radically new way in human social relationships, rather than simply attempting to solve society's problems on the world's terms. Going beyond mere institutions of social service (worthy as these may be), going beyond mere programs of social action (strategic as these may be), the messi-

anic community with its witness to a radically new way in human relationships serves society by raising consciousness in relation to social injustices and by contributing to the creation of social conscience. (This would seem to be the justification underlying the various forms of protest-witness such as symbolic actions, and the like.)

3) The social strategy of the messianic community is determined concretely by the form that Jesus' messianic strategy took. According to the theocratic option, the church acts in the world to change society. Christians see themselves as God's agents for ending injustices and bringing about social justice in the world. According to this vision a Christian minority, if it has access to power, can change society for the better. However, the messianic community is limited in the instruments which are at its disposal (those which the Messiah used) for bringing social change. Violence, defamation, falsehood, deceit, disrespect for persons, and so on, are among the instruments society has found to be most effective in expediting change. These are the instruments that have often been used (albeit grudgingly) by theocrats as well. But they are not at the disposition of the messianic community because they do not partake of the essence of the messianic kingdom.

Negatively, the fact that the social strategy of the messianic community is determined by the form of messiahship Jesus took upon himself implies that coercive means that do violence to a person are not at the disposal of the church. Positively, it means that the "form of the servant" is the form the messianic community takes. This fact, of course, determines the content of social concern as well as the forms that the social strategy of the messianic community takes in the world.

4) The form of social concern in the messianic community is "servanthood." In our identification with Christ and his mission we become servants. However, we should not confuse this servanthood with service. Service tends to mean that which is done in the interests of a noble and just cause for which one is struggling. In reality, this may represent a theocratic orientation even though the means may be nonviolent. Servanthood is symbolized in the church by the basin and the towel and really amounts to a *form of being* more than a *strategy for doing*. Servanthood is the form that the community's concern for persons takes. Therefore the church will struggle to serve where social injustices are greatest and where human need is most acute. The lure to struggle at those points where the greatest strategic influence can be exercised may be, in reality, a theocratic temptation. The messianic community is moved to struggle for social justice not so much because of the amount of "good" that can be accomplished, but predominantly because she *is* a servant community. Being a servant community is the concrete way by which conformity to the messianic posture of Jesus in the world is realized by the church. The mission of the church, insofar as it is authentic, will be cruciform.

5) The church is a sign, or a paradigm, of the kingdom in which concern for social justice is of necessity central. Therefore the struggle for justice moves us intensely, even though we resist the theocratic temptation to construct the

kingdom in the world now by what appear to be the most efficacious means. (Perhaps we can say that the watershed between the theocratic option and that of the messianic community in the struggle for social justice lies at the point of willingness, or unwillingness, to sacrifice persons in the interests of a just cause.) We live and serve, we suffer and struggle in the confidence that God's kingdom will come. Meanwhile the messianic community furnishes models of God's justice in its radically new relationships, its servanthood service, its patient suffering—the price of its costly discipleship. The church does not merely carry out these activities in order to pass the time until the kingdom comes. Rather, the church is convinced that the form of the coming kingdom is already determined by the form of its historic coming in the person of the Messiah. Therefore the coming of the kingdom will not be realized by means of coercion or violence, but in the actualization of the social relationships that correspond to the kingdom. A community that practices on a small scale the kind of social justice which is an essential part of the kingdom contributes a paradigmatic value to secular society. The role of the church is to be a foreign body within the larger body politic, whose mission is to show what the intention of God is for all of humankind. Far from social irresponsibility, this is the only way in which the community of the Suffering Servant can be responsible.

CONCLUSION

Radical Anabaptism shares liberation theology's concern for social justice. While the latter has generally tended to emphasize almost unilaterally the Exodus paradigm as a point of departure for understanding God's liberating intention, the former has historically insisted on the relevance of the peoplehood motif found in the Abrahamic covenant, foundational in the Exodus experience of liberation, further developed in the prophetic vision of the renewal of God's salvific activity (reflected with special clarity in Isaiah 40–66), and most fully revealed in the Messiah.[12] It is this messianic community, in which the signs of the new order have begun to become reality, that is called to participate with God in the liberation of all humanity, as well as nature itself, from all bondage.

In our common concern for social justice, radical Anabaptism and liberation theology may increasingly find that they have much in common in their mission. The temptation to fall back into new forms of Constantinianism (implicit or explicit) is powerful and must be resisted by both at all cost. The theocratic temptation to see ourselves as God's agents for the establishment of his reign on earth by what seem to be the most efficacious means at our disposal is likewise attractive, but must be resisted.

A contemporary version of the Anabaptist vision of social justice can be found in Christian communities whose existence is more often than not institutionally precarious, but which are characterized by a common commitment to minister to those who are on the margins of society. These communities, scattered throughout the "three worlds," are a minority movement whose only claim to existence lies in their dependence on God's provident grace for their life, and in the authenticity of their mission for their reason for being.

For many Christians in Latin America whose concern for social justice is oriented by liberation theology, as well as the communities characterized by an Anabaptist vision, the prophetic promise of messianic justice continues to be a cherished hope.

> "Behold my Servant, whom I uphold. . . .
> I have put my Spirit upon him,
>   he will bring forth justice to the nations . . .
> He will not fail or be discouraged
>   Till he has established justice in the earth" (Isa. 42:1–4).

NOTES

1. Walter Klaassen pointed this out in a lecture, "Social Currents and Early Anabaptism," given at Goshen College (1975).

2. Schleitheim was the site of an early Anabaptist synod held in February 1527 in which the fundamental identity of the emerging movement was established. The bases of congregational life were articulated and a clear vision of a non-Constantinian church in its relationship to the secular establishment was set forth.

3. Like Luther, the Anabaptists held to a doctrine of two realms, or kingdoms. However, there was a fundamental difference between them. While Luther insisted that it was necessary for Christians to participate in both realms, in one as a Christian and in the other according to the generally accepted norms for secular society, the Anabaptists held that Christians are called upon to consistently apply the Gospel to all of their participation in both realms.

4. Reported by Bartolomé de las Casas in *Historia de las Indias*, Book 5, ch. 4, quoted by Lewis Hanke, *The Spanish Struggle for Justice in the Conquest of America* (Philadelphia: University of Pennsylvania Press, 1949), p. 17.

5. Gustavo Gutiérrez, *A Theology of Liberation: History, Politics and Salvation*, trans. and ed. Sister Caridad Inda and John Eagleson (Maryknoll, N.Y.: Orbis Books, 1973), p. ix.

6. "Justice in the World," Doc. II.1, a statement prepared by the Catholic bishops of Peru. "The Future of the Missionary Enterprise," *IDOC-North America*, 51 (March 1973), pp. 21–24.

7. Ibid., p. 23.

8. Of course this is also generally true of the exponents of a "doctrine of national security."

9. Father Domingo Lain, "An Open Letter to the People of Colombia," Doc. II. 8, *IDOC-North America* 51 (March 1973), pp. 35–37.

10. Johann and Hildegard Goss-Mayer, "Efforts for Liberation by Nonviolence in Latin America," *IDOC-North America 51* (March 1973), p. 26.

11. Joseph S. McCullough, a letter published in *IDOC-North America* 51 (March 1973), p. 28.

12. See LaVerne A. Rutschman, "Latin American Liberation Theology and Radical Anabaptism," *Journal of Ecumenical Studies* 19:1 (Winter 1982): 38–56.

9

The Relevance of Anabaptist Nonviolence for Nicaragua Today

C. ARNOLD SNYDER

This paper is based on a broad comparison between the Peasants' War of 1525 and the Nicaraguan Revolution of 1979. It is plain enough that there are many significant differences between these two events—not the least of which is the span of 450 years that separates them and all the concrete differences such a historical distance implies. But there are also some very striking similarities between the Peasants' War and the Nicarguan Revolution—not the least of which is the appearance in both of a theology of social justice that allows armed resistance. Furthermore, in response to the peasant upheaval the sixteenth-century Anabaptists at Schleitheim (1527) explicitly rejected armed resistance and called for a nonviolent response.

Thus the aim of this presentation is broad and exploratory. First, we will outline how the theologies of social justice have explained and justified armed resistance, concentrating, of course, on their similarities and congruities. Then we will discuss the theologies of social justice and nonviolent Anabaptist theology. Third, we will outline the nonviolent response of Schleitheim. And finally we will ask the central question: Is this nonviolence "relevant"[1] to Nicaragua today; that is, is it an adequate guide for a situation such as Nicaraguan Christians are currently facing? Needless to say, no final words will be said here. My hope is only to encourage further thought and dialogue on these questions.

SOCIAL JUSTICE AND ARMED RESISTANCE

While there have been many radical theologies in the history of Christanity, the sixteenth century produced a particularly interesting one. Martin Luther had made use of a very dangerous tool—the Bible—during his struggle with the

Roman church. *Sola scriptura,* or the "Bible alone," became the rallying cry across Germany, but it was a cry that meant different things to different people. To some radical theologians and a good many simple people it meant that the Bible was to be read simply and accepted at face value; only those things that the Bible commanded were to be allowed, and whatever was not commanded in the Bible was not genuinely Christian.[2] This simple approach to Scripture led to radical results.

When the poor and simple people in sixteenth-century Germany turned to Scripture to find out what it said, they found a Gospel that spoke directly to their condition of economic hardship and social disadvantage. They discovered a God who led his people Israel out of political bondage into the promised land.[3] They found that Jesus was born to a simple working family, his birth announced to humble shepherds rather than to the nobility[4]; that Jesus ate and lived with common people and had hard words for the wealthy and pretentious religious people of the day[5]; that he singled out injustices and taught that all men were brothers who should love and care for one another.[6]

The central teaching that resulted from this naive Bible reading was not a doctrine of salvation by faith through grace.[7] That was an emphasis appropriate to a theologian at leisure like Martin Luther. By contrast, Bible reading in the countryside resulted in a demand for social and economic justice that caused a great uproar and finally ended in a full-scale war between the "common man" and the nobility. This "Peasants' War" raged throughout the year 1525, and it is estimated that one hundred thousand commoners were slaughtered by the troops of the nobles. In the end the feudal system remained in place, the peasants were put back in their place, and biblical interpretation became the property of the theologians and preachers once again.

What makes this story interesting today is that a very similar set of events is unfolding in Latin America, on a much larger scale. Most of us in North America mistakenly consider Latin America to be just a backward version of North America, not realizing that Latin America inherited, and still labors under, an entirely different social and economic system. In the words of the Mexican author Carlos Fuentes, Latin America was "founded as an appendix of the falling feudal order of the Middle Ages."[8] What Fuentes is pointing out is that, unlike the liberal and democratic order that shaped North America, the social and economic order operating in Latin America today was transplanted intact from feudal Spain in the late sixteenth century and in many ways still resembles the social and economic structure of Luther's Germany much more than it does that of Ohio or Manitoba. Latin America has not been able to break the feudal pattern of concentrating land and power in the hands of a small elite class, and it is this small, privileged minority that has dominated the political and religious institutions.

Oddly enough, just as the church's participation in feudal abuses helped stimulate a church reform in the sixteenth century, and just as there was a radical turning to Scripture in Luther's day, so also today in Latin America.

The dramatic change for the Latin American Catholic Church came in the wake of the Second Vatican Council, with the historic meeting of Latin American bishops at Medellín, Colombia, in 1968.[9] The Latin American Catholic Church, which for so long had given its blessing to the status quo and had been part of the ruling order, now became a promoter of lay Bible reading and study, and here and there began to encourage the building of small, committed Christian communities of Catholic laypersons.

When the poor and simple people in twentieth-century Latin America turned to Scripture for the first time to find out what it said, they found a Gospel that spoke directly to their condition of economic hardship and social disadvantage.[10] They discovered a God who led the people of Israel out of political bondage into the promised land.[11] They found that Jesus was born to a simple working family, that his birth was announced not to the high and mighty but to humble shepherds[12]; that when Jesus announced his mission, he said he was bringing good news to the poor[13]; that Jesus worked with his hands and rubbed shoulders with the common people, and had hard words for the wealthy and the pretentious religious people of the day[14]; that he singled out injustices and taught that all people were brothers and sisters who should love and care for one another.[15] Except for the fact that the sixteenth-century radical literature is little known and was written in German, one might suspect that some plagiarism had taken place, for the similarities are striking.

One result of this naive Bible reading by the poor in Latin America has been a persistent demand for social and economic justice. In some cases, this has resulted in an alliance between Christians and revolutionaries. In fact, the Nicaraguan revolution can almost be seen as a kind of modern day peasants' war with the Gospel providing a rationale for destroying the old order of oppression and providing the model for a new society of equality and economic sharing. The fact that the Bible was interpreted in much the same way three hundred years before the birth of Karl Marx should help us see that although the theology emerging in Latin America is radical, it is also authentically biblical in origin and inspiration. It cannot be casually written off as a Marxist deformation. In fact, if we are objective about this, the real question is whether it is not we, the wealthy and privileged, who are guilty of deforming the Gospel message, for Jesus' own hearers were also primarily the poor and the downtrodden.

But let us return for a moment to the sixteenth century and the aftermath of the bloody Peasants' War. There was another group of Christians who went underground and continued to agree with the peasants in many things. They too thought that the Gospel needed to be read and interpreted by all church members, and not just by experts and theologians. Furthermore, they insisted that the Bible spoke of love, of the sharing of earthly possessions with the needy, and of social equality among Christians.[16] For these and other beliefs these sixteenth-century Christians, called Anabaptists, were hunted down and martyred in great numbers, the few survivors managing to escape to less perilous areas. Their descendants today are known as Mennonites, Brethren,

Amish and Hutterites—groups that certainly are not noted for revolutionary theology.

Although the sixteenth-century Anabaptists continued the peasant tradition of group Bible reading and worship, of economic sharing and social equality,[17] they disagreed on some fundamental points. The group of Anabaptists that met at Schleitheim in 1527 explicitly rejected violence and the attempt to create a new society according to biblical norms. Instead, they insisted on following the life of Jesus as their model and example, and furthermore, they insisted that this meant nonresistance in the face of evil and separation from a sinful world. And so the Anabaptists and most of their descendants, with some notable exceptions, soon became a nonviolent, withdrawn group, living quietly and migrating frequently.

Once we become aware of the radical sixteenth-century roots of Mennonite nonviolence, and then note the emergence of many shared themes in Latin America today, we are confronted with a new and interesting set of questions. Since the Anabaptist nonviolent tradition is post-revolutionary in origin, does it have anything relevant to say to Christians actively involved in revolutions today? Is Anabaptist nonviolence a step forward toward justice, peace and love, or a step backward toward oppression, exploitation and grief? To take a concrete example, is Anabaptist nonviolence relevant in a situation such as Nicaraguan Christians find themselves in today, or will it become relevant only if they too are forced underground, only if their version of the Peasants' War meets defeat at the hands of North America's heavily armed and financed mercenary troops?

In order to examine these questions we must look in more detail at some central points of agreement and disagreement between, on the one hand, the two theologies of justice and, on the other hand, nonviolent Anabaptist theology. We then will be in a better position to evaluate our own Mennonite nonviolent response.

THEOLOGIES OF JUSTICE AND NONVIOLENT ANABAPTIST THEOLOGY

When we focus on the question of violence and the Christian, we find that the pivotal concept that impels the German peasants and the Nicaraguan liberationists is the recognition that God is a God of justice. Furthermore, in both cases this justice is not to be awaited in some sweet by and by, but is to be sought in the here and now. In 1525 an anonymous peasant author wrote that the political cannot be separated from the religious because in both spheres God demands actions that will result in the common good of all.[18] This insistence that the spiritual and the secular realms are essentially only one realm, that God's activity takes place *in* history, and that he demands justice from his children is also characteristic of Nicaraguan liberation theology,[19] but there is a central point of difference between these theologies of justice and Anabaptist theology, as we will see later.

Along with the recognition that God demands justice in the here and now, the theologies of justice also stress God's creation of a people, the *Gemeinde* in German, or the *pueblo* in Spanish. The German peasants saw with particular clarity that God's will as revealed in Scripture had been the establishment of a community in which God's natural gifts would be *gemein,* or shared together in love. In 1525 a furrier-turned-theologian wrote, "In the Apostle's time . . . all things were owned in common. Now those were good Christians! It would be good if we did this ourselves. Christ the Lord certainly warned us about wealth in Luke 6, saying 'Woe to you, rich people.' . . . So now we can see who are the true preachers of God's word."[20]

For the German peasants, God's chosen agent for establishing this divine order was the *gemeiner Mann* or the common man. Likewise in Ernesto Cardenal's community of Solentiname in Somoza's Nicaragua, a farmer commented on the parable of the mustard seed by saying, "It doesn't seem . . . that there's any connection between some poor *campesinos* (peasants) and a just and well-developed society, where there is abundance and everything is shared. [But] we are the seed of that society. When the tree will develop we don't know. But we know that we are a seed."[21] So it is by means of common, ordinary people gathered into communities that God works out God's will in this world, and God's will is justice, equality and love among brothers and sisters.

When the focus and center of divine justice is seen in the community and in the sharing of those things that are common to all, sin is understood as being social rather than personal. Sin is selfishness, or the destruction of community. A central text supporting this social view of sin is the judgment in Matthew 25:31ff, which, Nicaraguan theologian Juan Pico points out, says unequivocally that Jesus condemns those who have not fed, clothed and visited the poor and needy. The damned are rejected not merely for failing to *believe* in Jesus, but rather for failing to maintain the community with concrete acts of Christian love.[22]

This shift in emphasis from individual belief to social practice is significant, for it marks an important point of agreement between the liberation theologies and Anabaptism, and a point of disagreement between these traditions and most of the rest of Christendom. The primary emphasis in Christianity following Constantine has been orthodoxy, or right teaching and belief. But the sixteenth-century peasants, and the Anabaptists after them, were not much impressed by the *Maulchristen* or mouth-Christians, who continued to mouth their faith while they misused others.[23] A young man in Solentiname had the same insight and expressed it very well: "Doctrine alone, the knowledge of Jesus' words, the Bible itself: These are things that have no value by themselves. Building just on that is building on the surface. You have to build on actions, on love put into practice."[24] In short, it is orthopraxis, or right action, which makes Christianity genuine, rather than mere orthodoxy, or right teaching.[25] Or said another way, it is doing justice, not simply believing that one is justified, that is the mark of a Christian.

The legitimacy of armed resistance by the oppressed follows from the principles we have just outlined. In the sixteenth century the peasants first attempted to negotiate nonviolently with their lords, but the nobility would have none of it. Eventually the peasants spoke of tyranny. It happens sometimes that persons in authority insist on oppressing those under their authority. This is a sin, a violation of the law of love, and a destruction of community. When a community loses all hope of the ruler changing for the better then, in the words of an anonymous German peasant, "a community can remove its harmful ruler."[26] God's law for rulers is that they are ordained to care for their subjects, not to impoverish or oppress them; and the violence of tyranny, being against God's ordering, must be opposed by defensive counter-violence, as when cattle gather in a defensive circle to defend themselves against marauding wolves.[27]

In Nicaragua the question of violence is framed in the terms first posed by the bishops' conference in Medellín, which identified different types of violence.[28] The "first violence" is the violence routinely perpetrated by the power structure, usually quite within the law. This is the institutionalized violence that kills the innocent by starvation, disease and malnutrition. It was this first violence that led many Christians in Nicaragua to nonviolent protest and action in the sixties and seventies. Originally many more people were involved in such nonviolent protest than were involved in violent resistance.[29] But Somoza responded with increased repression rather than with reforms. Those who demonstrated and worked with the poor were called communists; they were jailed, beaten, tortured and killed. The young people especially became the targets of Somoza's extermination squads. Eventually some Nicaraguan Christians decided upon the response of counter-violence. A Baptist teacher whose two young nephews had been kidnapped and killed by Somoza's Guard said to me that it was certain that killing another human being with a rifle is a crime, but wasn't it also a crime to permit starvation? How could we as Christians agree to participate, he asked me, in a social and economic structure that was killing people day by day in an organized and systematic way?[30]

To summarize, we can note how the concern for justice eventually led some Christians to attack the agents of injustice with counter-violence. When nonviolent attempts to change an unjust structure were met with repressive violence, this was met with counter-violence on the part of some Christians. Since, they argue, God's will is a just society on this earth, a brotherhood of equality, love and sharing, and since this just society is being destroyed by the sin of selfishness on the part of a few at the expense of many, then the people of God have a right to overthrow the ungodly and tyrannous system. For it is on *this* earth, and not in some sweet by and by, that Christians must live out their communal life of love and sharing.

The above, in outline, is the peasant position justifying violence that the sixteenth-century Anabaptists knew, understood and rejected; here too is the twentieth-century position held by some revolutionary Christians in Nicaragua and other parts of Latin America. We next need to examine the reasons given by the Anabaptists for their rejection of such counter-violence.

THE NONVIOLENT RESPONSE OF SCHLEITHEIM

The most complete and explicit Anabaptist rejection of peasant violence came in the Schleitheim Articles, written in 1527 by Michael Sattler.[31] The heart of the rejection of violence is twofold: first, a stress on following the example of Jesus; and second, a reinterpretation of the concern with justice.

The Nicaraguan theologian Juan Pico has placed the question of Jesus in the forefront of the discussion, for he notes that the image we have of Christ is an absolute image that lies at the heart of our faith and our action.[32] Michael Sattler would have agreed.[33] So a central question becomes this: Who is this Jesus whom the believer is to follow and what example does he give us?

On the whole the German peasants do not appeal to Christ's example as being definitive for the Christian. The Nicaraguan theologians, on the other hand, do make an effort to develop a fuller image of Christ; for them Christ is a liberator. For Nicaraguan theologian Roberto Mendizábal, the story of the life of Christ is a story of "radical opposition to injustice and inequality, to the accumulation of goods and despotic power.[34] This Jesus did not identify himself with power. He could have identified himself as God, but instead he identified himself as the lowliest of men, a servant of others. He is a Christ who can be known only by those who are also seeking God's kingdom of justice and equality in this world.[35]

The appeal to the example of Jesus, however, creates some problems for a theology of justice, for despite the episode in the Temple, Jesus' life and example is one of nonviolence rather than armed resistance. For example, far from joining the Zealots in their fight against Roman imperialism, Jesus refused even the token resistance of Peter's sword when the soldiers came to arrest him.[36]

Juan Pico recognizes the difficulties of appealing to Jesus' example, but, for Pico, Christ's humanity means that his actions were limited by his time and place in history and so are not binding on the disciple. Pico wrote in 1979, "The fact that Jesus was a man also confirms the fact that there are a thousand other ways that a person can die for others which Jesus could not fulfill. And it signifies that there are a thousand ways a person can live for others that Jesus could not live."[37] So the crucial difference is that in Nicaraguan liberation theology, Christ's actions are just one example of sacrificial love, not the one and only blueprint for ethical action. This, of course, has immediate consequences for the question of nonviolence. For radical Nicaraguan Christians, the taking up of arms in a cause of justice is also a way of following Jesus, for it remains true to Jesus' larger aim of establishing a community where justice and charity prevail.

The end result, then, is that for many Nicaraguan Christians participating in the insurrection to overthrow a tyrannous dictator was a Christlike action. It was a way of following Jesus' footsteps, even though Jesus himself did not take up arms, because self-sacrificing actions that lead to greater justice for the people as a whole are Christlike actions.[38]

Like the Nicaraguan theologians, the Anabaptists who met at Schleitheim insisted that Christianity must be practiced, not just recited in church, but they spoke of a submissive and spiritual Christ, not a liberator. The Christ whom the believer is to follow is the Christ who submitted to the will of the Father, who did not become involved in political matters, who suffered rather than retaliated, and who said that his kingdom was not of this world.[39] The fullness of the kingdom must await Christ's return. However, the true disciples have a foretaste of the kingdom in their separated communities, for that is where love and justice are practiced.[40]

Although the Anabaptists rejected the political project of reforming the world according to the pattern of Scripture, they preserved the vision of justice, economic sharing and social equality within their church communities. We can see this not only in the Hutterites, who still practice community of goods today, but it is also evident in the earliest known church order of the Swiss Brethren. This order states, for example, that "of all the brothers and sisters of this congregation none shall have anything of his own . . . as the Christians in the time of the apostles held all in common."[41] The demand for a Christlike life, for economic equality and justice, is maintained within the Anabaptist group and community, which becomes the focus of Christ's presence in history.[42]

But what becomes of justice in the larger world? The Schleitheim Articles completely change the scope of the question, for they assert a strict polarity and division between what is of Christ, which is to be found in the Anabaptist community, and all the rest of the world, which is of Satan. So the non-Anabaptist world falls entirely outside the "perfection of Christ," and is an abomination that we should shun.[43] The Schleitheim Articles do go on to speak of justice in the wider sense, but God, not man, is responsible for this justice. This is the justice of judgment on that final day when Christ returns and, as Michael Sattler wrote to his friends from prison, that day is very near. The conclusion is, then, that the true believers should separate from the sinful and unjust world, follow Jesus by doing no violence and practicing justice among themselves, and thus prepare themselves to be the Lord's pure bride, for according to the signs of the times, the Lord will not tarry.

Such, in broad outline, is the opposition between the Anabaptist doctrine of nonviolence and the theologies of justice. The two foci of the disagreement are, first, the understanding of Christ, and second, the understanding of the role Christians should play as promoters of justice in the wider world.

IS THE ANABAPTIST UNDERSTANDING OF NONVIOLENCE RELEVANT AND APPLICABLE TO NICARAGUA TODAY?

When I arrived in Nicaragua in the summer of 1983, two fleets of United States warships were closing in on that country from the Atlantic and the

Pacific coasts. Their presence there, and the presence of thousands of U.S. Marines in Honduras, was being described by the American president as "routine," but no one in Nicaragua, myself included, could miss the intent of this "routine" exercise in military intimidation. Events in Grenada have since demonstrated that Nicaraguan fears of an invasion were and are very much in order. How relevant is Anabaptist nonviolence in such a setting? Should we counsel Nicaraguan Christians to accept nonviolently the re-establishment of a dictatorship and to give up the gains they have paid for in blood? Is Anabaptist nonviolence a step forward toward increased justice, peace and love, or is it a step backward toward oppression, exploitation and grief?

When we imagine applying the separatist, eschatological and passive nonviolence of Schleitheim to such a situation, I fear that we must say that such passive nonviolence would result in an increase in oppression and exploitation. In fact, what imperialist power would not sincerely encourage all of its colonists to believe in passive nonviolence of this kind? They would be obedient and quiet subjects, a little on the boring side, to be sure, but certainly not people to worry about. Generations would come and go, concerned only with giving a passive witness, waiting patiently for divine justice to descend from heaven. Machiavelli in his wildest dreams could not have devised a better formula.

The Achilles' heel of the Schleitheim position of nonviolence is its lack of concern with matters of justice in the wider world. Rather than teaching an ethic of justice, it preaches an otherworldly ethic of purity and holiness in expectation of Christ's imminent return. Already in the sixteenth century the radical dualism of Schleitheim was not accepted by all nonviolent Anabaptists. Pilgram Marpeck and Menno Simons, although they rejected the sword, both had positive views concerning the legitimacy of the state and the possibility of active participation in political life.[44] From the start the Anabaptist tradition contained within itself the contradictory tendencies toward quietistic separatism and direct involvement in affairs of government. This is especially true when we take Balthasar Hubmaier and Bernhard Rothmann into account. And it is clear enough from our history that there are dangers at either end of the pole.

The problem has always been how to maintain a creative tension between being Christ's church and living in the world. The North American Mennonite experience, however, suggests that in this historical context, the quietistic temptation has been the stronger of the two. While there are some notable exceptions—and the work of the Mennonite Central Committee is probably the most concrete expression of this—in general the descendants of Sattler and Menno have chosen to be "the quiet in the land." There is a strong temptation to continue grasping the passive and separatist side of the church/world duality that is so much a part of the Mennonite heritage.

Perhaps it is time to make a more explicit rejection of this "pure church/evil world" polarity. Perhaps we need to say publicly and often that there cannot be, nor has there ever been, a pure, believers' church apart from the world. There has only been an all-too-human people trying to be Christ's faithful church in the middle of the world, meeting God in *all* human reality, be it "church" or "world." If this can be admitted, we have taken a giant step toward the relevance of nonviolence for a situation such as exists in Nicaragua.

If we can take the crucial step of recognizing that the doing of justice in the wider world is not something God meant us to leave entirely in the hands of his divine providence, if we can see that God left a good part of the task in our human hands, we will find that we have been moved out of the possibility of complacency and passivity. Because if God calls on us to *do justice* in the wider world, and if we respond to his call and command, the only question that can remain will be the when and the how of doing justice. Has God also revealed the means and the methods of justice? The Anabaptist tradition maintains that the answer is yes, and the means and the method is revealed by the life of Jesus Christ, which is also the point of focus for Nicaraguan liberation theology.

The Achilles' heel of the liberation justification of violence is the appeal to the incarnate Christ as example. While it is clear that Jesus gives us no example of passivity, neither does the life of Jesus provide a convincing example of revolutionary violence. It is not our place to say that the life of Christ as we understand it is the only possible guide to life for each and every Christian. But surely Christ's life is one legitimate guide, and it is probably the one *sure* guide, for it has the great merit of restricting self-serving interpretations of the Gospel. And with this observation we must leave the matter of Christian revolutionaries in the hands of our Nicaraguan brothers and sisters in Christ with the prayer that they may search the Scriptures diligently and honestly for the message and example of Christ concerning violence and reconciliation. We share a common point of focus, namely the life and work of Christ, and there can be no firmer foundation for further dialogue than that.

But the matter is not ended when we ask our Nicaraguan brothers and sisters to search the Scriptures diligently, for the situations of violence faced by Christians in Nicaragua are in large measure being forced on them by the economic, political and military policies of the United States. Have we in North America also searched the Scriptures diligently in this matter of the exportation of misery, starvation, armaments and invasion? Have we honestly understood the meaning and the challenge of Christ's life and example? Are we committed to following after Christ in all things, or have we been seduced by a life of ease, wealth and conformity? Have we really read those passages where Jesus challenges our comfortable economic assumptions? Are we being totally honest when we say that our kingdom is not really of this world?

Recently a Central American brother, a leader in the Mennonite church of that region, stood before a group of North American Mennonites and asked: "Is the North American church interested in sacrificing itself, or not?" He wanted to know if we in North America were ready to help provide a third option in Central America, but he warned that this would mean getting into the game as participants, rather than being content with watching and cheering from the sidelines. Jesus Christ, he reminded us, was not a passive escapist; rather, he actively, but nonviolently, confronted the injustices of his day. The risks being run by nonviolent Christians in Central America are clear. What risks is the church in North America taking, he wanted to know, in order to challenge the commerce our government is conducting with the lives of brothers and sisters in Central America?[45]

Is our nonviolence relevant for Nicaragua today? The answer to this question is not abstract or theoretical. Unless we fully understand that silence and passivity in the face of violence are actually complicity in violence, we will not be disposed to act. And in that sad case, our nonviolence will not be relevant to our Nicaraguan brothers and sisters, regardless of how fine and correct our conception of Christ may be. They can do very well without us and our nonviolent theological concepts. In a word, they cannot *afford* our nonviolence, because they are not being protected by great naval fleets, thousands of marines, nuclear weapons and constitutional guarantees. Our nonviolence will not be relevant, for we are speaking mere words rather than acting to prevent the violence suffered by our brothers and sisters.

On the other hand, if we have realized that Christ's call to love is a call to act for justice in this world, we will be challenged to find avenues for nonviolent and reconciling action. If we are convinced that the life of Jesus is the unfailing blueprint for his disciples, so much the better. This will simply mean that we continue to seek Christlike avenues for direct action, that in Christ's name we continue to seek ways to prevent the violence of injustice, starvation, disease and murder from taking place and to respond with loving concern after it has taken place. For it is not the radical following of Christ that holds us back from action, but rather the temptation of ease and conformity and the comforting half-truth that our kingdom is not really of this world anyway.

There are countless strategies for reducing violence, from the peace witness on the Honduran border to tax resistance to the declaration of sanctuary and the opening of churches to Central American refugees. These actions, and many others we could name, are all appropriate because they say: "I do not consent to this violence; in Christ's name I will not consent to this violence, and I place myself here as one prepared to take the consequence."

This is a nonviolence that is relevant to Nicaragua and to all the world, and it is relevant because it actively teaches and demonstrates a committed, nonviolent concern with the welfare of our neighbor in need. As Miguel d'Escoto has noted, nonviolence was never included in the process of evangelization of Nicaragua until the people rose up and began to fight for greater justice, at which time it suddenly became wrong for them to use violence. His conclusion is simple, and should go directly to our hearts: "We have no right to hope to harvest what we have not sown."[46] And, he might have added, the seeds of nonviolence are sown by example or they are not sown at all. If there is an Anabaptist vision that we should recover for the future surely it is the totally engaged Anabaptism that dies to self only to rise fearlessly in Christ. Such discipleship will not shrink from acting on behalf of the powerless and violated, as we know Christ himself did when he was among us. God grant us the conviction to search together for the truth in all sincerity, and then the strength and courage to follow our Lord in life and deed.

NOTES

1. The focus on "relevance" is meant to indicate a point of departure that takes seriously the ethical demand that Christians experience *as followers of Jesus* when confronted by real and present human suffering and injustice in the world. Such real situations demand action that aims at relevance in history. If nonviolent Christians are actively profiting from the misery and suffering of others, the question of the "relevance" of their nonviolent witness and proselytization becomes even more acute. In the end the demand for "relevance" rests on the suspicion that the dichotomy between church and world has been idealized and exaggerated, and that it obscures a more fundamental human reality that unites church and world under the lordship of Christ.

2. Sebastian Lotzer, lay preacher and author of the *Twelve Articles* of the peasants, wrote that no Christian has need of a church council to help in interpreting Scripture: "Dear brothers! Listen to the Word of God, buy the New Testament, that is Council enough. Pray God for grace; he will give you enough grace for understanding what is needful for your salvation" (*Christlicher Sendbrief*, 1523, in Alfred Goetze, *Sebastian Lotzers Schriften* [Leipzig: Teubner, 1902], pp. 45–46, 40.)

3. The *Twelve Articles* of the peasants say, "Did [God] not hear the children of Israel crying to him and deliver them out of Pharaoh's hand? And can he not save his own today as well?" (In Peter Blickle, *The Revolution of 1525*, trans. T. A. Brady and H. C. E. Midelfort [Baltimore: Johns Hopkins, 1981], p. 196.)

4. "God almighty has always given and announced his holy Word only to simple, pious and unaffected people, as when he was about to be born, it was announced to the shepherds, not to the learned men and Pharisees" (Lotzer, in Goetze, p. 33.) The general examples we will cite here will be drawn from Lotzer's writings, which are representative of the sentiments expressed elsewhere in the peasant literature.

5. Lotzer notes Jesus' hard words for the Pharisees, who are compared to the preachers of Lotzer's day, and he also observes how Jesus ate with common people and sinners. See the *Ausselegung* of 1524 in Goetze, pp. 77–78.

6. For Lotzer, true brotherhood is sharing wealth with the poor, and in this connection he cites Matthew 25:31, also a favorite in Nicaragua today. Lotzer, in Goetze, p. 34.

7. Although Lotzer follows Luther in emphasizing faith and denigrating the "works" of Catholic penance, he strongly stresses that works "prove" faith: "For here is the proof of our faith: where the love of our neighbor is not followed with works, there faith is dead. We wish to be fully evangelical with our mouths, but [the Gospel] is nowhere to be found in our actions" (Lotzer, *Beschyrm Büchlin*, 1524, in Goetze, p. 50). The egalitarian proofs of faith are even more pronounced in other peasant writings.

8. Quoted in John Rothchild, ed., *Latin America, Yesterday and Today* (New York: Bantam, 1973), p. 371.

9. "The Conclusions of the Conference represent the most important document in the history of the Church in Latin America" (Enrique Dussel, *A History of the Church in Latin America*, trans. Alan Neely [Grand Rapids, Mich.: Eerdmans, 1981], p. 147). See pages 138–47 for a discussion of Medellín. Appendix 2, pages 306–42, provides a useful periodization of events in Latin American church history.

10. A peasant in Solentiname, in Somoza's Nicaragua, commented: "The examples of Jesus are very clear for simple people. They say nothing to proud people, who despise this language of Jesus because it is simple . . . It's so simple that only the simple understand it" (Ernesto Cardenal, *The Gospel in Solentiname*, 4 vol., trans. D. D. Walsh [Maryknoll, N.Y.: Orbis Books, 1982], V. 2, p. 43). Our general examples will be

drawn from the Solentiname community. Rosemary Ruether has commented that many Latin Americans today "read the Bible much as medieval and Reformation radicals read it, as a critical and subversive document. They find in it a God who sides with the poor and with others despised by society; who, at the same time, confronts the social and religious institutions that are the tools of injustice" (Ruether, " 'Basic Communities': Renewal at the Roots," *Christianity and Crisis* 41 [September 1981]: 234).

11. Ernesto Cardenal commented to his community at Solentiname that God "urges Moses to take Israel out of Egypt, where the Jews were working as slaves. He led them from colonialism to liberty" (*Solentiname* II, p. 27).

12. A young man in Solentiname commented on the shepherds: "They were watching over their sheep which is like taking care of cattle today. They were workers, laborers, poor people. The angel of God could have gone to the king's palace . . . but the angel didn't go where the king was but where the poor people were, which means that this message is not for the big shots but for the poor little guys, which means oppressed, which means us" (*Solentiname* 1, p. 52). A woman in Solentiname noted that Mary "was a woman of the people like us" (*Solentiname* 1, p. 18). Concerning Joseph, one of the men comments: "He was a carpenter, one of the people, one of us poor people. And later they threw it in Jesus' face that he was the son of these people. He couldn't teach people anything because he was the son of poor people" (*Solentiname* 1, p. 23). Or again, "The Scriptures are perfectly clear, man. The fact is that Christ was born as a poor little child, like the humblest person. The Scriptures keep telling us this and I don't understand why we don't see it" (*Solentiname* 1, p. 42).

13. "His good news is for the poor because this new kingdom is the triumph of the poor and the humble" (*Solentiname* 1, p. 128).

14. A young woman in Solentiname commented on Matthew 23:6-7: "And this thing that Christ attacked is still going on, because those church people are still at the head table at banquets and guests of honor at the big festivals and receptions and they like to be treated with great respect: Monsignor So-and-So." To which a young man responded, "And they think that they're there to teach the people and that the people can't teach them anything and that the commentaries on the Scripture have to be made by them, because they are the teachers of the law, the teachers of the Bible, and the people are ignorant" (*Solentiname* 3, pp. 294-95). God being present with the humble and judging the wealthy harshly is a constant theme at Solentiname.

15. "If you want to achieve a spiritual life, you have to achieve it through material things. Because if I love God, to prove it I have to do something for my comrades and share what I have, be brothers and sisters with everyone. If I don't achieve it in material things, I'm not loving; it's more like I'm hating" (*Solentiname* 3, p. 115).

16. For a fine early example, see the anonymous Swiss Brethren congregational order, which circulated with the Schleitheim Articles, in John H. Yoder, *The Legacy of Michael Sattler* (Scottdale, Pa.: Herald Press, 1973), pp. 44-45.

17. Hans-Jürgen Goertz, *Die Täufer: Geschichte und Deutung* (Munich: Beck, 1980), pp. 20-23.

18. "An die Versammlung gemeiner Bauernschaft," in *Flugschriften der Bauernkriegsziet,* ed. A. Laube and H. W. Seiffert (Berlin: Akademie-Verlag, 1975), pp. 112-34; 128. This anonymous and radical document originated and circulated near the Swiss/German border, that is, in the very area where Anabaptism and the Peasants' Revolt interacted. We will rely on this writing and those of Sebastian Lotzer to represent the viewpoint of the peasants. We have made no attempt to be exhaustive.

19. Phillip E. Berryman quotes a central conclusion from Medellín: "Without falling

into confusions or simplistic identifications, there ought always to be made manifest the profound unity which exists between the salvific project of God realized in Christ and the aspirations of man; between salvation history and human history; between the church, People of God, and temporal communities; between God's revealing action and man's experience; between supernatural gifts and charisms and human values" (Berryman, "Latin American Liberation Theology," in *Theology in the Americas,* ed. S. Torres and J. Eagleson [Maryknoll, N.Y.: Orbis Books, 1976], p. 22. Miguel d'Escoto is even more direct: "We believe that humanity has been created in the image and likeness of God, created to be a co-creator with God in the unfinished task of making this a world after God's own design" ("Nicaragua: An Unfinished Canvas" *Sojourners,* [March 1983]:15).

20. Lotzer, *Entschuldigung,* in Goetze, p. 84.

21. *Solentiname* 2, p. 54.

22. Juan Hernández Pico, S.J., "Qué Significa Jesucristo en un Proceso Revolucionario Como el de Nicaragua?" in *Fe Cristiana y Revolucion Sandinista en Nicaragua,* ed. Alvaro Argüello, S.J. (Managua: Instituto Histórico Centroamericano, 1979), pp. 68-69. Cf. note 6 above.

23. The word is used by the anonymous peasant author of *Versammlung,* p. 126. The Anabaptist position is well known. Menno Simons says, "Whoever boasts that he is a Christian, the same must walk as Christ walks" (*The Complete Writings of Menno Simons,* ed. J. C. Wenger [Scottdale, Pa: Herald Press, 1956], p. 225).

24. *Solentiname* 2, p. 139.

25. "The first thesis of Liberation Theology is that Christianity is charity—which means action. It is not what he says that saves a man but what he does. . . . The true knowledge of God is in action" (Berryman, p. 43).

26. *Versammlung,* p. 125.

27. Ibid. p. 129.

28. Summary in Berryman, pp. 28-29.

29. Pat Murray and Julie Miller, Maryknoll sisters in Nicaragua for the past thirteen years, described the situations as follows: "We knew villages where one person, or even nobody, could read. . . . When they tried to do anything about that, have demonstrations, go down to the courthouse, people were arrested, they were beaten when they were put in jail, they were threatened—and these were just simple campesinos. . . . The unfortunate thing was that there just was no alternative [to violence]. They tried peaceful protest." Interview with author on August 5, 1983.

The extent of nonviolent protest leading up to the insurrection has not been adequately studied or documented thus far. The observation of Nobel peace prize winner Adolfo Pérez Esquivel, that the insurrection succeeded because of nonviolent resistance on the part of the people, contains a helpful hint but does not qualify as an adequate analysis of the events leading up to the full-scale armed revolt. See Adolfo Pérez Esquivel, *Christ in a Poncho,* trans. R. R. Barr (Maryknoll, N.Y.: Orbis Books, 1983), pp. 29-34.

30. Interview with Gilberto Aguirre, August 4, 1983.

31. Text in Yoder, pp. 34-43.

32. "The image we may have of Jesus Christ . . . an absolute image, an image that ennucleates all our faith" (Pico, p. 64). The theme of following the incarnate Christ is pervasive in Nicaraguan theological writings. Fernando Cardenal says, "It is the goal of my life to live and die in conformity with the model that Jesus taught us in the Gospel" (*Ministros de Dios, Ministros del Pueblo,* ed. Teofilo Cabestrero [Bilbao: Declée

de Brouwer, 1983], p. 85; Eng. trans. *Ministers of God, Ministers of the People,* trans. Robert R. Barr [Maryknoll, N.Y.: Orbis, 1983]). A member of a Christian base community in Managua said after the victory in 1979 that "We see in Jesus' actions a series of models which provide the key for such a difficult time as this" (Argüello, p. 112).

33. "The foreknown and called believers shall be conformed to the image of Christ" (Sattler to the Strasbourg Reformers, Yoder, p. 22).

34. Roberto Mendizábal, "Revolucionarios no Creyentes y Cristianos Revolucionarios en Nicaragua: Profundización en la Alianza Estrategica," in Argüello, p. 15.

35. Mendizábal, pp. 23-25.

36. Juan Pico says that Jesus did not choose the violent revolutionary option of the Zealots because they were too narrow and nationalistic, although Jesus accepted former Zealots among his disciples and did not rebuke the movement as he did the Pharisees. Furthermore, in confronting the power of the Pharisees, says Pico, "Jesus was opting against a power that was truly political at that time" (Pico, p. 77).

37. Pico, p. 70.

38. "The God of revolutionary Christians is a God hidden in history; we know that we can meet Him only by following in Jesus' footsteps. . . . Jesus explained God not only with his words, but with words that harmonized with his life. . . . Without the practice of that justice that seeks a new society and a new man the God of Jesus hidden in history will not be discovered" (Mendizábal, pp. 24-25).

39. Schleitheim says the following: "Now many, who do not understand Christ's will for us, will ask: whether a Christian may or should use the sword against the wicked for the protection and defense of the good, or for the sake of love. The answer is unanimously revealed: Christ teaches and commands us to learn from Him, for he is meek and lowly of heart and thus we shall find rest for our souls. . . . Christ did not wish to decide or pass judgment between brother and brother concerning inheritance, but refused to do so. So should we also do. . . . Peter also says: 'Christ has suffered (not ruled) and has left us an example, that you should follow after in his steps.' . . . Since then Christ is as is written of Him, so must His members also be the same, so that His body may remain whole and unified for its own advancement and upbuilding" (Yoder, pp. 40-41).

40. Sattler writes to the church at Horb, "Be mindful of your predecessor, Jesus Christ, and follow after Him in faith and obedience, love and longsuffering. Forget what is carnal, that you might truly be named Christians and children of the most high God. . . . Forget not the assembly, but apply yourselves to coming together constantly and that you may be united in prayer for all men and the breaking of bread, and this all the more fervently, as the day of the Lord draws nearer. In such meeting together you will make manifest the heart of the false brothers, and will be freed of them more rapidly" (Yoder, pp. 61-62).

41. Yoder, p. 45.

42. The *Congregational Order* goes on to speak of the Lord's Supper, which warns each member to commemorate "how Christ gave His life for us, and shed His blood for us, that we might also be willing to give our body and life for Christ's sake, which means for the sake of all the brothers" (Yoder, p. 45). Here the theme of Christ being incarnate in the members of the Anabaptist brotherhood is unmistakable.

43. The sword of government is described as "an ordering of God outside the perfection of Christ" (Yoder, p. 39). Given Schleitheim's uncompromising dualism, this means that the sword of government is of Satan. "Now there is nothing else in the world and all creation than good or evil. . . . God's temple and idols, Christ and Belial, and

none will have part with the other. . . . [God] admonishes us therefore to go out from Babylon and from the earthly Egypt, that we may not be partakers in their torment and suffering, which the Lord will bring upon them. From this we should learn that everything which has not been united with our God in Christ is nothing but an abomination which we should shun" (Ibid. p. 38).

44. Speaking to rulers, Menno Simons says, "Your task is to do justice between a man and his neighbor, to deliver the oppressed out of the hand of the oppressor" (*Complete Writings*, p. 193). See all of Chapter 12 for the variety of views on this subject. See also William Klaassen, "The Limits of Political Authority as seen by Pilgram Marpeck," *Mennonite Quarterly Review* 56 (October 1982): 342-64.

45. Presentation made by a Guatemalan Mennonite church leader and pastor at the Symposium on Anabaptism, Oppression and Liberation in Central America, Chicago, Illinois, October 14, 1983.

46. D'Escoto, p. 17.

PART II

DIALOGICAL INTERFACE AND IMPLICATIONS

10

On Discipleship, Justice and Power

JOSÉ MÍGUEZ BONINO

The depth and level of scholarship, and the significance of the challenge presented in the articles that Daniel Schipani has collected in Part 1 of this volume deserve a detailed discussion article by article. This is impossible within the limits of this brief response. Rather than referring to the individual essays I have therefore chosen to grapple with what seems to me to be the basic thrust of the whole collection (granting that there are specific points and directions that differ among the authors). One must gladly acknowledge that the image of "liberation theology" (at least inasmuch as it relates to Latin America) is fair and accurate. The authors have not worked with the superficial and frequently distorted caricatures which are, alas, too frequently found even among reputed scholars. If some of the authors of articles seem to limit themselves to early writings in liberation theology (probably because they are more readily available in English translation), others are evidently familiar with the wider body of literature. The central questions, in any case, seem to me well-founded and relevant.

My very simple plan for this article is, first, to explore briefly the basic points on which there is fundamental agreement between the Anabaptist and liberation models of theology and, secondly, to debate what seems to me the two basic points of contention (which, in fact, turn around one fundamental question).

SISTER THEOLOGIES AND SPIRITUALITIES?

The Latin American theologian who begins to explore the Anabaptist territory soon becomes puzzled. The language is different, and the categories of reflection are drawn from other forms of discourse. The atmosphere, however, is strangely familiar. This is contrary to what frequently happens in relation to traditional academic theologies where language and categories frequently coincide but the atmosphere is alien. Can we account for this more accurately? I think there are at least four closely interrelated centers around which we can gather the common elements that create this sense of unity.

1. As several of the articles (Rutschman, Swartley, Driver) point out, there are analogies in terms of the *social context* in which these theologies were born. It is a critical point in history when a long-established social and economic order (feudalism in the sixteenth century, the traditional and neo-colonial model in Latin America in the twentieth) begins to crumble. Culturally and in religious terms, the Christendom model is in crisis. Both movements find their base in the poor—although in both cases part of the leadership comes from the cultured. There are, of course, vast differences between the two situations. But when one compares both with the birth of the nineteenth-century liberal theology or modern academic theology, the kinship of the social matrix and the theological subject between Anabaptist and liberation theologies appears noteworthy.

2. *The "poor"* refers not only to the social condition of the peasants who responded to the Anabaptist challenge. They also become a *theological locus*. All the articles in the symposium make clear that, granted that the biblical poor cannot be simply assimilated to a social class in the modern sense, the fact of economic deprivation is constitutive of the concept. God's concern for and vindication of the poor is in both theologies a decisive watershed in the theological "discernment of the spirits." Poverty is not only a socio-economic condition and a theological locus but an *epistemological principle*. "God almighty has always given and announced his holy Word only to simple, pious and unaffected people," comments Lotzer in the sixteenth century. And a peasant in Solentiname echoes it in the twentieth: "The examples of Jesus are very clear for simple people. . . . It's so simple that only simple people understand it" (cited by C. A. Snyder).

3. *Discipleship* is the only epistemological location for understanding Jesus Christ. In traditional Protestant theology discipleship, when discussed at all in systematic theology, was seen as an ethical consequence or, at best, as part of a sanctification conceived as a "second moment" after justification. For both Anabaptist and liberation theology, discipleship (*"seguimiento,"* to use Sobrino's vocabulary) and faith are a single reality. Rutschman has compared the two christologies, and while he finds differences (and even distinguishes different strands in Anabaptist christology), he points out what seems to me the two fundamental coincidences. On the one hand, Jesus Christ cannot be understood unless and until the believer enters a personal relation of active commitment to his "way." On the other hand, following implies a "conformation" to the "story of Jesus," to his "active obedience." There is, in Rutschman's words, a common commitment "to the life and work of Christ." The central place given to discipleship makes the life and ministry of Jesus, the liberator of the poor, constitutive of christology and not simply a presupposition. This is not a mere rearrangement of theological concepts: it creates a totally different atmosphere for theological reflection. With the "pietists," it

locates it within the believing community, as the testimony of a "disciple." But, beyond pietism, it does not leave it as a subjective religious category, but ties it indissolubly with the kind of life and the historical self-definition of the Christ as he gives it in his actions and words. Jesus' option for the poor and his identification with the helpless and defenseless belong now to the heart of any authentic theology. Christ did not *also* do that: he *was* that . . . and so his disciple!

4. *Justice* is, to be sure, a fundamental category for the whole Reformation. Luther himself makes it clear that it does not only refer to the "alien justice," the righteousness of Christ, imputed to us by faith, but also to the active justice (the works of righteousness) to which the believer is called and for which he or she is empowered by the Spirit. But the two came to be so distinguished in Reformation theology as to become dissociated (and not seldom opposed). This dichotomy, it seems to me, is fundamentally abhorrent both for Anabaptist and for liberation theology. The fundamental place of the righteousness of the kingdom (Jesus as the announcer and inaugurator of God's Jubilee) in the ministry of Jesus and the ministry of justice in actual works in his disciple forbid any separation between faith and life. "In short, it is orthopraxis, or right action, which makes Christianity genuine, rather than mere orthodoxy, or right teaching. Or said another way, it is doing justice, not simply believing that one is justified, that is the mark of a Christian" (Snyder).

Such a vision of justice is not confined to single actions but looks for a new organization of life. "Both movements are radically oriented to the vision of a new order, rooted in the conviction that God is doing a new thing" (Swartley). Or, in the words of Sider: "It will not simply do to spiritualize Jesus' message and overlook the fact that right at the heart of the mission of the Incarnate One was a concern for justice for the poor and oppressed."

These similarities can be further developed. We would find, to be sure, significant differences between the two theologies due to historical circumstances and to the religious experience and language of the two communities. But it is difficult not to perceive that these analogies are not artificial but express a common ethos, a basic kinship in the way in which the Christian faith and life are conceived and embraced. When we see this basic commonality, it is easier to look into the difference that also exists. I shall not try to look at it historically, but I shall try to discuss it as it appears expressed in the articles in this book.

CHRISTENDOM, COMMUNITY AND POLITICS

It seems to me that C. Arnold Snyder has stated the nature of our problem in two brief sentences. The first speaks of difference within unity: "Although Anabaptists rejected the project of reforming the world according to the pattern of Scripture, they preserved the vision of justice and social equality within their church communities." The second is a question: "But what becomes of justice in the larger world?" These are the issues we need to explore.

1. The Rejection of "Christendom"

The concern with a non-exorcised tendency to build a new Christendom seems present behind most of the criticisms addressed in the book to liberation theology. Practically all authors refer to it explicitly. The history of Catholicism in Latin America and tendencies present in it now justify the questioning. In fact, Christianity has become so involved with the idea of Christendom that we all would do well to examine ourselves in this respect.

What is at stake here? It seems that it has to do with the relation between faith-discipleship and the understanding of the church that goes with it. Discipleship in this vision—the following of Christ, or more profoundly, the conformation to Christ in his servant and suffering role—is not conceived as the acts of isolated individuals but of a community, "a gathered, disciplined, sharing and discerning community of believers who feel reponsible for each other but whose desire to serve extends to all" (Rutschman). This is a correct description of the base ecclesial community that is, in the last analysis, the subject of liberation theology. "This community concept of the people of God," says Rutschman, "has much in common with early Anabaptism."

But our authors seem to fear that such an idea is endangered in liberation theology by the tendency to simply equate this community with the poor or the people. When this happens there is a twofold danger. On the one hand, the reference to Jesus becomes blurred. Poverty or peoplehood is substituted for active and committed following of the concrete Jesus of the Gospels as constituting the church. This is not a misplaced observation. In fact, some language used by theologians can convey this impression. But the problem is a deeper one. Most Latin American people—particularly the poor—understand themselves as Christian. Their faith, created in and by the conditions of an imposed Christendom, is frequently mixed with superstition, alienating and diffuse. But can we simply write it off as false? When our people invoke the name of Jesus Christ—out of their need and hope—can we say that he is absent? Few of us, if any, feel ready to do that. "Our people are poor *and believer,*" says Gustavo Gutiérrez. It is as such that they belong to the church. Or rather, the church belongs to them. Was it so different with the Anabaptist peasants?

From this point onward theologians differ. In the more secularized River Plate area, Juan Luis Segundo believes that the time of this "popular religiosity" is gone. The church must admit—and celebrate—the end of "mass Christianity" and gather the community of "adult Christians" who assume the faith of Jesus Christ the liberator and commit themselves to it. The rest continue under the saving grace of God but cannot properly be called the church. In areas where this widespread faith permeates the masses of the poor—frequently Indians or mixed bloods—other theologians believe in the growth, from within that faith, of the committed community, which becomes, so to say, "condensers" of this wider church. This is so, not only for pastoral motivations but because in that diffuse faith one can identify genuine elements of the Christian identity (generosity, trust, solidarity, an identification with the crucified Christ, a stubborn hope and resistance) that, however manipulated or imprecise, are the seed of a committed discipleship. Experience in the growth of faith communities (basic ecclesial communities) tends to substantiate their claim. Whatever the dangers lurking in the pastoral venture inspired by this viewpoint, and without forgetting or minimizing that danger, we cannot perceive in it any neglect of the specific reference to Jesus Christ as the center of the identity of the Christian community. It is Jesus Christ, and not some vague idea of "poverty" or "peoplehood." Jesus claims this people for himself; they, in turn, claim him as their own. We are not entitled to draw hard and fast limits!

On the other hand, are we not thus blurring the distinction between world and church? Such limit is clearly marked in the New Testament. But what is the "world" in the New Testament? Is it simply the lack of a personal acceptance of Jesus? Is it not also—and even mainly—the realm of lies and arbitrary power, the murdering hatred, domination (frequently by precisely the more "religious" and "churchly" people)? Jesus himself, at the same time that he demands discipleship and cross-bearing, seems to see inheritors of his kingdom in this unenlightened and confused *ochlos* who is rejected and exploited by the "world." Serious consideration of these questions does not lead necessarily to the clear and precise distinctions we love so much. But I believe that refusing to separate Jesus' sternness in calling to totally committed discipleship and his identification with and embracing of the poor, the despised, the *ochlos* will lead us to a deeper understanding both of the church and of the Gospel. I think that misunderstanding this refusal because of a desire to keep a Christendom complex misses the living center of liberation theology.

Christendom, on the other hand, is something else. It is a "worldly religion"—in the sense of world that we have indicated above. It is a power structure that "christianizes" from the top, that enforces submission, that uses the institutions of a society for the benefit of the church. This is the sign of theocracy and has nothing to do with a church built from below, in the realm of freedom and love. I will not deny that the Christendom reflexes die hard and that we have to be on guard against this temptation—particularly when Christian leadership participates actively in the struggle for a new society and consequently Christian leaders' influence and power as social leaders are not clearly distinguishable from their Christian leadership in the communities. The temptation to build a Christian society and to equate it with the kingdom is a real one to which we are, alas, too prone. But I think the real world will help keep us alert to it.

2. What Becomes of Justice in the Larger World?

Christians cannot ignore this question. They cannot do it because the world is not only the world of falsehood, oppression and death, but also the whole cosmos and the whole humanity that God loves and cares about.

How to understand this ambiguous reality of the world? Snyder indicates (discussing the Schleitheim Articles) that "they assert a strict polarity and division between what is of Christ, which is to be found in the Anabaptist community, and *all the rest of the world, which is of Satan"*(emphasis added). We know this view, which is common to many religious groups and not without support in biblical passages. It is widely held in Pentecostal churches in Latin America, which in many ways resemble the base communities in social composition. Sociology will tell us that such a perspective is psychologically understandable in a people whose experience of the world is that of an oppressive, adverse reality. But in the whole biblical picture it is difficult to square such a view with the Christian faith in the triune God. On the one hand, it would force us either to equate creation with sin or to say that creation has been totally destroyed and deprived of meaning through sin. On the other hand, it would deny the universal lordship of Christ (however, a contradicted and hidden lordship) that the New Testament claims. Christ has conquered the evil world and Satan, and he has dethroned the powers of evil, not only in the believing community. That victory will only be "publicly" revealed eschatologically, but it is already operating in the world. Finally, the Spirit is still at work in the world and the meaning of the Spirit's action is revealed in Jesus Christ. Only by divorcing the "right" and the "left" hands of God can we establish such a dichotomy—and consequently the total separation of the believing community and the world.

This latter solution seems to have at times crept into the Lutheran understanding of the doctrine of "the two kingdoms." In these interpretations, which cannot quite be ascribed to Luther himself, the realm of the world gains a total autonomy in relation to the soteriological realm. Christians, therefore, dwell in two cities: the believing community in which the Gospel of love and mutual submission holds sway, and the earthly kingdom where they have to follow the autonomous laws of reason . . . which easily become assimilated to the "ways of the world." It seems to me that in practice Anabaptists have found only two ways out: either to circumscribe their life to the believing community, creating a sort of world of their own, self-sufficient and as closed as possible (without being successful either to achieve complete sufficiency or to fully exorcise the "ways of the world" in the community itself), or to accept in practice that one has to deal in the world in a different manner. Neither of the two solutions seems to me satisfying.

To this way of posing the question, the writers offer a very important and significant answer: the parabolic significance of a community that testifies to "the way of Christ." Such presence is by itself a call to change, a witness to justice and peace. "The Anabaptist experience suggests that religion can also function as a counter-cultural force. . . . It may take the form of testimony. Countercultural groups may provide the nuclei for a new society, as light and leaven in a fallen world, that demonstrate God's intention for all humanity" (Rutschman). This seems to me a perfectly legitimate answer and one that corresponds to the New Testament pattern. This is what a base ecclesial community tries to be. I have myself underlined that "parabolic" role of the disciples' community, and I continue to believe it is a central one. But I am convinced that it does not cover the totality of the question. This is partly due to theological reasons—which I mention earlier—related to the doctrine of creation, the lordship of Christ and the operation of the Spirit in the world. It is also due to the experience of the meaning and legitimacy of the prophetic function that the churches fulfill in Latin American life and that Christians play in social change, not only in Latin America.

Let me put this very simply. The community of believers is not only that—a community of believers. It is also, whether it wants it or not, a sociological entity, part of "the religious field" and as such has its own weight in society and plays a role—willy-nilly—in the conflicts that affect the whole society. It can responsibly consider and assume this role, or it can simply let the interplay of societary forces "use" it. It cannot avoid taking sides in the basic contradictions of a society. Believers, on the other hand, not only live in the community but also—and more and more, mainly—in the world. They buy and sell, teach and learn, work and travel, and—in democratic societies, at least—vote. None of these are neutral activities. Either they assume this non-neutrality consciously or let other sociological powers (class or group determinations) take over their behavior. That this happens seems to me abundantly visible. Yoder indicates: "The nonconformity remains." Certainly. But nonconformity to what? To everything that happens in the world? To some things more than to others? And nonconformity how? Through passive withdrawal? Through active proclamation? Through denunciation? Through participation to change that to which one does not conform? Every one of these possible options—and any other that one might devise—are forms of *power*. In the end, no Christian person or community can escape the fact that they exercise a measure of power in society. The least one can ask from Christians is that they exercise it responsibly.

Most writers in Part 1 of the book emphasize the question of violence as a critical point in the relation of Anabaptism to liberation theology. I think it is a real question. But I also think it is wrong to begin there. The question of violence can only be meaningfully discussed if one takes at least two steps backward and looks at the question of power and that of politics. Power is not a mythological entity but a way in which relations between individuals, classes and groups operate. It relates to economic relations, to knowledge, to political organization, to ideology and also to force. It crystallizes in structures and develops its laws and conditions. Nobody *can* opt out of such relations. It seems to me that, in biblical terms, we *should* not opt out. Nor are we, again in biblical terms, justified in thinking that God has opted out or that God operates in these relations outside the participation of human beings—Christians included. But this means, if I see it correctly, that there is a realm (call it a kingdom, a sphere, a secular reality, a structural dimension of reality, or anything else) in which the disciple and the believing community *are included* (and cannot and must not opt out) and where they will function according to the nature of that realm.

Force, including physical compulsion and violence in its many forms, is part of that realm. We cannot will it out of existence. But some Christians and Christian communities—and I feel personally drawn in that direction—have consistently refused to accept this mode of participation. We cannot avoid it altogether—at least as long as we live a corporal existence! But we can make a lucid and consistent decision to refuse participation in systematic use of force in that sense. We can be pacifists! When this decision is taken in the context of a Christian witness that includes responsibility for the realm of the world, I find it legitimate. But it is always also a political decision (for instance, when Yoder takes the option of "intrasystemic change", which has also a human cost and determines certain forms of action). But can it be made into a compulsory, *sine qua non* option for all Christians?

The reference to "the nonviolent way of Jesus" cannot answer the question. We all know that the example of Jesus cannot be invoked historically by mere transposition. We are all faced by decisions that Jesus did not face and immersed in relations that were not his (the attitude of Jesus toward the Zealots, a fact on which we all seem to agree, does not cover the total problem). We can, and must, conform to "the form of existence of Jesus" at a deeper level. Whether that includes or excludes the possibility of the use of force seems to me still an open theological (and existential) question to which there cannot be ready-made answers.

The question is not whether we accept violence or not, but what do Christians do with the reality of violence in which we are all actively involved. This book makes a significant contribution to the effort and puts an acute question into the dialogue of Christians, in Latin America and elsewhere, as they strive to witness significantly in the world to the "jubilee" of our Lord.

11

Response from a Baptist Biblical Scholar

GEORGE V. PIXLEY

The authors of the collection of essays in Part 1 explicitly address the issues posed by liberation theology from within the Anabaptist tradition. What is even more important, some of them address the issues posed by the Latin American popular movement that struggles for its liberation in a world dominated by capitalist oppression. The fact that such a collection is possible in our time is to be celebrated. The fact that the engagement of Anabaptists with liberation struggles poses problems, some of them apparently intrinsic and others of a personal or local nature, should not detract from the importance of engagement. All Christian communities and all Christian traditions have difficulty in assuming the struggles of poor people for their liberation, and each community and tradition must explore these difficulties. The exploration must be guided by a concern to be faithful to our founders and their teachings, but of course we will want also to be humanly concerned for peoples who are dying slow deaths as a consequence of exploitation and marginalization. And it might be that the exploration would take us even farther, to examine the life and practice of our founders and of our communities in the light of the Gospel. Should this prove to be a result of the challenge of peoples in the process of liberation, any tradition that stands under the banner of the Gospel of Jesus Christ would have been confronted by the Lord himself! This would be difficult but valuable, and not too surprising in the light of what our Lord said about coming to us in the least of our brethren (Matt. 25:31–46).

My concern in this response is a fraternal one. I have been invited as a Baptist to offer a response to this inter-Anabaptist discussion from the perspective of a brother from a tradition that is a near relation within the free-church wing of Protestantism. We are a younger movement, which arose a century later out of some of the same concerns as Anabaptists, but in a different setting, that of seventeenth-century England. We share the view of the church as a gathering of believers, which we too express in believers' baptism. We share also the concern that religion not become tied up with the coercive thrust that is intrinsic to the state, and so have a long history of the defense of the separation of church and state. Our most notable difference from Anabaptists is surely the absence in our midst of a strong commitment to pacifism, an element so notable in the Continental origins and later development of the Anabaptists. Related to this is quite a different view of discipleship, a more worldly view that typically expects the Christian to follow his or her Lord within the structures, even the political and military structures, of this world.

Now we as Baptists have our own troubles in listening faithfully to the cries of the oppressed. It is certainly not my concern to argue for the superiority of our Baptist tradition, which besides being ungracious, would also be something of which I am not fully convinced. But since this is a very explicitly tradition-based discussion, it seems necessary for the reader to know from what position outside of the tradition in question I am reflecting. It is as if a cousin were invited by a small family to comment on the attempts of the family to reach an agreement on a strategy for facing a serious issue in its life.

Secondly, my response is that of a biblical scholar. Both the Anabaptist and the Baptist traditions recognize the privileged authority of the Holy Scriptures, which stands for both of us above all other authorities. Both of us are still struggling to come to terms with the effects of historical research on the question of biblical authority. As a teacher of Bible who is professionally trained in historical and literary research, I approach the question of the ultimate authority of the Bible with great respect for the historical relativities that went into the formation of the biblical texts and also with a heavy dose of skepticism toward received traditions of interpretation both confessional and academic.

Having thus situated my response to this family discussion, let us now proceed to substantive matters. The first issue we shall discuss is one of clarification, but a clarification with substantive implications. There is a certain tension running through these Anabaptist essays as to whether the question at issue is a theological one or a practical one. The tension is already revealed in the title of the exchange as compared with the subtitle. "Freedom and Discipleship" suggests that the issue under discussion is the practical one of how to follow Jesus Christ so as to maximize the freedom his preaching promised his followers. The subtitle, which narrows and further defines the subject, puts the emphasis rather on the theoretical, "Liberation Theology in Anabaptist Perspective." This subtitle suggests that the issue for Anabaptists is how to "baptize" a theological current so that it will not escape the confines of what is truly Anabaptist.

Now it seems clear that both of these issues are valid, but that the practical one surely takes precedence over the other. Responding to the cries of the oppressed is a matter of faithfulness to our discipleship to our Lord, and our eternal salvation is at stake, as Ron Sider puts it so well. And with respect to the struggle for liberation in Latin America, which seems to be the focus of these essays, not only is our salvation at stake as we respond to the cries of the oppressed but the very lives of thousands and perhaps millions of men, women and children are at stake (in the struggle if not in our response to it). We are here facing one of the major issues of humanity in our time, and ultimately the survival of the human race on this earth may be at issue. Faced with an issue such as this one, everything important depends on our faithfulness, where "our" must necessarily be much broader than the Anabaptist community but must include it. In dealing with this issue of life and death for millions of Latin Americans, Asians and Africans, and of the eternal salvation of Anabaptists (and other Christians), our authors assume the role of prophets and pastors to the people of God. This is far and away the most important thing that happens in this collection of essays, and some of the authors assume the mantle of the prophet more clearly than others, but none of them ignores this responsibility, which is implicit in the title of the collective work in which they are participating.

Still, there is a subordinate theoretical issue at stake in the discussion, the one the subtitle points to. The way the subtitle poses this question it would seem to be an internal issue within the Anabaptist perspective. I believe that, in the light of the primary practical issue posed by the title, this is the correct and evangelical way to pose the theological issue. The question for any Christian tradition is not whether it will *do* liberation theology, but rather of the specific shape that reflection on the struggle for liberation will take within that tradition. For Christians it can hardly be a live issue whether we take the side of the man beaten by the side of the road to Jericho. It is a live theological issue to discuss how we can best be of service to him in the particular conditions of our world today and with the situation that we as the believing community occupy in that world, and also how our service to him can be integrated with the other activities our discipleship has led us to assume. Much of the discussion in the essays in this collection falls into this valid theological concern. But at times our authors slip over into another and less legitimate way of posing the issue, that which tries to believe that liberation theology is something external to Anabaptist theology and that the question is how these two mutually external ways of reflecting on discipleship relate to each other. Because the response to the cries of the oppressed is a Gospel imperative, the reflection on that response cannot be external to any tradition of reflection that claims to be evangelical. So that even from our fraternal perspective outside of the immediate Anabaptist family we reject this as an illegitimate way of posing the issue.

The next issue I would like to raise with the Anabaptist brethren who have written for this collection is that of the nature of *discipleship,* and especially of the persecution which our Lord told us would be a part of this kind of life. Here my reaction is that of a biblical scholar. Jesus told us that in order to follow him we would have to take up the cross. This requires that we look at the cross and what it is that caused Jesus to be executed, and which presumably also leads his followers to the same unpleasant fate.

Perhaps the best way to approach this issue is to look at the Servant of the Lord in Second Isaiah. There is a very misleading perception of the Servant that was created by critical biblical scholarship, a perception condensed in the title (a modern title) "the Suffering Servant." The Servant, according to Isaiah 42:1–4 and 49:1–6, has the specific mission of making known to the nations the justice of the Lord. It is as a result of the faithful execution of this mission that the Servant must experience persecution (Isa. 50:4–9) and finally be led to the slaughter by the nations (Isa. 52:13–53:12). Suffering is, hence, a consequence of the Servant's mission and has no independent meaning or value. The Servant is not such because he suffers. Rather, he suffers because of his mission of making known the justice of Yahweh. Those who have no interest in the establishment of justice will always persecute the spokespersons of justice. So justice is the key, and suffering is not a virtue of discipleship but rather a consequence under the conditions of history of being a faithful servant of the Lord of justice.

The case of Jesus is not much different. Jesus did not, as a certain theological and exegetical distortion would have it, carry out his ministry in order to die. His judicial murder was related to his ministry of proclaiming the kingdom of God as the effect is related to the cause. The cross derives its meaning first of all from the ministry devoted to the preaching and the realization through healing of the kingdom where the poor are blessed and those who are hungry shall be filled. It is in this context that we can validly claim that God sent the Son also to die and that we can claim that his death was "for us." It is also as a consequence of mission in a historical world where sin is a fact that suffering is a necessary part of discipleship.

Some of our authors appear to attach a value to suffering in the course of discipleship that treats it almost like a virtue as virtues were understood in medieval ethics or in Puritan theology. It has been the experience of the Latin American peoples as they struggle for liberation that suffering imposed by the authorities is part of the struggle. Christians within the struggle have seen this (rightly, I believe) as persecution for the sake of Christ and his kingdom, and presently have quite a considerable list of martyrs produced by this persecution. But it is no virtue to suffer. A Christian does not desire suffering, but will accept it as part of his or her mission should it prove impossible to escape it after all strategies of defense fail. This suffering is then seen, according to an interpretation that is biblical in its origins, as a witness, martyrdom. Through suffering brought on the disciple by the enemies of the kingdom, the Christian seals in blood his or her witness. Perhaps this is one area where the experience of Christians in Latin America can help Anabaptists recover the biblical roots of discipleship.

For Anabaptists and for all Christians the historical relativization of biblical interpretation that has taken place during the past two centuries still causes considerable distress. In a useful way René Padilla poses the issue in his contribution, and I quote:

> Something is wrong if theology is asked to eschew objectivity in biblical interpretation and to be guided by the Marxist claim to scientific objectivity in the socio-economic analysis. As a human work, that analysis is

not exempt from the relativities of the human situation any more than biblical interpretation; both the reading of the Bible and the reading of the historical situation are limited by social conditioning.

It is indeed helpful to compare the relativities of biblical interpretation to the relativities of social analysis. For the Christian of any tradition both biblical interpretation and social analysis are essential to a life of following Jesus Christ. In each case we do indeed have to read a text, a written text in one case and one made up of events in the other. The fact that we seek a "scientific" reading of both texts indicates that we seek to be explicit and systematic in our criteria for producing knowledge. In this way we may achieve objectivity, which in our humanly relative situation does not mean a knowledge that is not time-bound but rather a knowledge whose criteria are publicly shared so that it is not suspect of being an idiosyncratic imposition of meaning on chaotic facts. Others who share our position and our methodological assumptions can verify the knowledge thus produced. And, in fact, this view of the matter does apply to both the social sciences, Marxist or otherwise, and biblical interpretation.

Our inadequate assimilation of the historical relativity of all knowledge in the theological field leads to desperate attempts to bracket biblical interpretation from this general rule. There appears to me to be some of this in certain of the essays in this collection. Now we may, like Padilla, wish to exempt the text itself from relativity, both the social text and the biblical text. This would mean that in God's mind there is one meaning to both texts. This meaning would count as the true meaning. The catch, of course, is that we must deal with our human readings of the text, which will attempt from their historically conditioned science to approximate the true interpretation, that, in principle, is beyond human grasp. Or, we may prefer not to assume that there is one absolute truth beyond our relative sciences. From a scholar's point of view either position is acceptable, just so long as we do not make the mistake of attributing to our scientific knowledge the absolute truth that could only be God's.

The importance of this discussion of the scientific roots of our knowledge is to make sure that we avoid the curse of fundamentalism, both in our social science and in our theology. Fundamentalism is the logical error of attributing to our interpretation the authority that would only apply to God's knowledge, whether of social reality or of the Bible. For Marxists this usually comes to imposing a scheme on history and adjusting the facts to fit the scheme, much as happened with Stalin's fivefold scheme of the necessary steps of historical development. In this case the result was to impose on the Chinese Communist Party a disastrous alliance with the Kuomintang in the belief that China had to go through a capitalist stage before it could become socialist. For evangelical Christians it leads to forcing on the oppressed the schemes of our interpretation of Scripture as if our science were of the same authority as God's knowledge. The result can be as disastrous in terms of the lives of Christians as was the Long March on China's communists.

This leads naturally into the discussion of the use of violence by oppressed peoples to achieve their liberation. The question is especially difficult for Anabaptists because of their historically pacifist interpretation of the Gospel and the life of Christian discipleship. Does the absolute core of the Gospel (supposing it has one) require of Christians a commitment to nonviolence? A related question is whether Jesus himself was committed to such a principle. And, finally, is this principle entirely independent of practical results (in the setting of our discussion, of the fruits of liberation that it might achieve)?

Arnold Snyder is to be commended for the honest manner in which he addresses this issue in the concrete context of the Nicaraguan struggle against imperialist domination. It would be improper for me as a nonpacifist Christian who represents a nonpacifist interpretation of the Gospel in a Baptist key to argue the issue in response, a fraternal response, to Anabaptist brethren. So I will just point to some of the alternatives.

Not all biblical scholars would agree that Jesus was a pacifist on principle. It is true that he rejected the armed struggle against the Roman occupation of his land. This could be because he rejected violence in any form. But it could also be because he did not feel that the Roman oppression was the most serious oppression burdening his people. He apparently felt that the Temple was the center of the harshest oppression in Palestine and that Pharisaic teaching was the means through which it was internalized by pious persons. So the warfare he waged was largely ideological, though he did attack the Temple once and he did advise his disciples to carry swords with them in his final instructions before the crucifixion. This is not to say that the pacifist reading of the Gospels is not respectable, but only that it must not be assumed to be the only "scientific" reading of the texts.

The practical results of nonviolence are relevant to some versions of Christian pacifism and not to others. The nonviolent struggles of Gandhi are indeed impressive. But one must also look at the more impressive results of the armed liberation of China under the leadership of the Communist Party. Gandhi left India in the hands of a capitalist class of Indians who have continued enriching themselves while grinding poverty and chronic malnutrition remain the fate of most Indians. China has been able under the leadership of the Communist Party to practically wipe out hunger in the most populous nation in the world. Of course, there is another side to recent China and the issue is not cut and dried. That is, in fact, the only point I wish to make.

But is pacifism an absolute demand of the Gospel? It is here that we get to the core of the matter. If this should be the case it would be irrelevant should we prove that Jesus was not a pacifist and even less relevant to prove that pacifism is an ineffective policy for achieving liberation. Should we find that only armed resistance has any hope of maintaining the freedom Nicaraguans have achieved, and which is threatened by an army formed and maintained by the wealthiest nation on earth, a Christian pacifist position comes under a severe strain on its credibility when it is held by communities that live within that wealthiest nation. Perhaps the only way to continue to bear witness to the Gospel in such a bind would be to emigrate. Anabaptists, I know, have often taken that option, so I am not telling you anything new. My own way to solve the dilemma would be simply to take nonviolence as a recommended but not an absolute value of the kingdom. But I am a Baptist and this is not my problem. Perhaps this way is not really open to Anabaptists, in which case the avenues open would seem either a radical evangelical questioning of Anabaptism as a form of Fundamentalism or emigration for the sake of maintaining the purity of the witness of the community to the Gospel.

This leads up to the final and most difficult question posed by this whole discussion, that of *ecclesiology*. As in the previous question, my role as a fraternal respondent is extremely difficult to maintain on this question. The key issue of *ecclesiology* is present in some way in each one of these essays, though perhaps most developed in Willard Swartley's piece. The Anabaptist tradition views the church as a highly committed body of believers who do not share the values of the world. The world is seen in principle as an alien sphere, which can only be restored to health and salvation by the heavenly intervention of Christ. The kingdom of God, which Jesus preached, is seen as a reality that surpasses history in such a way that it can never be realized except in a partial manner within the separated community of believers gathered in the church of Jesus Christ.

As a Baptist my first inclination is to argue with the biblical basis of this church-world dualism and its strictly imperative character. Of course it is true that the Gospel of John in particular can become the basis of a strong case for the Anabaptist view of the matter. But probably such argument is irrelevant to an inter-Anabaptist discussion. It is probably best to thank these Anabaptist theologians for dealing so honestly with what looks from the outside like a devilishly difficult issue: How can we as Christians both show our concern for the survival of so many millions of people who are struggling to achieve livable conditions in a hostile world and still be faithful to the principles of a faith that can only be lived in a highly disciplined community of persons who keep themselves separate from the world. The considerable difficulty of the position is a practical one that must be solved by a communal pastoral strategy. It has been engaged by some of these essays, and I can only urge that it be continued.

There is one further issue I would like to raise, this one a fairly easy one because it rests, it seems to me, on a misconception. Some of our essayists think that what is happening in Latin America could lead to a new hierocratic society, a modern form of the Constantinian establishment. Should this be the case it would be a matter of concern to the whole free-church wing of Protestantism, Baptists included. It seems to me, however, as someone who has been related to the popular movement in Latin America through its more Christian elements, that this is not a real danger. Implicit in the popular movement is a commitment to what in Nicaragua is called *poder popular*, "people's power." Issues that matter to ordinary people are to be solved by the people themselves or by those whom they empower to carry out their will. This applies in the economic, the political, the cultural and the religious spheres. This raises no small tensions within such a hierarchical church as the Roman Catholic Church, as clearly illustrated during the pope's mass in the main plaza of Managua. The pope preached that day on the need for obedience to the hierarchy in order to preserve the unity of Christ's church. But most of the seven hundred thousand Christians gathered there were concerned most of all for peace, focusing their concern on the mothers of the seventeen boys who had been buried the day before after being killed in the defense of their country and their revolution. When the pope ignored the mothers, who held pictures of their sons in the front section of the crowd, a spontaneous chant began of *"poder popular."* Even before that moment the Vatican has seen the principal threat of Christians within the popular movement as being a threat to hierarchical authority in the church. It is a mistake to interpret the Vatican's diplomacy in Latin America as mainly guided by a fear of Marxism. It is rather guided by a fear of a large number of Christians who feel that the church is the People of God, as the Second Vatican Council claimed, and in that light view the clergy, including the pope, as servants of that people. This, it seems to me, is deeply imbedded in the popular movement in Latin America. Insofar as it remains the view of that movement, never will church institutions be able to negotiate the fate of believers at the base, so there can never emerge a new establishment of the church.

It remains for me to congratulate the Anabaptists here represented for undertaking to put their most dear traditions to the test by confronting the issue of the liberation of the oppressed people of Latin America and the world. I pray that Baptists and others will follow their example!

12

Responding to the Challenge: Renewal and Re-Creation

RICHARD SHAULL

As an outsider to the Anabaptist Movement and to recent developments in Roman Catholicism in Latin America, but an outsider who has a deep appreciation for and has been profoundly influenced by both, I greatly appreciate the invitation to contribute to this volume.

My association with Anabaptists goes back to four formative years spent at Elizabethtown College. While living there in the spiritual and ethical milieu of the Church of the Brethren, that church contributed tremendously to my religious orientation and played a major role in my decisions about what I would do with my life. More recently, I have taken an increasingly critical stance toward what is happening in our society and the direction in which present policies are leading us at home and abroad. I have felt compelled by my faith not only to stand over against these trends but also to seek a community of faith that lives by a different set of values and witnesses to an alternative future for this nation and for the world. This has led me to turn once again to the Anabaptist tradition, to learn from it and be nourished by it.

After having spent more than two decades as a missionary in Latin America, I realize that the spiritual renewal I have yearned to see on that continent is now coming primarily from Roman Catholic circles. The theology of liberation and the Christian base communities are part of a movement of the Spirit that could lead to a New Reformation. The fact that these developments relate the Gospel directly and dynamically to the sufferings and struggles of the poor, who constitute the vast majority of people in the Third World, means that they may have something to say to all of us in the years ahead. Because of this, I have been urging Protestants in this country to take these movements more seriously and engage in dialogue with them. This volume represents an important step in the direction of such interaction and may encourage others to follow the same path.

From the start I want to be very clear about the approach I take to the theology of liberation. As an outsider I look at it from a certain distance; I approach it critically, as I would any other theological movement, attempting to assess its strengths and weaknesses in light of the Gospel as I can best understand it. At the same time, I cannot escape the fact that the theology I am examining confronts *me* and calls *me* into question. Because of its message, I have been compelled to read the Bible in a new way and hear a word I had not heard before. My eyes have been opened to see new dimensions of the Gospel message about God's concern for the poor and Christ's proclamation of the advent of a kingdom in which the poor and marginal will have a new life and a special place. My relationship with God has been enriched and transformed, and I have been forced to hear a new call to obedience. In other words, the theology of liberation has offered me a rich gift of grace and that fact has a decisive influence on my critical approach to it.

TOWARD THE RECOVERY OF OUR OWN HERITAGE

A major development in twentieth-century Christianity, Catholic as well as Protestant, has been the realization that our heritage has to be *rediscovered* from time to time in order for its richness to be available to us. As a Calvinist from a conservative rural community, I was brought up in a church that considered it had a rich heritage that it was bound to preserve. Great Calvinist divines of previous centuries had grasped the fundamental biblical truths about sin and salvation, life and death, and had articulated them in a system of doctrine that later generations had the responsibility to guard vigilantly.

And then my generation was confronted by a disturbing word from neo-orthodox theologians and biblical scholars. They demonstrated that, in the very process followed by earlier generations to preserve the right doctrine, important elements of the message had been lost. The repetition, from one generation to another, of the theological formulations of traditional Calvinism really meant that each generation preserved less of it. Neo-orthodox scholars, on the other hand, demonstrated that, by reworking and rethinking the theology of the church in dialogue with a new historical situation, they were participating in a process of rediscovery through which that heritage spoke to us once again in a compelling way.

I'm convinced that the theology of liberation is now calling us to move to another stage in this process. These theologians challenge us to rediscover what the Scriptures have to say about God's concern for the poor, the kingdom of God and our calling to practice justice; they thus challenge us to open our eyes to elements in our theological heritage and events in our history that we may have lost.

In the essays in Part 1 of this volume I find encouraging signs that Anabaptists are experiencing something of this sort. Ronald Sider stresses elements for an Anabaptist theology of liberation that can be found in the writings of many Latin American biblical exegetes: God's action to liberate the poor and oppressed; Jesus' identification with the poor and marginal; the Magnificat, with its message that God casts down the wealthy and the powerful; and the declaration that "neglect for the poor is punished eternally." LaVerne Rutschman recognizes that the theologians of liberation "have made discoveries not unlike those of the radical Anabaptists of the Reformation period." Willard Swartley provides quite an impressive list of elements the two movements have in common: God's activity in the world "is essentially political, social and revolutionary." Both Rutschman and Swartley protest against the evils of existing political orders and contain a variety of responses, from violent revolution to nonviolence, and both follow a hermeneutical circle in their study of Scripture.

As I read and reflected on these and other similar statements, I was reminded once again of the fact that Anabaptists have indeed found and preserved elements in our biblical and theological traditions that we more mainline Protestants never grasped, or at the very least, never considered of crucial importance. For this reason Anabaptists have an advantage over others of us when it comes to responding to the cry of the poor and of those persecuted because of their involvement in the struggle for justice. They are able to appeal to elements in their social autobiography as a people that are largely lacking in many other Christian movements.

At the same time, I wonder to what extent the present emphasis on some of these elements may be the result, directly or indirectly, of the work and witness of liberation theologians. Have they, by any chance, helped Anabaptists to rediscover their own heritage? As an outsider I can only raise the question, but I think it is a legitimate one. I have no doubt that Anabaptists have emphasized what the Bible has to say about God's concern for the poor—and its implications for us—but the Latin Americans were the ones who communicated this to me most powerfully. I learned early on, from the Anabaptists, something very important about discipleship, cross-bearing and Christian community, but the persecution and martyrdom of members of the Christian base communities in Latin America have become the most compelling witness for me as to what that can mean today. The Brethren at Elizabethtown College awakened in me a deep concern for peace and international justice, which has grown over the years, but the Latin American theologians of liberation were the ones who led me to see what this meant in terms of relations between the United States and the Third World and the cost of Christian discipleship.

Sider concludes his chapter with a strong plea to Mennonites to examine the extent to which they may be in danger of allowing surrounding materialistic values to become the decisive factor in their lifestyles and calls on Mennonite leadership to revamp their church organizations so that they reflect "the same concern for the poor and oppressed described in the Bible." I share this concern not only for Anabaptists but for all North American Christians. I also believe that the theology of liberation can be of great help to us as we pursue these goals, and that it is important for us to recognize this fact.

TOWARD THE RE-CREATION OF OUR HERITAGE

In my encounter with the theology of liberation something else is happening: I find that I am hearing a *new* message; I am confronted with dimensions of Christian faith and life I have not known until now. Because of this, I am forced to deal with what I consider to be one of the most central, and at the same time, one of the most difficult aspects of the Gospel: the fact that it is, by its very nature, the *Good News of tomorrow,* not the Good News of yesterday.

Time and again in Christian history men and women in a desperate human situation have turned to the Bible and, often to their surprise, have been grasped by a new and compelling word that brings them life and hope. This amazing Good News then becomes for them, in each case, the key for rereading the Scriptures and rethinking the faith; a new experience of Christ becomes the source of a new life of faith and the foundation for a new community. Through the presence and power of the Holy Spirit, truth present yet hidden in a tradition becomes a living word, capable of reinterpreting human life and destiny. Those of us in the Lutheran and Reformed traditions claim that this is what happened as a result of Luther's discovery of justification by faith; I assume that the witness unto death of the Anabaptists is the result of a similar experience. And in each instance I believe that a crucial dimension of the Gospel was discovered and made available to all Christians from that time forward.

Only future generations will be able to judge whether the theology of liberation represents such a new hermeneutical principle, capable of reinterpreting and enriching our faith. But one thing I know to be true: for many people in Latin America, and for me, the theology of liberation has done precisely that. As the poor and those who share their suffering and struggle have brought their burden of pain and death before Jesus Christ and earnestly searched the Scriptures, they have come to a new depth of understanding of God's concern for the poor as well as of God's liberating action in history on their behalf. They have discovered that God's saving work means liberation of the oppressed, the offer of abundant life, spiritually and materially, as sin is overcome and social structures are transformed. As the poor study the Bible in the midst of their pain and struggle, God's word speaks to their situation with new clarity and power; out of the dialogue taking place in the base communities between the history of redemption in the Bible and the struggle of the poor for liberation today, a new way of doing theology makes it once again an exciting adventure. The Gospel has become the Good News of tomorrow; those who respond to it choose the path of costly discipleship while bringing into existence and being sustained by a new community of faith.

This encounter with the theology of liberation and the Christian base communities in Latin America has been a profoundly disturbing one for me. I usually approach other theologies confidently, from the security of my own position; using the categories provided by my theological paradigm, I judge them and decide where I find them wanting. But in this case I'm confronted by a theology that calls my own categories into question and points to elements of the Gospel message to which I have not given attention. It challenges me to re-examine and re-think my whole theological perspective and, in so doing, to be open to the possibility of being changed. It throws me into a new and tough struggle about the meaning of the Gospel and of Christian obedience. The ultimate issue is not whether I agree with the theologians of liberation or whether they are right or wrong on one point or another, but whether I am open to the leading of the Holy Spirit, in order to become more than I now am, in and through this engagement.

Approaching these essays from this existential vantage point, my reaction is somewhat mixed. I'm encouraged to see a number of signs of openness to critical interaction, which I rarely find in discussions of liberation theology in academic circles in this country. At the same time, I'm disturbed by the apparent ease with which some of the contributors judge liberation theology without seeming to struggle with the challenge it might present to the very categories they are using so confidently, and without exploring the possibility that God might be calling them to be transformed in and through this encounter. I can best illustrate what I mean by several examples:

1. It's quite easy to continue to speak of the central Gospel message of salvation in purely "spiritual" terms, while recognizing that, thanks to the theologians of liberation, we must *also* be concerned about social issues. In this way we can speak of salvation as we have always done, while adding that "God also acted to liberate the poor and oppressed." We can insist that people must first enter into a right relationship with God by confessing their sins and accepting Jesus Christ as Savior, and then also be concerned about the poor. Or we can declare that the sin of Israel, according to the prophets, was idolatry, but that God destroyed Israel "not just because of idolatry . . . but also because of economic exploitation and mistreatment of the poor" (Sider).

I rejoice that such concerns for the poor are being voiced so strongly in evangelical circles. But the theologians of liberation are saying something more. They claim that any understanding of God's saving work that separates the individual and the social, the spiritual and the material, is contrary to the biblical witness. In other words, God's *salvific* action embraces the fullness of human life in history and focuses specifically on the liberation of the poor and oppressed. An essential element in our relationship with God is participation in the struggle for justice for the poor; in fact, many Latin Americans witness to a new depth of experience of God in and through their relationship with the poor. And for the prophets, economic exploitation and mistreatment of the poor provide important clues as to what idolatry is all about. The theologians of liberation could be wrong on this point, but if our ultimate authority is the Bible rather than our own doctrinal formulations, are we not compelled to re-examine our theology in the light of the biblical witness, urged on by their claim?

2. It's easy to compare the community life of the early Anabaptists with that

of the Christian base communities in Latin America today and see a number of parallels, without becoming particularly disturbed by it all. As LaVerne Rutschman remarks, "This community concept of the people of God has much in common with early Anabaptists, a gathered disciplined sharing and discerning community of believers who feel responsible for each other but whose desire to serve extends to all."

However, I have experienced in the base communities some extraordinary things that I have rarely found elsewhere: an amazing willingness on the part of the poor to share material things; an affirmation of the most marginal as worthy and responsible human beings; relationships in community in which those who minister contribute to the empowerment of others; and a commitment to the struggle for justice, which often leads to persecution, imprisonment or death. The base communities may indeed have much in common with the early Anabaptists. But it could be that the Church of the Poor in Latin America is engaged in *re-creating,* in a new historical situation, something of the quality of community life found among the Anabaptists in the sixteenth century.

3. As someone brought up in a Calvinist church that placed great emphasis on the authority of the Bible and the central place it should have in our lives, I value highly the Anabaptist concern for this same thing. I agree with Willard Swartley when he says that "we must stand ever firm on our commitment to the biblical text as the final arbiter and guide to our lives," and I would like to see, in my own church, more emphasis placed on direct engagement with the Bible and less on abstract doctrinal systems.

But I'm disturbed when I hear Anabaptists or Presbyterians stating confidently that they are the ones who are maintaining the centrality of the Bible, while the theologians of liberation tend to allow the analysis of the social situation "to take precedence over Scripture study itself" (Swartley); or that Anabaptist theology is "inherently anti-ideological" because it relies only on the Bible, while liberation theology is in danger of falling victim to Marxist or other ideologies.

I'm disturbed by this because it is the liberation theologians who have led me, in recent years, to give greater importance to the Bible as God's word, and to hear a message from it that interprets my life and my world in a way that had never happened before. Frequently, as I have participated in Bible study with members of Christian base communities, I have perceived that the struggling poor often have a depth of insight into the meaning of that word which I don't find among biblical scholars or contented North American Bible readers, no matter how strong their emphasis upon biblical authority. Latin American Christians who risk their lives in the struggle for justice for the poor and maintain a living dialogue between the biblical stories of liberation and the situation in which they find themselves have introduced me to a "hermeneutical circle" that brings me closer to God's living word than the more traditional exegesis. And when the liberation theologians tell us that the Bible does not give us any clear-cut categories for understanding social reality, and that therefore our faithfulness to the biblical message compels us to risk expressing it in contemporary terms, that simply makes good sense to me. It is, in fact, quite in line with God's choosing to be present in the world through the incarnation, and with the Hebrew prophets, who risked expressing God's message to them in very concrete and highly political terms, time and time again. In other words, I can't escape the possibility that liberation theology is challenging us all to affirm the authority of the Bible and discover more of its richness *by exploring new approaches to it.*

Convinced as I am that we remain most faithful to our heritage when we take the risks involved in re-creating it, I am especially happy with the essays in this volume that, in my judgment, not only do this but demonstrate the contribution it can make both to understanding the Gospel and to Christian discipleship.

1. Having lived in Nicaragua, in close contact with groups of Christians whose faith and sacrificial witness stirred my soul, I responded very positively to Arnold Snyder's reflections on Anabaptist nonviolence in relation to the experience of Nicaraguan Christians. What struck me about this chapter was the author's deep concern to hear what the Holy Spirit might be saying in and through this witness of suffering Christians today, to take into account their concrete historical situation as well as that of the early Anabaptists, and to establish a dialogue by means of which both Anabaptists and Nicaraguan Christians might continue to grow and be transformed. Thus he can raise the issue of nonviolence for Nicaraguans while declaring that "we must leave the matter of Christian revolutionaries in the hands of our Nicaraguan brothers and sisters in Christ with the prayer that they may search the Scriptures diligently and honestly for the message and example of Christ concerning violence and reconciliation." He sharpens the focus on faithfulness to the Anabaptist heritage on the part of North Americans by laying before them the fact that many Nicaraguans have been led, by Jesus Christ, to a passionate concern for justice. And he ends up by asking: "Have we in North America also searched the Scriptures diligently in this matter of the exportation of misery, armaments and invasion? Have we honestly, understood the meaning and the challenge of Christ's life and example, . . . or have we been seduced by a life of ease and conformity?"

2. The exegetical study of John 8:31-32 by Hugo Zorrilla is another example of this same type of creative work. This text deals with the theme of radical discipleship, which has occupied such a central place in the Anabaptist witness over the centuries. In order to capture the richness of its meaning, Zorrilla does his own exegetical work, drawing on a wide range of scholars, including a few Latin Americans. He never discusses liberation theology directly, but his language shows that he is very much at home in that world of thought and draws upon it. Here is someone who has heard the cry of the poor as well as what the liberation theologians have to say, and whose scholarly work contributes to enriching our understanding of the biblical message and the tradition within which we stand.

As I read this paper, a number of things caught my attention: The author looks carefully at the social and political realities of the situation in which Jesus, and later the Johannine community, found themselves, especially the structures of domination and repression. His study of the text leads him to conclude that Jesus' message of salvation embraces the whole of life, that human sinfulness has a social and collective dimension to it, and that Jesus' messianic practice aimed at the "liberation of the poor of the earth." He claims that "knowing the truth is not the result of some academic exercise; ... the truth responds to the practice of service." And in line with this Gospel, the criterion for identifying a true disciple is the practice of justice toward the poor.

You might say that there is nothing here that Anabaptists have not been saying all along. Perhaps that's true. But as I reread the eighth chapter of John guided by Zorrilla's reflections on it, my eyes were opened to elements of its message I had not perceived before, and consequently God's word broke through to me with new power.

3. My third example is not limited to one particular study, as are the two mentioned above; it rather refers to a theme which emerges, in one form or another, throughout this volume. It is, I believe, an issue raised sharply by serious encounter with Latin American Christians, yet nowhere do I find a response to it as clear or as sharp as those to which I have just referred. But the issue is a burning one, and the undercurrents of concern with it that come through here suggest to me that the interaction with the theologians of liberation on this point has begun and will continue. I refer to the question: How does the individual Christian and the gathered community of faith live out a faithful witness to the kingdom of God *at this point in history?*

For Anabaptists this is a compelling question, given their concern for the kingdom of God and for radical discipleship that stands in the sharpest contrast to the values and way of life of "this world." But now a movement has arisen among Latin American Christians that has essentially this same concern, yet declares that God is calling us today to respond in a somewhat different way.

For Anabaptists and for Latin American Christians committed to liberation, the Christian life is one of sacrificial service to the neighbor. But for Latin Americans this neighbor is identified as the poor and marginalized victim of an oppressive economic and political order, and *concern for this neighbor must lead to participation in the political struggle for liberation.* Liberation theologians would claim that this responsibility is laid upon them because the historical movement away from absolute hierarchical structures of power toward democracy gives all citizens of a nation the opportunity and the responsibility to work for the transformation of structures of exploitation and injustice. They would also insist that this responsibility is a consequence of the influence of Jesus Christ in history. Redemption is a historical process; as we share in the hope for the coming of God's kingdom, we are compelled to do everything in our power to make the first-fruits of it accessible to the poor, to whom the Good News of its coming has been proclaimed ever since Jesus began his preaching.

Both Anabaptists and Latin American Christians live by an intense eschatological longing for the establishment of the kingdom of God; both movements are committed to the building up of a community of radical discipleship, which becomes a sign and first-fruits of that kingdom. As a consequence of their faithfulness to this vision, early Anabaptists and contemporary Latin American Christians have been denounced as highly subversive and have paid a tremendous price in suffering, persecution and martyrdom.

Anabaptists in sixteenth-century Europe living out their vision of the coming Kingdom saw the established Church of Christendom as the incarnation of evil: owner of one-third of the real estate of Europe; a hierarchical structure of social and political domination buttressed by its close alliance with imperial power while at the same time conferring a divine sanction on that power; a hierarchical structure claiming control over the life and eternal destiny of all Christians through the medieval sacramental system. In this context the Anabaptist communities—practicing *real* baptism, living close to the peasants and articulating their discontent, reading and following the Bible as they radically re-structured human relationships in their disciplined congregations—were seen by authorities of both church and state as highly subversive elements, to be eliminated at any cost.

It's easy for descendents of these dangerous men and women to respond to what is happening today within this same frame of reference and to claim that they are faithful to this heritage when they sustain their witness to the separation between church and world-state. But the theologians of liberation and the witness of the Christian base communities suggest another possibility: that this new Church of the Poor might represent an authentic expression of this same vision and commitment in today's world.

For the theologians of liberation, the real structure of oppression today is no longer the church of the Constantinian era but the social, economic and political system of domination and exploitation existing in South—and North—America. As they have shared the suffering of these poor victims of this system and read the Bible with them, they have heard God's call to radical discipleship. And as the base communities become a new center of rich, biblically based spiritual life and create a new quality of life—in which the poor share almost everything and learn how to affirm their worth and empower each other—Christian communities are once again seen as highly subversive forces to be eliminated at any cost.

When I visited the refugee camps in El Salvador and talked to the older women survivors of military and para-military violence in their communities, one after another of them told me the same story: their husbands, sons and daughters had been killed because of their Christian faith and their role in forming a new community of faith. They had been involved in efforts to bring together small groups of peasants or urban poor to read the Bible and discuss its message, share their sufferings and struggles, form small cooperatives in order to work together to keep their families from starvation and lay a new economic base for subsistence. Because of this, thousands of them had been killed and hundreds of thousands forced to leave their homes and wander across the face of the earth as refugees.

As I read the essays in this volume and my own historical memory was stirred once again by the witness of the early Anabaptists, the simple stories from El Salvador and elsewhere came back to me and I asked myself: Is it possible that the Holy Spirit is at work in these communities, re-creating the quality of life and costly discipleship that I have so much admired in the early Anabaptists? For here I see the same intense Christian passion for social justice, the same biblically motivated movement toward the poor, the same willingness to respond to fundamental social and economic dissatisfaction; the same commitment to a life of radical discipleship; and the same faithfulness unto death that I have recognized as the great gift of the Anabaptists to the world church. If this is true, then greater contact and interaction between Anabaptists and Latin American Christians might not only lead to new developments in ecumenical solidarity but also challenge those with such a rich heritage to embark on new ventures of re-creation.

CONDITIONS FOR FRUITFUL CRITICAL INTERACTION

The fact that the theologians of liberation present us with a new hermeneutical principle leading to a rereading of the Bible and a reinterpretation of the faith means that their thought will be subjected to vigorous criticism. But what kind of criticism will be of real value to them and to us? Given the limitations of space, I want to make only two brief comments:

1. Constructive criticism can take place only when each person involved makes a serious effort to enter into and understand sympathetically what the other is saying. When we fail to do this in our engagement with the theologians of liberation, we dismiss their challenge too easily and so distort what they are saying that we lose the opportunity to be heard by them.

I can best illustrate what I mean by this by referring to several statements made by René Padilla:

Padilla implies that, for the theologians of liberation, "political relevance is the only criterion for the verification of theology"; that they are unable to evaluate praxis on the basis of a norm outside praxis itself, and consequently the question must be raised, "Does that mean that biblical revelation has nothing to offer in terms of criteria to test our historical praxis?"

What Padilla really wants, I suspect, is to guarantee a clearly defined and unquestioned "cognitive content" of faith "outside praxis itself." What the liberation theologians are proposing is a biblically based faith that is just as compelling, but is based on something quite different than theological statements given absolute value. Rather than struggle with that challenge, Padilla makes accusations that simply do not hold up:

It is not by accident that liberation theology is extremely inadequate when it comes to questions that have no immediate bearing on politics or point to the supra-historical and personal dimensions of the Gospel. It has nothing to say, for instance, on the question of the ultimate meaning of a person's life.

What the liberation theologians have done is challenge an understanding of God's redemptive work that separates salvation as having to do with "the ultimate destiny of the individual" and participation in the historical struggle for liberation. Rather than confront the implications of that challenge, Padilla removes it by making claims that make a caricature of the new communities of faith emerging in Latin America. Of course, some Christians involved in intense political struggles for liberation are going to be carried away by that experience and pay insufficient attention to other dimensions of the Christian life. In that sense they are no different from Christians in other times and places who have been carried away by the excitement of their discovery of something compelling in the Gospel. But what Padilla has to say here is simply not true of the movement as I know it; more than that, anyone who believes it need not face the possibility that it is precisely this understanding of the Gospel that is producing a new spirituality and giving meaning to the personal lives of many.

Padilla wants a theology "that reads the Bible on its own terms and refuses to force it into an ideological straitjacket," which he sees the liberation theologians doing because of their reliance on Marxist categories of social analysis. Sider puts it more bluntly: "Mennonites want to ask whether liberation theologians are willing to let the Bible rather than Karl Marx provide the decisive definition of the proper Christian attitude toward the oppressed."

Once again, these critics are touching on a crucial issue. I too am concerned about the risks involved in any attempt to express the meaning of the faith in contemporary terms and have challenged and will continue to challenge any assumption about the objectivity of the social sciences in general or of Marxist social analysis in particular. But I can't earn the right to be heard by the liberation theologians on this issue if I accuse them of being locked into an ideological straitjacket. The power of liberation theology lies in the fact that it is the Bible rather than Marxism that has brought forth a profoundly Christian concern for and response to the suffering of the oppressed. Moreover, authentic critical interaction with the theologians of liberation on this point will be fruitful only if we realize that preserving biblical language does not guarantee that our thought is any less ideological than theirs, and only if we take seriously their challenge to us to relate the word of God to the concrete social, economic and political realities, that is, to structures of domination and oppression, under which we live.

2. I find that I especially value the type of criticism that not only takes seriously what I'm trying to do but forces me to go beyond where I now am. This, I

believe, will be the real test of our future engagement with the theologians of liberation.

For example: They claim that European theology, ancient and modern, is metaphysical rather than historical, as in the Old and New Testaments; it uses a type of rational conceptualization that is deductive rather than dialogical; and it is elitist and part of a total system of domination. But if we accept this judgment and involve ourselves in a theological dialogue between the biblical story and the stories of struggling oppressed peoples today, we may soon discover that we are being challenged to raise more critical questions for ourselves and for the theologians of liberation about the type of reason we and they use. When I take part in Bible study groups with poor Hispanics, I find that they have a history and a culture, a language and a way of thinking about things, all of which are radically different from those which have produced our traditional and contemporary theological discourse, Catholic and Protestant. And when I try to engage in theological reflection with women who are developing their own more organic and intuitive thought, I realize that the theology of liberation has hardly begun to deal with the fact that it is still very much a part of the oppressive male system.

Various contributors to this volume have criticized the liberation theologians for being too ideological and have insisted on the need to keep closer to biblical language and remain more faithful to a biblical perspective on social and political issues. They may be right, but they must demonstrate their rightness by dealing with social and political realities in our society with as much seriousness, concreteness and passion as the Latin Americans have. This means, I believe, that those making that claim will be heard only as more Christians take on the struggles for liberation in this country as Latin American Christians have done in theirs, develop their own categories of social analysis and demonstrate how their study of the Bible in the midst of their praxis can orient and sustain them. As this involvement and theological reflection develops further among communities of Blacks and Hispanics, Christians committed to the struggle for peace and for a new United States policy toward Third World countries, and among women who are exploring a new world of life for themselves and their sisters, Christians in North and South America will be able to challenge each other as they hear and live out the Good News of tomorrow and contribute to a rebirth of hope.

13

Orientation in Midstream: A Response to the Responses

JOHN H. YODER

The texts before us demonstrate both the promise and the limits of the kind of ecumenical approach they represent. As the subtitle of the collection would have it, a specific theology is being seen from a specific perspective. It is not clear how a theology and a perspective are thought to differ, nor does that seem to matter. In any case there are two different sets of thoughts, which are named, juxtaposed, compared and contrasted. This is done with a high level of fairness and competence, as all three respondents testify.

The shortcomings of the process and of the collection are not due to anyone's being obtuse or superficial, even less to misrepresentation or caricature. We have before us a specimen of the dialogical ethos at its best, reaching about as far as it can go in reciprocal listening, comparison and clarification. What then are the limits of this idiom?

Denominational reification is an obvious limit. Ever since Paul scolded the Corinthians for it, the temptation to claim a worthy identity in the name of one's chosen teacher has beset us. Although Padilla begins by saying that there is no such thing, and while Míguez recognizes wider variations when he says that the essays' portrayal is fair "inasmuch as it relates to Latin America," the bulk of the dialogue (or, more precisely, of the reporting about a dialogical situation) continues to ascribe to the theology of liberation a degree of homogeneity that does not obtain. Shaull reprimands Padilla for not describing the base communities Shaull has known, when Padilla was not pretending at all to be describing them; he was citing the writings of Assmann and Miranda, who had no intention in their writing to describe base communities.

One dimension of reification is the difficulty it creates in handling growth and change. Shaull assumes, as we noted, the identification of liberation theology with the base communities he has associated with. But the confluence of these two movements goes back only to Puebla. Before that they represented separate bodies of literature, separate thinkers, separate institutional streams, separate sources in Medellín.

The base community movement (beginning mostly in Brazil) and the great expansion across Central America of the ministry of lay catechists *(delegados de la palabra)* had arisen under the impetus of creative thinking in pastoral theology (what in North America would be called "home mission strategy" or "Christian education"). It moved in quite different circles from the early writing in "liberation theology," even when the "liberation" writers were themselves pastorally active. The non-sacerdotal, non-episcopal, so to speak cryptoprotestant quality of both of these innovations in the early 1970s has not been adequately analyzed. Their flowing together at Puebla represents a providential movement beyond what either set of thinkers had projected, which most observers have failed adequately to celebrate.

The limitation (I call it a limit, not a flaw) of overdoing the homogeneity of liberation thought arises in the present collection precisely from the intention of the Anabaptist interlocutors to be fair. They do not point to internal debates and open agenda within liberation thought, and the protagonists of the varied views on those matters are not present within the debate. Our texts lift up the major, most widely shared affirmations and leave the "yes, but then what about . . . ?" questions for another setting.

"Yes, but then what about . . . ?" applies not only within but also beyond the context of Latin America. God's partisanship for the victim is no less clear in Asia or Africa. All our concern to have theological reflection be close to context does not free us from the need for it to be at the same time global. The agenda of liberation, especially when it is juxtaposed with that of the radical restructuring of nation states (as it almost always is in the current debate, but has not always been in history and need not always be in logic), could be enormously enriched and sometimes corrected by reference to the very different contexts in which partisanship for the poor has been incarnated around the rest of the world, even the rest of the Third World.

Reification also tends to decrease the internal potential of a movement or of a study for enrichment and critique. There is in this collection no reference to the very significant subcurrent among Protestant liberation thinkers from lower South America, notably Rubem Alves and Miguel Brun, challenging on both biblical and pragmatic grounds the dominance of the Exodus imagery over that of the Diaspora. There is no reporting on the indigenous nonviolent movements (Helder Camara, Hiber Conteris, Adolfo Pérez Esquivel and his *Servicio Paz y Justicia),* thereby perpetuating the mistaken idea that only Anabaptists have doubts about the capacity of killing to liberate. There is no reporting on the prehistory of ecumenical conversation about the phenomenon of revolution in the perspective of faith, in which most of the arguments discovered by Catholics in the 1970s had been run through by Protestants two decades before. Each of these dimensions of variety could fruitfully have qualified the bipolar mode imposed on the collection by the way it was set up.

In a similar but different way, there is no such thing as "Anabaptism." As Rutschman notes, even the use of the term as a self-designation is barely a half-century old. Before that it had been a term of reproach used by mainline Protestantism, while Mennonites, Brethren, Baptists and Disciples had refused to acknowledge it, on the consistent grounds that what their founders had practiced was not a rebaptism. Only in this century have (some) Mennonites accepted the term, as part of the "coming of age" of an established sect, purchasing respectability on the interchurch scene by agreeing with the mainline churches (a) on their name, (b) on the normativeness of sixteenth-century forebears for defining denominational identity into the present, (c) on the justification of the denomination itself on the grounds that it serves as the vehicle of a distinctive identity, (d) that the way to define a minority group is to focus on the reasons for its differentiation from the "main line"; and (e) that the shadows and the texture of the interim experiences of four centuries (Mennonite ethnicity, cuisine, migration patterns and acculturation styles) are downgraded in favor of the more "original" "pure type." The interpreters of Anabaptism in the present collection generally follow J. Horsch and H. S. Bender in assuming this approach to be usable, with some updating and nuances. I would not.

In the sixteenth century (as our texts recognize somewhat more adequately) there was no such thing as a univocal Anabaptism. The "type" one distills out of that story, whether its use be pejorative as with Zwingli and Bullinger, apologetic as with Horsch and Bender, outgroup friendliness as with Tom Sine and Franklin Littell, self-critical as with Walter Klaassen or *Concern,* or ecumenical as with Donald Durnbaugh or here with Rutschman and Snyder, is the product of a particular modern encounter. *Any* selection of sixteenth-century traits that one chooses to avow or to be embarrassed about is unfair to the fact that most of the substance of Mennonite identity in North America or South has been derived from mainline Protestantism and pietism, not from any Reformation roots. The books Mennonites study, the hymns we sing, the experiences we preach toward and the lifestyles we educate toward are more like Wesley or Moody than like either Sattler or Menno.

If Mennonites in 1988 are quietist or dualist, it comes not from Schleitheim (whose text was unknown among us until the 1920s) but from the Holiness movement, where we got the rejection of the necktie and the wedding ring, or from Campbellism, where we got the rejection of musical instruments. If we are insufficiently critical of the injustices of the specific systems under which we live, it is not so much because we have been pursuing to the hilt a Sattlerian dualism, as because we have assimilated the establishment convictions of our Reformed hosts in the Netherlands, or Lutheran hosts in Hamburg or Danzig, or our Methodist and Baptist and United Church neighbors along the North American frontier. The debate is among the several strands of mainline Protestantism, not between Anabaptism and anything it was conversing with before.

The conversation with liberation is not helped by bringing into it the embarrassment of intra-Mennonite identity confusion as if that were a worthy ecumenical conversation partner.

Not only is conversation hardened by reifying each "theology" or "perspective" it juxtaposes to another, but also behind the images of groups or stances there are habitual definitions of what the underlying axioms are, which are equally rigid. Even when all the authors want to overcome Western patterns of abstract logic, they do not cease to analyze their differences in terms of the traditional axioms. Míguez lists in rapid succession creation, the lordship of Christ, the operation of the Spirit of God in the world, and the unity of both hands of God, as if all these general slogans counted on one side of a classical debate. Each of those slogans would merit careful definition, followed by testing as to where it fits in the debate and what validation it can claim either from Scripture or from the setting of our present struggle. In any case their use is part of a classical, Western, rational way of doing theology, not a new method nor an escape from historical stereotypes.

I started the analysis apophatically, saying that there is no such thing as one coherent normative "liberation theology"; neither is there such a thing as a coherent, normative "Anabaptist identity." That is why "reification" deceives. We could turn the telescope around for the equally true obverse. Each "theology" or "perspective" is much broader than what is represented here. "Liberation theology" is a whole world. There are within it angry and gentle options, doctrinaire ideology and self-critical distance. There are positions with a more or a less accountable attitude to the Scriptures, or to the ecclesiastical hierarchy. There are "evangelicals" and "liberals." Likewise the sub-subculture of those free-church communities using the code name Anabaptist is a whole world. It has its ghetto fundamentalists and its urban conformists, its communitarians and its Muppies, its cryptocatholics, its cryptocalvinists, its ivy-league liberals, its open charismatics and its romantic ethnicists. The two "whole world" systems overlap more than they collide. Over against most other historically derived theological and ecclesiastical systems, over against most major macropolitical systems, they agree far more than they differ. The symposium papers do not deny this, but they attend to it less than to the differences.

The two "perspectives" or "theologies" have in common their major adversaries both in the world (war, oppression, empire) and in the church (ritualism, sacerdotalism, spiritualism) and therefore should be comfortably allied, if they were to be situated on the entire ecumenical theological scene, and if their real activity on that scene were to correspond to their frontier statements of what they stand for.

In the absence of the adversaries and of the respective in-group constituencies for whom the Anabaptist and liberation writers work, the tendency exemplified by the collection before us is to magnify the differences which should matter less and to downplay the commonalities, which in this setting seem hardly worth saying.

The Anabaptists feel obligated to describe a countercultural rigor that

Mennonites have not known for centuries; the respondents will make sure they hang just a little to the mainline themes (focus on the notion of a social ethic based on creation or on the legitimacy of national violence), which most of the time they criticize.

Such a predilection for teasing out the remaining differences between largely parallel positions is the standard role of historians and ecumenists. This collection is in that sense part of the academic game, not part of the discipleship or the liberation to which the "perspective" or the "theology" itself would give priority.

Two of the major still-contested "classical" themes, which these essays lift up, namely how the church's distinctness from the world should be expressed and whether violence (routinely undefined) can (or, if Jesus be Lord, should) liberate, seem to me to have made no progress through the exchange. Neither the Anabaptists' commitment to justice (routinely little-defined) nor the commitment of all parties in the conversation to theologizing from the context seems to have changed the conversation at the points where the parties still feel they should differ. I think we can do better on both themes, but if we can, it will probably be by doubting rather than by accepting and retreading the classical formulations.

The three respondents agree at one point, namely in downplaying the danger of a new Constantinianism, which several of the Anabaptists had thought they could discern in the liberation literature. Pixley says this cannot happen because *poder popular* will not let it, Míguez because the world will not let it, Shaull (if I understand him) because the temptation of state power is less perverse if the church is not behind it and the poor are. These reassurances seem to me to contradict each other, and to fall short of realism about the power of sin and the nature of the principalities and powers, whether that realism be articulated in a Marxist, a biblical or a historical frame of reference.

The respondents are not to blame for thus underestimating the weight of the Constantinian question. It is, after all, not their language. It is the code language of radical reformers at least since Waldo, and designates threats to a Gospel ethos more deep-seated than what our respondents assure us will not happen. The Constantinian adjustment means a change in Christian ecclesiology and eschatology[1] and an according change in metaethics.[2] The various reassurances given by the respondents are not on the level of this grasp of the problem.

If we were to maximize flexibility rather than polarization, we would note within the literature before us: that the texts least acceptable to the respondents were those of Sider and Padilla, who at the same time are the least specifically "Anabaptist," the more generally "evangelical"; that Zorrilla's text and my own were written with no intention to be typologically "Anabaptist." They simply surveyed critically a finite segment of the biblical record. The *praxis* reference to the contemporary world of oppression, like the denominational loyalty of both writers, was implicit in both studies, but making those references self-consciously explicit would not have improved them.

If we are to try doubting traditional formulations, we will note that neither "separation" nor "responsibility" is clear, either in what it affirms or what it denies. Some identify responsibility with a formal commitment to a consequentialist mode of reasoning, whereby costs and benefits can be quantified and the right action validated by a utility calculus. Only when that assumption is made (though it is usually made tacitly) can it seem to follow self-evidently, as it so often does in the dialogue about political violence, that all that it takes to justify killing on one side is the preponderance of guilt or threat on the other.[3] There is, after all, a long history of moral philosophy and theology challenging the consequentialist reduction.[4] If those who say that violence is not the moral issue, that the goals for which it is used is what decides, had demonstrated their acquaintance with that classical heritage, their position would be at least worthy of serious dialogue, but generally the appeal to "necessity" and "efficacy" is made so self-confidently as to deny that claim. Only in the posture of dominion presupposed by the established traditions is that reasoning self-evident.

We have thus stumbled upon the connection between the respondents' two shared arguments: the undervaluing of the danger of Constantinianism and the retention of the classical confessional ideas of "separatism" and "necessary violence." Just as consequentialism is a Constantinian reflex in ethics, so is the reproach of separatism a Constantinian reflex in ecclesiology. Some free churches have been separatist, especially when (as at Schleitheim) the established Christian government had begun killing them. But that was not their first choice. Is not killing dissenters a worse offense against Christian unity than forming voluntary congregations? Is not any state church provincial by definition? Is not classifying certain segments of society as worthy of death, because they are on the wrong side of the justice question, a denial of the unity of God's people as a gift of grace or its reduction to a group with common interests? When surveyed across the whole gamut of history, instead of centering on the most traumatic points of schism, the radical reformation movements have pioneered proportionately more than the mainline churches in the creation of new forms of Christian ministry, mission and unity.

If we are to reach beyond traditional polar formulations, we may also read Christian history more broadly and creatively. There would be the entire span of liberation stories and church renewals between Jesus and ourselves: the *pauperes Christi* and the Waldenses, Chelcicky, the Friends and the River Brethren, Campbell, the Pentecostals. . . . The choice of only the Anabaptists to represent the antiestablishment tradition is itself the backwash of the assumption that the normative reformation around which we must all be oriented happened in the sixteenth century.

Beyond the exegesis before us there would be the contributions of those strands of the Scripture that we have been looking at less. Gutiérrez reads Exodus, the prophets and Romans; Miranda reads John; and so forth. The suspicion of ideologically biased eisegesis is not immediately allayed. It can be allayed, but at the price of a different kind of discipline. There would be more to learn from looking deliberately at holy war from Moses to Saul and its transformations beyond then, at the evolution and final abandonment of the royal states, at Wisdom, Psalms and the postexilic narratives. In the New Testament there would be the narrative substance of the synoptics, the sociology of the general epistles, and the vision of the apocalypse. Each would contribute something more to the spiral conversation ceaselessly linking modern setting and ancient Scripture.

Each of these efforts to transcend traditional dichotomies could help loosen the control of our minds by the assumption that polarizing pure types is the way to ecumenical progress. Those who thus polarize feel that they have done their job when they have shown that the old issues of "separatism" and "responsibility" are still there. A more creative, more ecumenical method would be to challenge that pat method rather than to accept its dilemma and choose one of its options. These other angles, ready to be retrieved through a broader biblical induction, may help to that end.

Appendix: Utilitarianism in Standard Ethical Theory

The above exchange of papers carries on a conversation between practical churchmanship on one end of the scale and biblical studies on the other, without equal representation of the ancillary and mediating disciplines of ethics, social sciences, historical theology. One specific set of issues is so evident that editor Schipani suggested that it may be functional to append to the collection a word of mainstream intellectual history in no way correlated with liberation or Anabaptist perspectives in particular. This matter of general Western intellectual history, however, underlies some of the exchanges in a tacit or taken-for-granted way.

RESPONSIBILITY FOR CONSEQUENCES IN MODERN WESTERN MORAL PHILOSOPHY

There are few more widespread mental reflexes in our age than to reduce action to its consequences: What matters is not whether violence is justified but toward what end. Similar arguments apply with equal self-evidence to questions of truth-telling, sexual fidelity or promise-keeping. What is at stake? Does it hurt anyone?

1. In terms of moral syntax, the simplest form of this argument is labeled *act utilitarianism*. It trusts that a given deed can be evaluated in terms of its positive and negative results; the right action is the one where that trade-off is the most favorable for all concerned. Rules about intrinsic or "deontological" moral values ("never lie," "never kill," "never surrender") are either swept aside in favor of utility calculation or transmuted into rules-of-thumb pointing to utility calculation but subject to exceptions dictated by utility.

Such utility readings seem self-evident in specific concrete settings. They occur in this form in the case for revolutionary violence as it is affirmed, for example, in the Snyder text. (In other contexts, the "intrinsic" or "absolute" or "principled" values at stake might be truth-telling or chastity. Here our documents have made for us the decision to take killing as the specimen.)

Moral philosophy has for centuries been pointing to the limits of consequentialism's unavowed axioms:

a) In the light of the uncertainty of all social events where multiple agents interact, how great must be the certainty of the causative links whereby it is predicted that the unavoidable evil acts will achieve the projected greater goods?

b) In the light of the incommensurability of various kinds of values, what rules of quantification serve to explain which values are lesser? How can individual human lives be weighed against desired/feared institutional changes? Are institutional goals ("freedom," "justice," "stability") always worth killing for? never?

c) Are the definitions of those values clear enough to yield effective norms of moral discernment? Does everyone have the right to define the social goal worth killing for? Is there any "objective" frame of reference apart from each party's self-righteousness?

d) Does not a punctual or "decisionist" concentration on the justification of a single decision or act neglect dimensions of length (past and future dimensions), breadth (communities) and depth (inwardness, virtue)?

Those who assume that the consequential system is capable of being made morally responsible have to be able to answer the above questions. Consequential arguments "work," that is, are *prima facie* convincing, within a given cultural setting, but they are notoriously unconvincing when the interlocutor, being from a different cultural location, does not share one's automatic tacit assumptions about the above questions a, b and c. They seem to "work" when applied to extreme cases (killing one maniac or terrorist to save a hundred innocent lives) but help little across the broad middle range of genuinely complex cases.

2. There is *intention utilitarianism;* an act or a decision is evaluated by its "goal," somewhat independently of whether that goal will be attained. This loosens the critical discipline of the questions of predictability (1a) above. It has strong claims from the history of Catholic moral casuistry:

a) There is the doctrine of "double effect," whereby an action that is clearly materially evil is not morally evil if the good results are greater, if the evil results are not the means to the good end, and if the evil results are not "intended," that is, not desired as part of the agent's motivation.

b) There is the pastoral concept of the misinformed conscience. It is better pastorally, that is, in terms of the integrity of the person's will, to do the (objectively) wrong thing for a (subjectively) right reason than the other way around.

c) There is the disavowal of responsibility for the actual results of a choice on the grounds that they were not intended. One says that World War II was justified to save the Jews from Hitler, although it did not achieve that; or to save Europe from dictatorship, although it gave Europe east of the Elbe to Stalin. The justification is by the ideal goals; it cannot be invalidated by their being unattainable or unattained.

This stance is also "teleological" or goal-justified, as it sets rules aside in favor of goals. Its concentration on subjective justification decreases its usability as an instrument of moral discourse for communities and institutions.

3. There is *rule utilitarianism;* it has rules but justifies them in terms of results. Instead of *act in such a way that your deed will produce the optimum tradeoff of goods and evils,* the standard is *act according to the rule whose observance by most people most of the time will make for the best possible world.* It is like deontological reasoning in vesting the claims of others, and is thereby able to think about larger wholes and longer terms than is act utilitarianism. It is capable of recognizing a basis for the kind of restraints on the justification of violence for which the "just war tradition" provides, and which if applied with integrity may enable strong moral restraints and substantial objectivity. Still it continues to make the same underlying assumptions as the questions in 1a, 1b and 1c above.

4. There is *role utilitarianism.* It says that certain persons, by virtue of their situation or office, are "responsible" to work toward a set of social goals at the costs of the claims of others who are opposed.

The role utilitarian may slip into "intention" reasoning, as when Che Guevara's failure in Bolivia is overlooked on the grounds that his goal was right, even though his strategy was disastrous. On the other hand, it may be rigorous and responsible, disciplining itself by taking seriously questions related to the just war tradition.

Although the person arguing such responsibility for obviously desirable social goals understands himself as a pragmatist or realist, he is in fact deontologically committed:

a) The assumption that I and not my adversary have the duty to *act* thus to direct the course of events is made not on pragmatic but on intrinsic moral grounds.

b) The assumption that I am qualified to make the moral evaluation to justify the act is again made on other than utility grounds.

c) The criteria whereby the preferred goals, by which I *judge* that I should *act* and that I have the right to sacrifice my adversaries' interests, lives, property ... (1b and 1c above), are justified intrinsically. Logically there cannot be an infinite regression of goal-justified arguments. Somewhere at the bottom the goal itself must be validated.

d) The choice of the population whose values are to be favored, the national (or larger or smaller) community whose interests count, and the relative weight of the conflicting communities (foreigners, enemies, neutrals) whose claims justify my historical initiative, is not made on utilitarian grounds.

The role utilitarian tends to claim that his critics are holding rigidly, in a way he thinks naive or obscurantist, to inappropriate moral absolutes at the cost of "practical reasoning."

A more careful analysis of the formal issues will show that the clash is not between moral absolutism (or "deontology" or "intrinsic values") and pragmatism (or "practical reason" or "consequences") but only between one set of "deontological" values that are avowed, often derived from a community's moral traditions, and another set of equally "absolute" values (those in 4a,4b,4c and 4d) that are more contemporary, more provincial, and less clearly avowed.[5]

NOTES

1. Cf. John H. Yoder, *The Original Revolution* (Scottdale, Pa.: Herald Press, 1971), p. 150ff; theme originally treated in a lecture at Montevideo, 1966.

2. Cf. John H. Yoder, "The Constantinian Sources of Western Social Ethics" in *The Priestly Kingdom* (Notre Dame, Ind.: University of Notre Dame Press, 1984), pp. 134ff.

3. Joel E. Tabora, S.J., offers an especially blatant form of this reduction of all moral discernment to ends/means efficacity, which he calls "rational necessity" (Joel E. Tabora, S. J., "On Violence, Force, and Rational Necessity," in *Pulso,* vol. 1, no. 2, 1985, Ateneo de Manila University, pp. l00ff. But the way he oversimplifies underlies many of the arguments, almost always presented with the same sense of self-evidence.

4. Cf. the section "Appendix: Utilitarianism in Standard Ethical Theory," pages 165-68, on the historic debate about consequentialism in moral argument. A perfect example of this is the article "On Violence, Force, and Rational Necessity" by Joel E. Tabora (see note 3 above).

5. This formal observation about the shape of the argument is similar to the point in John H. Yoder, *What Would You Do?* (Scottdale, Pa: Herald Press, 1981), pp. 14ff.

14

Freedom, Discipleship and Theological Reflection

GAYLE GERBER KOONTZ

I suspect that this invitation to include me in the theological circle is a way of pointing out, quietly, that paying attention to the situation of the oppressed involves listening to and feeling "reality" according to women as well as according to men. God's liberation through the Messiah, Jesus, involves the politics of women/men relations as well as the politics of state and class. So with some enthusiasm (my soul carries some small pieces of the weight of the suffering of women worldwide and is evangelical about a redeeming God who desires not only mutual respect between women and men but relationships characterized by genuinely self-giving love) and with some weariness (speaking once again not simply as a participant in a community of discourse but noticeably as a gender minority participant) I enter this dialogue.

As a Mennonite and a theologian and a woman I have come to appreciate and claim some of the elements that liberation theologians and believers' church theologians have identified as critical for theological reflection. I also believe that it is more difficult to absorb and appropriate in our own "professional" theological reflection some of these elements than we might think.

1. Both liberation and believers' church theologians call for high theological integrity, underlining the importance of faithful commitment and action as the context for theological reflection. I affirm this call.

As theological writers, teachers, preachers and leaders it is appropriate and important for us to be talking with each other and others in the church not only about the shape and content of our theological ideas, but also about our concrete commitments and actions in response to God in Christ. How we use our time and money, how we respond in attitude and action to a handicapped son, to racial prejudice in our town, to the death or unfaithfulness of a spouse, to poverty in Calcutta or to United States military policy are not simply personal and idiosyncratic factors to be transcended (ignored) in theological reflection. They are theologically relevant data that can and should be critically examined along with theological abstractions.

Our theological convictions not only illuminate and shape our responses to the problems of meaning and morality each of us faces daily, but our commitments and actions apart from intellectual reflection test and reform our theological convictions. Learning to be more vulnerable and accountable in our Christian theological conversation with respect to our *praxis* or discipleship commitments is not only a way to become more fully self-critical and responsible in theological reflection, but also a way to bring concern for "character" as well as "principle" into academic theological/ethical discussion at a strikingly concrete rather than theoretical level. Richard Shaull came the closest to demonstrating this approach in his response to the first essays.

2. Liberation theology, along with hermeneutic philosophy and cross-cultural experience, has graphically articulated and illustrated to me how conceptions of reality, biblical hermeneutics and theological understandings are standpoint dependent.

Such an awareness has been liberating to me as a Christian woman; it made possible and legitimate a hermeneutics of suspicion in relation to dominant theological understandings of what it means to be male and female before God, of the "maleness" and power of God, of leadership and authority in the church. I also affirm, at greater distance, how an emphasis on relativity in knowing frees racial and other minorities and the poor to challenge definitions of reality, self and God that are articulated by socially powerful, educated and wealthy persons.

While I have recognized the liberating power of a strong sense of the relativity of seeing and knowing, I have also been troubled by the movement toward individualistic relativism, which seems to be a primary alternative, at least in America, to traditional, more communitarian ways of identifying what is true, good and right. The system of meaning and values described by Robert Bellah and others in *Habits of the Heart* is essentially individualistic, even when specific people seek to respond to those suffering from injustice. In this context I have come to appreciate more deeply and appropriate the theology of the church that has been developed through the believers' church tradition. A strong emphasis on the visible church, which implies among other things the centrality of voluntary communities of believers gathered to discern the meaning of following Christ in particular situations, has its dangers, some of which have been noted here by others. But in a social context where individualism is dominant, a concern for a "hermeneutics of peoplehood"[1] and a theologically rooted commitment to build and care for an extended Christian family, a social structure through which God has been liberating and empowering many for the ongoing work of redeeming this creation, is an urgent and attractive corrective.

A further counterweight to individualistic relativism, which can arise from a strong awareness that the interpretation of experience and Scripture is standpoint dependent, is serious engagement with a common text that represents a common memory. Respect and love for Scripture permeates theological reflection in the Anabaptist Mennonite tradition, even though such respect and love has sometimes been preserved in a narrow "biblicism." While the Bible itself contains diverse perspectives, the biblical story is not so pliable that it can be made to justify just any interpretation or conclusion. It is striking when people from different historical, social, political points read the text and come to agreement about what certain biblical texts meant in historical context. While interpreters vary much more widely on the relevance of the theological conclusions they draw from the biblical material to current situations, such theologizing should be more fluid, it seems to me, since contexts differ. I find it helpful to look for a range of acceptable theological interpretations rising from and tested by a common text.

One critical implication of recognizing that our theologizing is standpoint dependent and of affirming the importance of "the church of disciples" in theological reflection, it seems to me, is to give greater attention to the constitution of the communities to which we are responsible as theologians. It is not enough to attempt to compensate for gaps of perspective in the North American theological guild or within Christian liberation movements or within particular denominational circles by taking some time to listen politely to those who, because of race, nation, class, sex or denomination, are absent or minority voices, and then proceed with writing, preaching, teaching and acting as usual. We must find ways to a) genuinely and intentionally engage ourselves over the long haul with specific conversation partners different from ourselves, and b) take extraordinary steps to empower representatives of the socially weak in whatever situation to serve as Josephs and Esthers and Daniels (see John Yoder's first essay) in the specific theological community in question.

One thing that struck me about the essays in this book by writers deeply aware of how nation and class can inform theological interpretation was the virtual lack of explicit reference to gender as another category that can profoundly affect theological and ethical perspectives. I noted that Richard Shaull was the first and only participant in this book to make explicit reference to potential conversation between Christian feminist liberation theology and Latin American liberation theology. The way that sentence itself is phrased illustrates the absence of Latin American Christian feminist theologians as serious conversation partners in this as well as perhaps other theological circles.

3. Liberation theology calls Christian theologians to keep the suffering of the poor and oppressed in the world in sharp focus in theological reflection. Believers' church theologians call Christian theologians to keep an ethic of peace and the visible community of disciples in sharp focus in theological reflection. I am grateful for these persistent voices; I believe both are consistent with Christian revelation. But again I note that from a feminist perspective most participants in the preceding discussion have not cast their nets widely enough in relation to these themes.

For example, to be thoroughgoing in a commitment to care for the suffering of the poor and oppressed, liberation theology of whatever variety must give explicit attention to ways in which sexism against women and related prejudice against racial minorities and the handicapped endangers the lives, health and wholeness of many female and other socially weak members of the human community.

A significant number of feminist theologians and ethicists, not all of whom are white or North American, share a number of the concerns highlighted in this book as characteristic of various Latin American liberation theologies. One such concern is methodological. Liberation theologians agree that analysis of the economic, political and social dimensions of the "situation" of the poor and oppressed in the world is a necessary component in theological reflection. If theological interprtetation is to articulate the relevance of biblical faith to contemporary reality, if it is to truly understand biblical faith itself, it must be able to understand and respond to the concrete realities of the socially weak.

Feminists press the claim that analysis of the "situation" is inadequate unless specific attention is given to the dynamics of women-men relations. Liberation from poverty and political exploitation is a priority for many women and men. But unless Christian vision and decision include an understanding of the ways in which issues of power and control affect our most fundamental relationships, poor women may be liberated into homes where they continue to be beaten by husbands, into workplaces where they continue to be economically exploited on the basis of sex, and into churches where their sense of self-esteem as well as their spiritual, moral and leadership gifts are restricted. In addition, in societies which exhibit sexism against women, social attitudes toward minorities and misfits, including male members of those groups, tend to parallel attitudes and practices toward women. In describing the problem of bondage, none of the participants in the previous discussion included specific reference to women-men relations. And while arenas for liberation included the lives of individual disciples and the church as well as broader social, economic and national groupings, no one mentioned the family.

Similarly, to be thoroughgoing in its own commitments, believers' church theologizing must learn to include cultural sexism as a peace and discipleship issue. In military organizations, governments, businesses and families where male identity or masculinity is related to being dominant—independent, competitively successful in relation to other males, in control of dependents or subordinates including women as a class—Jesus appears effeminate. He depended on divine rather than secular competitive power; he embodied servanthood, healing, inclusion of outcasts and women, repentance, mercy and self-giving love. Because the church is always a community of disciples *in* the world, Christian males who seek to follow Jesus in such cultures will face profound struggles of personal identity. I suspect the temptation to maintain "masculine" identity through successful competition with and benevolent control of others in the church, while dissenting from "worldly" models of aggressive militarized males, remains strong and affects women-men relations in our churches and institutions more than we realize.

I am concerned that while few question the relevance for "peace theology" of debating the possible necessity for violent action on the part of Christians in prerevolutionary situations or the rationale for conscientious objection to military service, we find it difficult to validate an examination of the dynamics of power and value in relationships between women and men as a genuine peace-related theological task. It is my conviction that for love of God and neighbor we need to protest and respond to domestic violence against women. For love of God and neighbor we need to name and respond to connections between poverty and prostitution. For love of God and neighbor we need to understand and disarm expressions of power through rape—in times of war *and* in times of peace.

Further, if Christian witness to the presence of God is to take a corporate form, if a genuine *community* of disciples is to testify to the saving, liberating, reconciling work of Christ in the world, then the shape of relationships between women and men in the church must also be redeemed. If relationships in the church of disciples are to reflect the spirit of Christ, there must be dissent from cultural patterns of power, control and male-female identity and behavior that permit violence against women, minorities, the handicapped, the poor . . . and against strangers from foreign lands.

4. While various liberation and believers' church emphases have been liberating and sustaining to me for some of the reasons noted above, they have also been the source of guilt and in some measure, ironically, of bondage. Both embody forms of prophetic spirituality. Both call for holy thinking and living, and do not fear to draw lines (though at different places) between the faithful and unfaithful. Both prescribe measures for theological accountability— though specific measures vary. In the bright light of prophetic theology and ethics, it is nigh impossible to be the kind of person who can speak adequately of God and the world. For next to the uncompromising love and justice of God, which prophetic spirituality holds forth for us, our finitude and our failure stand in sharp relief. It is not enough to bear the burdens and temptations of guerrilla warfare in Guatemala; theologians must be feminist. It is not enough to understand the pain and hopes of white congregations in North America; theologians must be in significant conversation with people of color. It is not enough to be conversant in classical and contemporary theology; theologians must be competent biblical scholars. Or conversely, it is not enough to spend time in careful biblical exegesis; theologians must be conversant with current sociological and economic debates. It is not enough to refuse to pay war taxes; theologians must sell all they have and give to the poor. It is not enough to teach peace theology; theologians must actively work for nuclear disarmament, pray for peace without ceasing, and make sure that congregational conflicts are dealt with fairly and peaceably. The prophetic spirituality that underlies our discussion, a spirituality which I love and respect, a spirituality that has been a source of liberation and of God's presence in my life, also wearies, undercuts and disempowers me. None of us, rich or poor, black or white, male or female, Protestant or Catholic, who purport to speak with theological insight and wisdom, can be "prophetic" enough, righteous enough,

comprehensive enough, to be free from further prophetic judgment.

It is important for me, therefore, as a participant in religious communities and theological climates that tend to encourage and sustain prophetic spirituality, to also develop aspects of incarnational theology present in the Gospel. As a North American, white, relatively wealthy, inadequately committed disciple, I need to hold prophetic theology in tension with incarnational theology. None of us who attempt to hear and do the word of God—even if we are in some measure sexist or racist, or overly mistrustful of the educated, rich or powerful—are so far from God that there is no hope for God's spirit and word to shine through. There is need for a hermeneutics of generosity as well as a hermeneutics of suspicion.[2] Patriarchal biblical texts may become a locus for the word of God to me. The spirit of Christ may be found embodied among the rich as well as among the poor. We need to recall a theology of grace as well as a theology of righteousness. Prophetic spirituality separates the holy and unholy. Incarnational spirituality holds them together in paradoxical love, which always runs the risk of blasphemy.

5. It is my conviction, as a result of the conversation in these essays and elsewhere, that believers' church theological scholarship in the future should hold onto the audacious vision of integrating careful biblical exegesis, theology and ethics. While at a congregational level exegesis, theology and ethics have not been clearly separated, believers' church scholars, trained according to academic disciplines, joined networks of mentors and professional societies that have increasingly drawn and defended boundaries between biblical scholars, theologians and ethicists. I suspect that to bridge the disciplines in a creative, fruitful and cooperative way—to become a genuine community of scholars—will require not only time and energy but the movement of the Holy Spirit.

Further, I think trained theologians should be more explicit than we have been in the past in our theological conversation and writing about the social, historical, economic, cultural, personal elements and perspectives that motivate and shape our reading of the Bible and our encounter with God. We need not pretend that any reading of Scripture, any theological picture or ethical program arises from a disembodied mind, or that God's word is more clearly available the further a theologian is or appears removed from the contingencies of historical existence. Theology is articulation of an understanding of God and world *by someone to someone,* both of whom are profoundly historical beings. I believe we would do well to re-emphasize the fact that theology is communication, testimony—a painting of a religious worldview by one member of a religious community at one historical moment, more akin to preaching or religious art than is usually noted.

Finally, and perhaps most important, I believe we must become more self-critical about our primary communities of theological reflection, and if necessary, work to expand, change or restructure them. Examination of method in theology includes not only such familiar questions as What is the authority of Scripture in relation to modern social science? but also Who is included in one's community of theological reflection? Who is listened to and why? Where are the voices of the socially weak? Is the community of discourse and action pluralistic enough?

As others have noted, I too am excited and encouraged by the interchange this book represents. It represents an extension of the communities of theological reflection of a few believers' church leaders (and perhaps of some other Christian brothers as well). But it is and will continue to be a struggle for most of us to learn to live lovingly and forthrightly with Christian pluralism, far greater pluralism than the brief exchange in these essays represents, to say nothing of those who are members of other or no religious communities.

Those of us who have been shaped strongly by a prophetic discipleship tradition (perhaps also a prophetic liberation tradition) find it difficult to legitimate those who differ in theological and ethical perspective. We have tended to equate difference with faithlessness or at least serious error. Precisely because of our already strong suspicion of difference, and given the warning in Jesus' reference to motes and beams, our particular task might be to practice a hermeneutics of generosity. If we have eyes to see and ears to hear, the gathering together of different selves and communities may well become an occasion for God's words of justice and grace to break forth. A genuine struggle to understand and respect one another's historical situations, situations that give rise to differing interpretations of Scripture and differing theological convictions, may well become a means of transformation, new insight, deeper faith and unexpected action.

NOTES

1. See John H. Yoder, *The Priestly Kingdom* (Notre Dame, Ind.: University of Notre Dame Press, 1984), ch. 1.
2. The expression "hermeneutics of generosity" is borrowed from Margaret R. Miles, "Hermeneutics of Generosity and Suspicion: Pluralism and Theological Education," *Theological Education* 23 (Supplement 1987): 34–52.

15

Implications for Peace and Justice Witness

LEROY FRIESEN

As one long-convinced that dialogue between representatives of a believers' church perspective and those of Latin American theologies of liberation could be a yeasty one, I greet the emergence of this collection of essays under the editorship of Daniel Schipani with subdued delight. Possible shortcomings have already been cited: premature declarations of agreement and inadequate awareness of what agreement on a given issue really entails; a level of politeness that is both predictable and ironic, the latter given the immediate applicability of virtually every page to day-to-day events in both halves of the Western hemisphere (particularly in Central America); imprecision and lack of agreement as to the meaning of *violence* or *theologies of liberation* or *Anabaptism* or *justice;* gender imbalance among contributors and some related insensitivites in use of language; varying degrees of focus on the central issues of the dialogue. And yet, the collection is the first of its kind and a rather strong beginning at that. Many of the crucial issues do emerge along the way.

The objective of this essay is to reflect primarily on the questions raised by the four respondents. This is done from the perspective of one whose theological journey, while having its source and principal nourishment in a believers' church context, has included growing restlessness over the last fifteen years in the face of the liberation agenda. The Mennonite people are my people; I have chosen this people, this story, this perspective as the context in which to be part of the living out of the way of God in the world.

It will be apparent that I direct more of the hard questions to my own present-day community than toward our contemporary advocates of theologies of liberation. Love for one's own faith community and tradition would seem to carry certain responsibilities within the context of embodied accountability to seek to speak the truth in love, and to do so first at home. That is what

I here seek to do. My responses to the questions of this volume will themselves often be questions, together with suggestions as to promising directions for subsequent stages of this dialogue that I hope will follow.

1. THE PERIMETERS OF CHRIST'S LORDSHIP

Perhaps the most foundational issue raised by the dialogue of this volume is this: what are the biblical teachings as to the nature and extent of the lordship of the Risen Christ, and what view of the *world* is rooted in the degree of expansiveness of that lordship? In his essay José Míguez Bonino asks, Is Christ's lordship understood as having present jurisdiction only within the church with the cosmic dimensions viewed eschatologically (futuristically)? Or is it understood as already operative *throughout* the creation although publicly acknowledged as such only in the *eschaton?* I would add, Is it possible for the church to hold to the latter view without a significantly different discipleship pattern than that characterizing commitment to the former? Does God's modeling response to human tragedy in Jesus the Christ allow the church so to delimit that lordship that faithful witness is envisioned largely in terms of the living out of an alternative politic, especially when that politic is so deeply (and often unacknowledgedly) compromised ideologically? What is the *world* from the perspective of commitment to the lordship of Christ? Is it some alien, unsalvageable (except for the *eschaton),* indeed, *abandoned* sphere (at least for the interim), one ripe for burning? Or is the world that which God "so loved," that which has become the jurisdiction of the Risen Christ? In short, in what sense is the lordship of Christ a reality outside of the faith community and before the *eschaton?*

Perhaps it need not be said that these questions reflect an ongoing believers' church intrafamily disagreement at least as much as they do one with the advocates of theologies of liberation. In fact, Shaull is surely right to some extent when he wonders whether the growing discussion within this family has not been nurtured by contact with developments in Latin America. There is a great deal for Anabaptist-Mennonites and the adherents of theologies of liberation to work on together if there is a common confession that Jesus Christ is functioning lord of all creation today. There is very little to work on together if there is not agreement on that point.

2. THE GOSPEL AND JUSTICE

Is invitation to justice-making in the larger society part of the Good News of shalom? (Justice-making understood in the biblical sense of God's call to the righting of relationships.) Is justice tangential, optional, although surely recommended? Can a "pacifist/nonresistant" (Swartley's term) reading of Jesus' call to love of enemy as a witness to God's kingdom of shalom be divorced from justice-making in the larger society? Or is justice-making to be supported as part of the kingdom only as long as it is God rather than the faith community who is doing it? Is one of the appropriate conclusions from this collection of essays that justice *now* is of concern to liberation theology and not the believers' church, that the issue *belongs* to the liberationists, that it is on their turf? If so, what about the Bible on justice? Can love for the enemy be made "a critical test," to use Swartley's term, but justice not?

The contributors to this forum who are most enthusiastic about Latin American theologies of liberation view justice as being at the heart of the message of the Bible; the contributors who are most critical of those theologies demonstrate varying degrees of ambivalence about the theological case for justice-making. Willard Swartley, for example, uses the word *justice* quite sparingly (as in "God's establishment of justice") in his section "Beyond Comparisons: Toward Liberation with Discipleship." In the early stages of his response Míguez Bonino is perhaps generous in the extent to which he sees Anabaptist use of "discipleship" and the liberationists' use of "orthopraxis" as reflecting a similar refusal to separate "justice" from "justification." However, later in his piece he quotes Snyder in identifying one of the central questions of the entire volume: "But what becomes of justice in the larger world?" "Fraternal respondent" George Pixley questions whether his "brethren" in the dialogue have not identified *suffering* as *the* central virtue of discipleship rather than as its consequence, and thus neglected justice. It must be acknowledged that the drift toward inwardness and quietism in the believers' church tradition is not only infrequently found, but the focus on cross-bearing and, Pixley contends, *suffering* has not been unrelated to an ambivalence regarding the biblical case for justice-making. So what (all) *is* at the heart of the Good News of Jesus Christ? Is the invitation to justice-making part of the Good News?

3. BETWEEN THE TRADITION AND THE NEW

Does faithfulness to a biblically rooted Christian heritage, whether emphasizing the first or sixteenth or yet another century, consist primarily in the contemporary repetition of the responses of that formative period? Or does faithfulness open itself significantly to the Spirit's *re-creation* of new responses for the new situations of our time? If primarily the former, what difference does the dynamic presence of God's Spirit finally make? If primarily the latter, what understandings of the received tradition better allow for the distinguishing of new responses which are of the Spirit from those which are not?

Two of the respondents, George Pixley and Richard Shaull, forcefully raise these kinds of questions, although in each case they tend to focus the application primarily on the descendants of the Radical Reformation rather than equally on *both* parties in the dialogue as they should have done. Shaull cites Calvinism and neo-orthodoxy as contrasting examples in making the point that mere theological recapitulation from generation to generation actually preserves *less* than a "reworking and rethinking" approach to the tradition. Thus, he contends, what is seemingly *more* theologically is actually *less*, the stance of emphasizing *rediscovery* more faithful to the tradition than that seeking to be *primitivist*.

Descendants of the Anabaptists are not strangers to this less-with-more experience in preservation; nor are the theologies of liberation uninitiated to the hazards of the heady evaluation of the "reworking and rethinking" emphasis. Is it not possible for the church to view the tradition as the bridge of continuity with both its biblical origins and subsequent revitalizations while at the same time remaining wide open to the break-through of God's *New?*

4. ABOUT TELEOLOGY AND CONSTANTINE

Should the church today seek to avoid incorporating significant teleological (consequentialist) elements into its discernment of justice-making strategy, particularly in situations where sensitivity to *consequences* has to do with whether people live or die? Does not *compassion* have a certain teleological flavor? Surely the biblical story of the compassionate God does not provide basis for an exclusively deontological understanding of peace/justice-making. The Good News is about the God who gave a damn and continues to do so, the God who is the *Affectable One* (Moltmann), the God for whom the life or death of human beings matters indescribably. Neither the centuries-long cataloging of the vulnerabilities of teleology in general nor the pervasive act-utilitarianism of our culture in particular must be allowed to deter the church from allowing itself to be profoundly *torn* by today's unconscionable wastage of human life in many parts of the world.

What may be one of the most promising theological developments today regarding the church's call to justice is a growing openness in many quarters to the image of the *Suffering God:* the one who has taken on the world's pain; the God who cares/grieves/dies over what *happens* to people; the God in whom, in the words of Dorothee Sölle, "there is no alien sorrow." The church is not called to any solidarity with the devalued and the socially discarded that God has not already, irrevocably, forged, for part of the meaning of the *enfleshment* of God in Jesus the Christ is "solidarity" with the entire human family. Sider is right when he contends that "the Bible teaches that God is on the side of the poor." But beyond that, I would emphasize that the pain of the poor (as well as the rest of us) has always been God's pain! The call to costly justice-making, then, is the call to join the ongoing, suffering work of God as glimpsed in the *eikon* Jesus the Christ. The real hazards of pragmatism for theology should not be allowed to eclipse the far-reaching significance for justice-making of the *compassionate solidarity* on the part of the God who has staked all on an alternative future for the creation.

Part of my vague sense of uneasiness about aspects of the believers' church contribution to this volume is the infrequency with which reflections of this divine passion and compassion are surfaced. Part of what Jesus teaches us is that *this* God is not characterized by disengagement in the face of human tragedy, and neither can being part of that One's kingdom be so construed.

Whatever the relative theological merits and deficiencies of Latin American theologies of liberation, they have been fueled by a passion for the well-being of human beings that must be acknowledged as having its source in God.

Several of the essays in this collection express varying degrees of uneasiness with what is perceived in the Latin American theologies of liberation as the danger of "a new church-world synthesis" (Rutschman), "Constantinian structured vision" (Swartly) or "a new Constantinianism" (Yoder). Such uneasiness is neither surprising nor without foundation. Some of the theological bases for it are reintroduced by Yoder in his second essay where he concludes that the exchange has resulted in "no progress" on the issue. (Note: the helpfulness of the volume's exchanges on this issue is reduced by confusion about how the term *Constantinianism* is used. Yoder and Swartley, for example, appear to use the term for a church-state alliance with a state rather than a believers' church; Pixley [and perhaps others], on the other hand, tends to equate the term with *hierarchical* and thus contrasts it with the popular church in Nicaragua.)

Conversely, the danger in focusing on the "Constantinian threat," in retreating, for reasons growing out of ecclesiology, from a role which assumes a significant degree of responsibility for history, is that the church *does* risk becoming quietistic and/or hypocritical. That such inwardness is descriptive of a significant portion of the descendants of the Anabaptists in North America today is not unknown to Míguez Bonino, Pixley or Shaull! Nor do they appear to be convinced that many North American congregations are sufficiently uncompromised to merit description as "post-Constantinian" or "inherently anti-ideological," terms which Swartley uses (the latter credited to Walter Klaassen) for the sixteenth-century Anabaptists. How is commitment to the Bible (rather than Marxian social analysis, for example) allowed to critique the ideologies in our own eyes that we are unable even to acknowledge? The contemporary challenge facing North American Christians is to embody a justice-making alternative more concretely committed to all bearers of the divine image than any Constantinian synthesis has been or could be. Apart from such *costly* discipleship the raising of the neo-Constantinian warning will continue to be viewed in the Third World with the question: Is this *also* part of North American ideology, the unique *believers' church* brand of North American ideology? It would appear implicit in Shaull's essay that in North/South Christian dialogue, any unilateral defining of the neo-Constantinian threat as of higher priority that the urgency of liberation needs to have its ideological rootage unpacked.

Perhaps we in the North American church have had it wrong; perhaps the onus is on *our* backs after all, perhaps the burden is on *us* to allow the Spirit of God to create out of the church a just and justice-making political alternative to the Constantinian compromises (both old and new) that we have decried. Perhaps an opening of ourselves to being transformed into a community in solidarity with the marginalized beyond what any Marxist (or any other) revolution has ever claimed to be is the prerequisite for raising the question of neo-Constantinianism. That such a church on the road to transformation would encounter massive opposition, both in the Third World and in the First, goes without saying. It would surely be, in Yoder's imagery, a church in exile. The integrity of North American Christians' criticism of both teleological ethics and Constantinian ecclesiology in the ongoing dialogue cannot be separated from *concrete* and *embodied* commitment to such a world-encountering alternative.

5. THEOLOGICAL INTEGRITY IN THE FACE OF NICARAGUA'S REALITY

The question is most clearly presented by Snyder: Can North American Christians in good faith appeal to our brothers and sisters in Nicaragua to refuse to bear arms? Or stated more frontally, Can we justify detracting attention from the beams of death in our own eyes to the motes in the eyes of Nicaraguan brothers and sisters in Christ? George Pixley troubles us in the Northern church when he allows but three responses of integrity to North American peace church efforts to propound nonviolence as an ethical absolute in the face of these questions: 1) emigrate, 2) de-absolutize nonviolence (his personal conclusion), or 3) candidly acknowledge a "radical evangelical questioning of Anabaptism as a form of Fundamentalism." What are we to make of Snyder's question whether the "pure church/evil world" polarity of the Schleitheim Confession makes it (and sixteenth-century Anabaptism) essentially irrelevant to aspects of life in Nicaragua today?

To take the issue one step farther, can the North American church with integrity carry on its own discussion regarding the theological basis of nonviolence in a business-as-usual manner in the face of the killing in Nicaragua and our complicity in that tragedy? It is not clear to me whether even this volume, an exercise in such theological dialogue, can be justified *apart from* simultaneous, personal engagement toward the *telos* of bringing an end to the killing and our own deep complicity in it. One would hope that these essays are more of an effort in that direction than would first appear. What is more clear is that the church has little reason to say "ah, ha!" in the face of the growing evidence that *evil will confound itself* if hitherto it has been enjoying and attributing to God and reading its Bible through its ill-gained privilege. It must be acknowledged that participation in at least some theological discussions in our time can only take place with integrity amid confession, repentance and commitment to justice-making. The church cannot do peace/justice theology today without facing frontally all of the tearing questions that the reality of Nicaragua raises.

6. "... AND THE SISTER NEAR AT HAND, IN THIS TOWN, AND IN THIS LAND"

There is need for additional confession in the face of the temptation to neglect injustice nearby amid the urgency of various Third World situations such as Nicaragua. In her essay Gayle Gerber Koontz raises the implications for female-male relationships of theologies of discipleship *or* liberation, whether in Latin America *or* North America, in a way which cannot be avoided. In the hymn we sing "I bind my soul this day/To the brother far away, /And the [sister] near at hand, /In this town, and in this land," but the truth is that we would often prefer to bind our souls to those *not* near at hand. (This is true even for us believers' church folk who have sometimes restricted our soul-baring largely to those inside the church.)

The costliness of obedience to the way of Jesus may well be inversely proportional to the geographical distances involved. And perhaps the most near at hand setting in which *everything* that this volume is about must be tested is the full range of female-male relationships. As Gerber Koontz suggests, this is the clearest example of how neither of the traditions represented in the dialogue has been sufficiently radical in responding to God's call to a pervasively new order. All of this raises additional questions that were not given extensive treatment in this volume, the second even less that the first: 1) What is the meaning of the liberating message of the Gospel of Jesus Christ for North American persons and groups devalued for reasons of color, sexual orientation, gender or degree of ablement? and 2) What is the meaning of that same message for those *even nearer* at hand, a still largely male-led, privileged, ideologically-compromised North American church? Is there a theology of liberation for *us?* And will *we* on this painful journey be receptive to the guides with which God has graced the global congregation?

7. THE CHURCH AS HARBINGER OF GOD'S FUTURE

On the one hand, Latin American theologies of liberation are frequently criticized for focusing on present socio-economic realities to the neglect of both past and future dimensions of Christian faith. On the other hand, we as North American Christians would have to confess that we have often spiritualized the kingdom of God into a distant and tidy future. Both the Anabaptist-Mennonite tradition and the theologies of liberation need to be called to *lean into* and *be energized by* God's future, the complete flowering of the kingdom of shalom, while at the same time standing firmly and engaging concretely in the present world. A Gospel of the present *only* is without vision and condemned to existing possibilities; a Gospel of the future *only* is simply irrelevant. Neither one is the Good News of Jesus Christ. Both, finally, are bad news and, ironically, cause for similar expressions of materialistic despair.

The church's fellowship within, as well as witness without, rests in the possibility of *itself* becoming an embodied *first-fruits,* an *aperitif,* an Easter community that, like its risen Lord, is *harbinger* of God's sure and mended future. Respondent Shaull rightly cites Latin American base communities as embodiments of such contagious hope. Often found amid systemic despair, the life of these communities has incarnated hope to innumerable communities and individuals around the world, including both Shaull and myself. A smaller although no less inspiring corporate expression of hope to me has been the Honduran Mennonite Church, which has been seeking to follow the way of Jesus with greater faithfulness. Both the older Anabaptist-Mennonite tradition and the much younger theologies of liberation counterpart contain substantial promise for this struggle for hope at the interface of future and present. That *we* and *they*, with our very dissimilar although perhaps equally compromising susceptibilities, would because of this project live a little more faithfully at that interface is one expression of my own hope.

Contributors

John Driver, Missionary with the Mennonite Church for theological education in Spain and Latin America.

LeRoy Friesen, Professor of Peace Studies, Associated Mennonite Biblical Seminaries, Elkhart, Indiana.

Gayle Gerber Koontz, Associate Professor of Theology, Associated Mennonite Biblical Seminaries, Elkhart, Indiana.

José Míguez Bonino, Professor of Systematic Theology and Ethics, Instituto Superior Evangélico de Estudios Teológicos, Buenos Aires, Argentina.

C. René Padilla, General Secretary of the Latin American Theological Fraternity and Pastor of La Lucila Baptist Church, in Argentina.

George V. Pixley, Professor of Biblical Studies, Seminario Teológico Bautista, Managua, Nicaragua.

LaVerne A. Rutschman, Professor of Biblical Studies, Seminario Bíblico Latinoamericano, San José, Costa Rica.

Daniel S. Schipani, Professor of Christian Education and Personality, Associated Mennonite Biblical Seminaries, Elkhart, Indiana.

Richard Shaull, Program of Theological Education, Instituto Pastoral Hispano in New York and International Subsistence Service Program of the Presbyterian Church USA.

Ronald J. Sider, Professor of Systematic Theology, Eastern Baptist Theological Seminary, Philadelphia, Pennsylvania.

C. Arnold Snyder, Associate Professor of History, Conrad Grebel College, University of Waterloo, Ontario.

Willard M. Swartley, Professor of New Testament and Director of the Institute of Mennonite Studies, Associated Mennonite Biblical Seminaries, Elkhart, Indiana.

John H. Yoder, Professor of Theology, University of Notre Dame, Indiana.

C. Hugo Zorrilla, Missionary with the Mennonite Brethren Church and Director of the Program of Biblical Studies in Spain.

Index

Abiding: in Fourth Gospel, 26-27; meaning of, 27-28
Anabaptism: Baptist response, 139-46; eschatology and, 63-64; Latin American liberation theology and, 57-64, 131-35; liberation theology and, 68-70; "People of God" concept in, 60-62; present day, 161-62; social justice and, 101-4
Anabaptist: historical meaning of, 3
Anabaptist perspective: meaning of, 3
Anabaptist vision, 108-110; definition of, 3
Anabaptist-believers' church tradition: pedagogical orientation, 1
Anabaptists: at Schleitheim, 115
Authority: in Anabaptism and liberation theology, 58-60
Batey, Richard, 90
Baum, Gregory, 4
Believers' church: definition of, 3
Bellah, Robert, 170
Bender, Harold S., 3
Christendom: rejection of, 133-34
Christology: in Anabaptism and liberation theology, 62-63
Cone, James H., 87-88
Constantinianism, 180; dangers of, 163
Discipleship, 132; biblical basis of, 141-43; Christian practice and, 30-31; in Latin America, 53; meaning of, in Anabaptism, 57-58
Ecclesial communities, 152; contributions of, 4; origin of, 61; scripture and, 69, 57
Eschatology: in Anabaptism and liberation theology, 63-64
Exodus, 76; as experience of liberation, 78-82, 104; liberation and, 19; and liberation of the poor, 88-90

Faith: ideology and, 39, 56-57
Feast of Tabernacles: context and symbolism, 18-19
Fourth Gospel: freedom and repression in, 18-20; theme of abiding in, 26-27
Free church: definition of, 3; traits of, 4
Gatti, Enzo, 87
Gutiérrez, Gustavo, 1
Habits of the Heart (Robert Bellah et al.), 170
Hermeneutical circle, 55-56, 60, 69, 73, 149, 152
Historical reductionism: danger in liberation theology, 43-44
Hutterites, 119
Ideology: danger of reducing Gospel to, 46-48
Jesus: as liberator, 17-22; as living example of nonviolence, 121; Lordship of, 177; repression and violence and, 20; theology of justice and, 118
John 8:31-32: context of, 18-21; narrative scope of, 21-24; redactional analysis of, 24-25
Las Casas, Bartolomé de, 103
Latin America: socio-economic structure, 113-14
Latin American Catholic Church, 114
Latin American liberation theology: Anabaptism and, 131-35; church leaders and, 53; nonviolence and, 106; radical Anabaptism and, 57-64
Latin American theology: Constantinian stance, 107; creative periods in, 51-53
Liberation: countercultural community and, 82-84; discipleship and, 27-28; Gnostic understanding of, 29; the

Gospel and, 73-74; life of sacrificial service, 154-55; meaning of, 84; truth and, 29; vision of, 76
Liberation theology: Anabaptism and, 68-70; approaches to study of, 53-54; authority and, 59; challenge of, 148-49; Christology and, 62-63; concern for social justice and, 104; danger of historical reductionism in, 43-44; danger of pragmatism in, 40-42; eschatology and, 63-64; lack of feminist voice in, 171-72; meaning of, 2-3; Mennonites and, 85-86; nonviolence and, 61-62; pedagogical orientation of, 1; "People of God" concept in, 60-62; priority of praxis in, 35-36; relationship of, to political theology, 10n7; scripture and, 58-59, 66-67; social science and, 44-46; violence and, 104-5
Littell, Franklin H., 4
Marxism: 76, 143; socio-economic analysis and, 56-57; importance of, to liberation theology, 37-38
Míguez Bonino, José, 46, 47
Miranda, José, 87
Montesinos, Antonia de, 103
Munsterites: and theology, 70-73; and violence, 73
Nicaraguan Revolution of 1979, 112
Nonviolence: Anabaptism and, 61-62; in early Anabaptism, 58; liberation theology and, 61-62, 106; Nicaragua and, 120-22, 181; questions about, for today, 115; response of Schleitheim, 118-19; scripture and, 66-67; weaknesses of Schleitheim position on, 120
Option for the poor, 63, 88-94; what it is *not*, 86-88; John 8, in, 22
Padilla, René, 142, 156
Peasant Revolt of 1524-25, 102, 112, 113
People of God: in Anabaptism and liberation theology, 60-62; option for the poor and, 95-99
Pico, Juan, 118

Poor, the, 132; scriptural meaning of, 90-92
Pragmatism: danger of, in liberation theology, 40-42
Praxis: meaning of, in liberation theology, 54-55
Qumran community, 97
Radical Reformation: Anabaptists and, 3; contributions of, 4; variations of, 108
Repression: Jesus' response to, 20
Schleithem position: weaknesses of, 120
Scripture: importance of, in liberation theology, 152-53; interpretation of, and praxis, 47; new understanding of, 150-51; relativity of exegesis, 46-47
Sexism, 172
Sin: social, 116
Social concerns: sixteenth century, 102-3
Social justice, 133; Anabaptism and, 101-4; for the world, 136; the Gospel and, 177-78; history of Latin American struggle for, 103-4
Social Sciences: liberation theology and, 44-46; theology and, 37
Theology: historical praxis and, 35; ideology and, 38-39; of justice, 116-18; Munsterites and, 70-73; social sciences and, 37; standpoint dependence of, 170-71; tasks of, 34-36. *See also* Liberation theology, Latin American theology
Utilitarianism: act of, 165-66; intention of, 166-67; role of, 167-68; rule of, 167
Violence: "guerrilla option," 105-6; institutionalized, 117; institutionalized, against Jesus, 20; liberation theology and, 104-5; Munsterites and, 70-73; power and politics behind, 137-38; question of, 143-45; weakness of justification for, 121; against women, 173

www.ingramcontent.com/pod-product-compliance
Lightning Source LLC
Chambersburg PA
CBHW050800160426
43192CB00010B/1587